Making Government Manageable

Making Government Manageable

Executive Organization and Management in the
Twenty-First Century

Edited by Thomas H. Stanton
and Benjamin Ginsberg

The Johns Hopkins University Press
Baltimore and London

© 2004 The Johns Hopkins University Press
All rights reserved. Published 2004
Printed in the United States of America on acid-free paper
9 8 7 6 5 4 3 2 1

The Johns Hopkins University Press
2715 North Charles Street
Baltimore, Maryland 21218-4363
www.press.jhu.edu

Library of Congress Cataloging-in-Publication Data

Making government manageable : executive organization and
management in the twenty-first century / edited by Thomas H. Stanton
and Benjamin Ginsberg.
       p. cm.
Includes bibliographical references and index.
     ISBN 0-8018-7831-4 (hardcover : alk. paper) — ISBN 0-8018-7832-2
(pbk. : alk. paper)
     1. Administrative agencies—United States—Management. I. Stanton,
Thomas H., 1944– II. Ginsberg, Benjamin.
     JK421.M338 2004
     351.73—dc21   2003012877

A catalog record for this book is available from the British Library.

*To Harold Seidman (1911–2002),
our teacher and friend*

Contents

Foreword, by Harold Seidman   *ix*

Preface   *xiii*

*Introduction: Executive Organization and Management
after September 11, 2001, by Thomas H. Stanton*   *xvii*

PART I: The Changing Context of Executive Organization
and Management

1   Citizens into Customers: How America Downsized Citizenship
and Privatized Its Public
Matthew A. Crenson and Benjamin Ginsberg   3

2   Governance Principles: The Neglected Basis of Federal Management
Ronald C. Moe   21

3   Inherently Governmental Functions and the New Millenium:
The Legacy of Twentieth-Century Reform
Dan Guttman   40

PART II: The Impact of Organization and Program Design
on Management of the Executive Branch

4   The Cabinet Officer as Juggler: The Accountability World
of the Secretary of Health and Human Services
Beryl A. Radin   69

5   The Future of the Postal Service
Murray Comarow   88

6   Professionalism as Third-Party Governance: The Function
and Dysfunction of Medicare
Sallyanne Payton   112

PART III: Improving Executive Organization and Management

7   Organization and Management of Federal Departments
    Alan L. Dean   143
8   Modernizing Federal Field Operations
    Dwight Ink and Alan L. Dean   175
9   Technocracies: Can They Bell the Cat?
    Barbara S. Wamsley   204
10 Program Design and the Quest for Smaller and More Efficient
    Government
    Thomas H. Stanton   229

    List of Abbreviations   245
    Notes   249
    Contributors   275
    Index   279

Foreword

The United States government is facing the challenges posed by the changing nature and role of government in the twenty-first century without a coherent organizational strategy. Instead of a generally accepted body of organizational principles, we now have slogans—"steer not row," "market-based government," "citizens as customers." In the absence of an organizational strategy, structural choices tend to be decided by short-term political criteria such as reduction in the number of direct-hire federal employees without regard for potential long-range consequences. Without effective guidance from the White House, congressional committees find it difficult to resist pressure from interest groups to manipulate government structure to their advantage.

Organizational design is likely to raise one of the most fundamental questions asked in a democracy: Who shall rule? Institutional location, administrative arrangements, type of organization, source of funding, processes, and procedures can raise significant political questions concerning the distribution and balance of power among the executive branch, Congress, and the judiciary; the federal government and state and local governments; organized interest groups and the federal government and its third-party agents. Decisions with respect to organizational design may determine who shall control and for what purpose.

The principles developed by the President's Committee on Administrative Management and the first Hoover Commission, which call for straight lines of authority from the president down through department heads with no entity exercising power independent of its superior, are not adapted to current circumstance. Straight lines of authority and accountability cannot be established in what has become in major degree a nonhierarchical system. Federal agencies now rely for service delivery on third parties who are not legally responsible to the president or subject to his direction. Federal powers are limited to those agreed upon and specified in grants and contracts.

The debate that surrounded creation of the Department of Homeland Security illustrates the problems of organizing according to major purposes when the purposes cut horizontally across federal departments and state and local governments. Senator Robert Kennedy identified the dilemma when he asked: "Do the agencies of government have the will, determination, and ability to form and carry out programs which cut across departmental lines, which are tailored to no administrative convenience but the overriding need to get things done?"[1]

Lester M. Salamon argues that "the great challenge is to find a way to comprehend and to manage the reinvented government we have produced." He proposes a new approach called "governance" which emphasizes the collaborative nature of current government and shifts the emphasis from hierarchic agencies to organizational networks.[2]

Agencies are most likely to collaborate and network when they are in agreement on common objectives, operate under the same laws and regulations, and do not compete for scarce resources. Without an accepted body of organizational principles and effective executive guidance, the congressional response to problems is to fragment the government by establishing independent agencies, autonomous entities within departments, and statutory offices. For example, central departmental responsibility for management that was once vested in career assistant secretaries for administration is now divided among inspectors general, chief financial officers, and chief information officers. If collaboration is the desired goal, then Congress is moving in the opposite direction.

The Bush administration is aggressively encouraging market-based competition throughout the government.[3] Competition may have many benefits, but it does not promote collaboration and networking. Contractors and contract employees are not subject to the Constitution and the same body of laws and regulations as civil servants and do not share the same goals. Contractors (except for nonprofits) necessarily have profit as a prime objective, and they have little or no incentive to collaborate with their competitors.

According to Salamon, "third party government poses immense management challenges, perhaps far more immense than those posed by traditional public administration."[4] Instead of recognizing the need for enhanced departmental capability to manage third-party government, recent administrations have done the opposite by cutting the number of employees not directly engaged in service delivery.

The challenges and implication of the changes in government's nature and role are discussed in the following chapters, which should contribute significantly to our understanding of the issues.

HAROLD SEIDMAN
MARCH 2002

Notes

1. Senate Committee on Governmental Affairs, hearings on Federal Role in Urban Affairs, 1967, 40.
2. Lester M. Salamon, "The New Governance and the Tools of Public Action: An Introduction," *Fordham Urban Law Journal* (June 2001).
3. The Budget of the United States Government, Fiscal Year 2003, 45.
4. Salamon, "New Governance."

Preface

This book is a joint product of the Standing Panel on Executive Organization and Management of the National Academy of Public Administration (NAPA) (www.napawash.org/eom) and the Center for the Study of American Government at the Johns Hopkins University in Washington, D.C. Thomas Stanton is chairman of the NAPA standing panel and a fellow of the Johns Hopkins Center. Benjamin Ginsberg is David Bernstein Professor of Political Science at the Johns Hopkins University and director of the Johns Hopkins Center.

The NAPA Standing Panel on Executive Organization and Management is a unique institution. Established in 1971, it serves as a meeting place and sounding board for NAPA fellows and others to exchange views on approaches to improving the structure, capacity, management, and performance of public institutions. The panel meets monthly and frequently hears presentations from leading federal officials and experts on public administration. Speakers at the panel have included David Walker, the comptroller general of the United States; two postmasters general of the United States; deputy secretaries and undersecretaries of cabinet departments; heads of agencies; and other senior officials. Panel members have testified on government organization and management issues on numerous occasions, including on the reorganization of the Internal Revenue Service and on legislative proposals to create a Department of Homeland Security.

Many members of the NAPA standing panel have expressed concern about the loss of management capabilities in the U.S. executive branch over the past several decades. The panel consists of experienced federal managers and management analysts who know that government can improve its performance and who in many cases have helped federal departments and agencies to increase the quality of their organization and management. The authors thus bring a combination of political and administrative principles and practical experience to this book.

The Center for the Study of American Government, based in Washington, D.C., provides an institutional perspective on government, with courses on political theory, the budget process, the law of public institutions, government and the economy, congressional and executive branch politics, foreign policy, social welfare policy, the role of the courts, state politics and policy making, and specialized courses such as on the role of the media. The center also hosts conferences, including a 2002 symposium on developing and implementing comprehensive identity management systems. Thus, many of the authors also bring an academic perspective to this book, albeit with a practical orientation.

The center and the NAPA standing panel jointly hosted a conference in June 2001 titled, "Is Government Manageable? Executive Organization and Management in the Twenty-first Century." The conference was convened in honor of Harold Seidman, a senior fellow both of NAPA and of the Johns Hopkins Center, and Harold's many contributions to public service. Harold served as a link between the two organizations and was responsible for bringing a number of NAPA fellows, including contributors to this book, to Johns Hopkins. The conference was timed to mark Harold's ninetieth birthday.

Much has changed since the conference. Harold passed away in July 2002. We miss him and the chance to share this book with him. And the world changed after September 11, 2001. A concerned American public began to demand performance from the government. As the conference papers were developed into chapters for publication, it was appropriate to move from the conference title to a more positive one for the book: *Making Government Manageable,* without a question mark. It is our intention that this book will provide useful guidance for those who now need to strengthen the organization and management of government to meet the challenges ahead.

As always with a book of this kind, there are many people to thank. First, we would like to express appreciation to the indefatigable executive editor of the Johns Hopkins University Press, Henry Y. K. Tom. Henry has provided valuable advice throughout the process, including numerous beneficial comments on the manuscript. We also would like to thank the unnamed Johns Hopkins University Press reviewer, who read the manuscript twice and provided valuable feedback to the authors and editors, and our excellent copyeditor, Elizabeth Gratch. William Shields of NAPA and Pamela Winston, Maria Mendez, and Tanya Jenkins worked hard to make the original conference a success. Finally, we are grateful to the two institutions, the National Academy of Public Administration and the Johns Hopkins University, which made this work possible.

Introduction

Executive Organization and Management after
September 11, 2001

Thomas H. Stanton

Since September 11, 2001, the nation has become much more interested in making government manageable than at any time in recent decades. In addressing the credible threat of multiple acts of terrorism, mere gestures are not enough. The responsible government departments and agencies are expected to carry out their missions effectively, and the public will judge the results.

On November 25, 2002, President George W. Bush signed legislation to create the Department of Homeland Security. The new department consists of a large number of organizations with responsibilities relating to homeland security, including major organizations such as the Coast Guard, the Border Patrol, the Customs Service, the Transportation Security Administration, the Federal Emergency Management Agency, functions of the Immigration and Naturalization Service, and over a dozen smaller entities such as the Secret Service and the Animal and Plant Health Inspection Service of the U.S. Department of Agriculture. The Department of Homeland Security combines twenty-two federal agencies with 170,000 employees and a total budget of $37.5 billion. Based on the number of people, this represents the second-largest department in the cabinet, behind the Defense Department; in terms of its budget it is fourth in size, behind Defense, Health and Human Services

(HHS), and Education. The president explained that the purpose of the reorganization was "not to increase the size of government, but to increase its focus and effectiveness." This book similarly concerns itself with the need to increase the focus and effectiveness of the federal government, with respect to national homeland security as well as the other important functions of government.

Coping with the Disaggregation of Government

The core theme of this book relates to what might be called the disaggregation of government—that is, the fragmentation of government organization and management structures—and ways to improve executive organization and management to overcome the consequences of this disaggregation. Disaggregation of government has occurred in multiple dimensions:

- the growth of what Matthew Crenson and Benjamin Ginsberg call "personal democracy" and a tendency for individuals to use courts, administrative procedures, and the administrative processes to achieve their advocacy ends;
- diminution, as Ronald Moe points out, of the capacity of the president to serve as the manager of the federal government, as reflected in the loss of capacity for management analysis and support in the Office of Management and Budget compared to earlier periods;
- the growth of agency-specific laws in areas such as personnel and budget, which reduce the ability of the president to manage a government-wide civil service or budget system;
- the expansion of the number and size of quasi-governmental organizations (such as government-sponsored enterprises) to carry out public purposes;
- the expansion of third-party government and especially outsourcing;
- an increased vulnerability to strategic weaknesses that may be based on design flaws from the inception of an organization, such as in Murray Comarow's case study of the U.S. Postal Service and Sallyanne Payton's study of the Medicare program;
- the growth and entrenchment of what Barbara Wamsley calls "technocracies"—that is, specialized fiefdoms such as chief financial

officers, chief budget officers, contracting offices, inspectors general, and, most recently, chief human capital officers. These units represent particular professional and functional specialties and often lack overall management guidance to help trade off specialized concerns of the office against the larger management needs of a department or agency.

Some of the authors call for reversing the trend of disaggregation, while others propose ways of coping. A core issue that recurs in several chapters is the loss of capacity of the Office of the President to enhance the president's ability to manage the federal government. In earlier years an office within the Office of Management and Budget (or yet earlier the Bureau of the Budget) would have provided high-quality management analysis as well as support for management improvements in many of the areas covered by this book. Of special importance, such capacity could have improved the design of the new Department of Homeland Security, which as Alan Dean observes, was prepared in haste and deficient in many respects.

Executive Organization and Management and the Disaggregation of Government

The first section of the book consists of three chapters that address the nature of disaggregation of government and the causes. In the first chapter Matthew Crenson and Benjamin Ginsberg present an analysis of the political context that fosters disaggregation of government. They begin their chapter, "Citizens into Customers: How America Downsized Citizenship and Privatized Its Public," by observing that grassroots mobilization of citizens behind political causes has been replaced by a "proliferation of opportunities for individual access to government."

The politics of individualized access, in turn, has implications both for the design of government programs and for their implementation. In the case of the National Performance Review of the Clinton administration, government adopted an explicit approach of customized responsiveness to citizens and an emphasis on customer service, in place of an earlier tradition of public responsibility. This approach leads to policy prescriptions that services formerly provided by government should be privatized or, if government continues to be involved, provided through vouchers or other market-based approaches.

One consequence of the politics of individualized access is that government officials, at least with respect to domestic programs, may possess less discretion than before. Implementation of federal programs is affected by an increase in the prospect of litigation, GAO investigations, targeted congressional oversight, and the need to observe increasing formalities of open meetings, administrative procedures, and public access to information. Individuals now have a capacity to probe the innards of program operations and envelop the administering agency in a web of protracted proceedings, congressional micromanagement, and litigation to a degree that was unknown in the earlier days of mass mobilization.

In chapter 2 Ronald Moe looks more closely at disaggregation of government generally and organizational disaggregation in particular. He presents a case for "Governance Principles: The Neglected Basis of Federal Management." For Moe the three premier political principles of American government are:

- The institutions of government shall be divided among three coequal branches, the legislative, executive, and judicial, and these branches shall be at once institutionally separate and interdependent.
- All administrative functions are to be located within the executive branch and responsible to the president and, through the latter, accountable to Congress.
- There shall be a governmental sector (agents of the sovereign) and a private sector, and they shall be kept separate and function under distinctive theories of jurisprudence.

Through the mid-1970s, Moe observes, organization and management were based on these three principles. Then, starting in the late 1970s, a period of organizational disaggregation began. Moe points to a number of factors behind this trend. The Executive Office of the President lost capacity, especially with the decline in the ability of the Office of Management and Budget to carry out policy and planning for government management and organization. Also, a growing disparity between demands and resources hollowed out much of the executive branch, which has been "forced to rely on an ever expanding army of contractors."

The result has been organizational disaggregation across the executive branch. Agencies such as the Social Security Administration have split from departments to become independent agencies. Other agencies, while remaining parts of their departments, have obtained separate control over their funding systems and revenues. The number of separate personnel systems has increased, with different agencies receiving authority to classify and pay their civil servants differently. Dissatisfaction with government leads to creation of new, hybrid organizations that appear less bureaucratic. Budget constraints encourage agencies to develop new sources of revenue, and with this revenue come renewed efforts to shift functions either to contractors or else out of the government entirely.

The consequences for executive organization and management have been profound. Government managers face greater challenges than ever before. Moe notes the difficulty of ensuring accountability when public functions are delegated to private organizations such as government-sponsored enterprises (GSEs). He also points to the entrepreneurial mind-set that has been encouraged by public choice theory and, in the 1990s, the National Performance Review. When translated into action, this entrepreneurial outlook creates the challenge of trying to maintain an agency's service to less remunerative public purposes when the opportunity exists to gain revenues from more profitable activities.

Moe concludes with a call for a return to the principles of the Constitution. The federal government should not become a loose collection of several hundred semiautonomous entities, officers, and quasi-private proxies, all seeking to establish their own missions, designating their own favorite customers, following their own management rules, and defining their own standards of success. Only by respecting law-based principles of governance can our administrative system continue to grow and respond to democratic values.

In chapter 3 Dan Guttman explores one important aspect of organizational disaggregation. This chapter, "Inherently Governmental Functions and the New Millennium," focuses on the trend, noted by Moe, to delegate much of the government's work to private contractors. Thus, Guttman cites a 1980 Senate subcommittee investigation that found that the Department of Energy's 20,000 federal employees were a small fraction of the 100,000 to 200,000 people whom the department employed by contract. The resulting management challenges can be immense.

Guttman focuses on aspects of this problem which further impede effective government oversight of contractors. A major issue of concern is the disregard in practice of the principle that certain governmental activities must be performed by agencies and officials and cannot be delegated to nongovernmental actors. As Ronald Moe, and Harold Seidman before him, have observed, the state is subject to a different body of law than that applicable to private individuals and, in a democratic society, is held to different standards of behavior. For example, contractors and their employees are not subject to the same pay caps as apply to federal employees or to the same conflict-of-interest rules.

Guttman notes that, already in the early 1960s, the Bell report ("Report to the President on Government Contracting for Research and Development") concluded that the cumulative effects of contracting could be debilitating. Salaries of contractor employees were not capped, and their work was increasingly more interesting than that performed in-house. Such differences would create a tendency for the intelligence of government to migrate from the official workforce into the third-party workforce—thus further eroding the capability of the official workforce to control the third-party workforce. Over the long run the intelligence of government needed to control contractors might only be found within the contractors themselves. The danger was compounded because of the divergence between the interests of contractors and those of the government and the limitations of the rules governing those interests.

Guttman follows the Bell report in focusing on the concept of "inherently governmental" functions as setting the limits on the types of activity which government should contract out or otherwise delegate. Yet this principle has been observed in the breach. First, it is hard to define an inherently governmental function, especially in the abstract. Second, government rules about the use of third parties have been adopted on an ad hoc basis; third parties themselves drive many of the laws and the rule making in this area, with courts also playing a major role. Third, the rules as they have evolved do not preclude private parties from performing governmental functions but, instead, oblige those who do so to follow some rules of the kinds that apply to officials in similar settings.

Guttman echoes Moe's call for reviving the tradition of applying a coherent body of public law to these questions. Otherwise, as the chapter asks, if we continue to blur the boundaries between officials and private workforces, is there danger that we may lose the very qualities we most value in both?

The Impact of Organization and Program Design on Federal Management

The next three chapters present case studies that highlight the impact on management of an organization or program's design. The three case studies—the Department of Health and Human Services, the U.S. Postal Service, and the Medicare program—each illustrate different aspects of the relationship of design to performance.

Chapter 4, by Beryl Radin, analyzes "The Cabinet Officer as Juggler" in the context of the Department of Health and Human Services (HHS) and the secretary who is supposed to manage the department. She begins by highlighting some of the changes that affect cabinet departments generally, including several that reflect the disaggregation of government: a diminution of the role of the federal agency as direct provider of services; an increase in the devolution of authority to states and localities; and a dramatic increase in the contracting out of services. Again, the reliance on third-party government makes accountability much more complex than it would be if federal staff actually implemented the programs.

Radin finds changes that were predicted by Crenson and Ginsberg: increased public expectations about performance of government agencies and an increased level of controversy surrounding many issues involving domestic programs. The result, she says, has been movement away from the norm of centralized organizations to various forms of decentralized systems, movement toward the use of multiple strategies that are appropriate for different agencies, and a shift in the boundaries of issues and growing expectations of interagency and crosscutting efforts.

Radin finds HHS to be beset by the same centrifugal forces of disaggregation which affect many of the other parts of government described by Moe and Guttman in earlier chapters. The department and its performance are shaped by the diversity and size of the operating programs, vague and difficult goals, fragmented accountability structures, fragmented program authority, varied program responsibilities, controversial issues, diverse constituencies, multiple policy perspectives, conflicting policy approaches, and staff-line competition. She points to what she calls a "web of accountability expectations" to describe external influences that make themselves felt in the manner described earlier by Crenson and Ginsberg.

The secretary of this large and diverse department faces a constantly changing and conflicting set of accountability expectations, in a context of values and premises that may be difficult to discern. Radin concludes her analysis with a practical test of her hypothesis that the cabinet officer must be a juggler. She contrasts the flexible and decentralized management approach of Secretary Donna Shalala with the more centralized approach of the present HHS secretary, Tommy Thompson, and concludes that increased centralization and a command-and-control approach from the top fail to recognize the realities of the department and its fragmentation.

In chapter 5 Murray Comarow presents a quite different case study, again with reference to a major federal agency, the United States Postal Service (USPS). The Postal Reorganization Act of 1970 is striking in its demonstration of the fact that sound design can reduce pressures for disaggregation and improve the manageability of an organization. The 1970 act also shows how design flaws, especially when exacerbated by poor management decisions, can have consequences that ultimately may threaten the viability of the organization and its ability to carry out its public mission.

Before the 1970 act the Post Office Department ran its operations at a substantial loss. The appointment of postal officials was a major source of political patronage. Moreover, congressional decisions concerning the Post Office were the focus of intense attention by special interests. The act converted the Post Office Department into the United States Postal Service, an organization with all of the attributes of a wholly owned government corporation. (In deference to labor, the USPS was not formally designated a government corporation.) The law created a board of governors to head the USPS and select the postmaster general. The new law also ended congressional control over appointments of postmasters and other postal officials. It depoliticized appointments, promotions, and management decisions. The law also removed from the Congress the authority to set postal rates. Yet, instead of allowing the board to set rates after a judicial rate-making hearing, the law created a new Postal Rate Commission to set rates. Finally, the law created a process of binding arbitration—unique in the federal service—to settle wage disputes.

The 1970 act had impressive results. The Postal Service became self-supporting, without need for the regular appropriations that had covered significant Post Office costs before 1970. The cost of a first-class stamp has remained comparable, in real terms, to the cost of an eight-cent first-class stamp in 1968. And patronage has disappeared. These substantial benefits have served the American people well for several decades. The 1970 Postal Reorganization Act stands for the proposition that a well-conceived organizational structure can substantially improve the effectiveness of a government department or agency.

The 1970 act also demonstrates the converse reality: Over time design flaws can cripple an organization and render it much less manageable than otherwise would be the case.[1] In the case of the USPS the two design flaws were major. The creation of the Postal Rate Commission deprived the USPS of the ability to price its services to meet market conditions. Even more important, the provision for binding arbitration deprived the USPS of the ability to control the costs of its 800,000-person workforce.

Comarow devotes much of his chapter to an analysis of the potential crisis confronting the Postal Service. "The lethal combination of statutory constraints on wages and prices and competitive technology," he says, "may ultimately reduce the Postal Service to a shell."

In an early version of his chapter, circulated to appropriate policy makers, Comarow urged the creation of a presidential commission to try to overcome the design flaws that threaten the viability of the U.S. Postal Service; President George W. Bush subsequently created such a commission. Comarow concludes the chapter by warning that its recommendations must be backed by a strong bipartisan constituency to be enacted.

In chapter 6, "Professionalism as Third-Party Governance: The Function and Dysfunction of Medicare," Sallyanne Payton looks at the delegation of medical decisions in the Medicare program to physicians. This is an important design feature that affects the entire program and its administration.

As Payton points out, Medicare is one of the oldest and certainly the largest voucher program in government. The benefit of borrowing the private delivery system for Medicare payments is that the program can acquire large-scale administrative capacity from the private sector; the Medicare program was up and running within a few months of its inception. The Blue Cross and Blue Shield payment systems fitted the preferences and existing relationships of the medical community and thereby—at least for a period of years—helped to avoid a clash of cultures between providers and the government that was paying for services. As Payton notes, these were not small accomplishments.

Also, the program arguably might run with a relatively small oversight presence. Yet, Payton warns, such a nominal administrative virtue also can be a defect. Congressional parsimony has turned the Centers for Medicare and Medicaid Services (CMS) into a "hollow" agency. The relationship of CMS to its contractors is a classic example of the problems noted earlier by Guttman: The thinly staffed government agency lacks both the legal authority and the capacity to carry out the tasks performed by its contractors; this lack of authority and capacity, along with other shortcomings, is then reflected in a weakness in bargaining power which limits the ability of the federal agency, here CMS, to ensure the quality of performance of the third-party contractors who are administering larger parts of the program (here the payment of Medicare claims).

The government's role in paying Medicare claims nicely illustrates the conceptual fallacy of what David Osborne and Ted Gaebler have called "catalytic government," in which government was supposed to act by "steering rather than rowing."[2] Thinly staffed government agencies end up abdicating much of the steering function to the private contractor rowers when they lose the ability to require changes in direction of the programs they are supposed to administer.

Payton closes by pointing to a basic strength of the Medicare program and its relationship to professional health care providers. She finds that a good deal of that strength results from the decentralized nature of the system of professional self-governance on which it rests.

Improving Executive Organization and Management

The final section of the book continues the theme of the case studies. These four chapters present principles of organizational and program design and generalize the discussion to a range of departments, agencies, and programs.

In chapter 7, "Organization and Management of Federal Departments," Alan Dean presents the distilled wisdom of over fifty years of designing, analyzing, and working with federal departments. Especially after September 11, 2001, and the creation of a new department to deal with homeland security, the analyses in this chapter have special importance. The chapter sets forth a clear organizational test: "An executive department is usually called for when programs related to some definable government purpose become so numerous, so large, and so complex that an official of secretarial rank with enhanced access to the president is needed to provide effective oversight and coordination of program management."

On the other hand, a department is not appropriate merely to serve a narrow public purpose supported by a client group. Chapter 7 provides an appendix that offers a list of criteria that ought to be considered in deciding whether to create a new department such as the Department of Homeland Security. Five broad issues are salient in making such a decision. Would creation of a cabinet department help achieve the following goals?

- Establish a national priority for an agency's programs.
- Improve program effectiveness.
- Improve program efficiency.
- Improve federal policy integration.
- Improve accountability to elected public officials.

For Dean proper organization of cabinet departments is an important step in improving government effectiveness. Here the U.S. Department of Transportation provides a valuable model. The Department of Transportation Act of 1966 embodied a carefully designed structure that built upon many of the constituent units that were transferred from other parts of the government. These statutory constituents were largely based on modes of transportation, including the Federal Aviation Administration, the Federal Highway Administration, the Federal Railroad Administration, and the St. Lawrence Seaway Development Corporation. Principal operations of the Department of Transportation are conducted through these administrations.

While the law specifies the responsibilities and powers of the modal administrations, the assistant secretaries function solely in a staff capacity; they do not have authority to direct the administrators who head each administration. The secretary is free to change the duties and functions of the assistant secretaries, which allows the department to adjust to changing circumstances and priorities over the years.

As Dean observes, a number of other departments have a similar approach to internal structure. Thus, the Department of Defense is organized so that the three armed services conduct principal operations, while undersecretaries and assistant secretaries carry out matters such as logistics, personnel, budgets, research, and technology.

By contrast, some other departments are not as well organized. The Department of Energy, for example, operates with strong centralization, in an effort to avoid the creation of bureaucratic "fiefdoms." The result, however, has been a weak management structure with insufficient capacity in the subordinate operating units of the department.

Chapter 8, "Modernizing Federal Field Operations," highlights an aspect of governmental organization that has been neglected in recent years. Dwight Ink and Alan Dean bring considerable experience to bear in describing how federal departments and agencies can improve their operations through decentralization and coordination of field operations across programs.

Ink and Dean view effective field operations as essential for departments and agencies that need to get closer to the people and communities that they serve. They begin the chapter with a basic statement about the appropriate division of labor between headquarters and the field: While headquarters offices have responsibility for formulating and evaluating policy, and also for overseeing field operations, the basic role of field offices is to administer programs and policies enunciated by headquarters.

As they point out, field offices are often better situated than Washington to administer programs. Once again, and this is a recurring subtext of this book, those concerned with homeland security will find these insights relevant to their work. Terrorist attacks, although directed at the nation as a whole, are likely to be quite local in impact.

In designing the field structure, there is no one-size-fits-all approach. The field structure must be tailored to the mission, size, and the needs of the constituents of a department or agency. The authors caution that effective program administration and the needs of those served by an agency or program are the paramount considerations in designing a field structure. They express concern at the tendency of a Washington perspective to predominate rather than looking at field operations from the perspective of program constituents.

One other major issue of special importance after September 11 is field coordination. Ink and Dean provide an example of large-scale field coordination involving active presidential support from the 1960s. While the example is not new, it provides insights that seem quite instructive for those who are trying to bring a myriad of federal agencies and programs into coordination to deal with potential terrorist attacks within the United States.

The final major aspect of field operations concerns decentralization. Decentralization can yield substantial benefits, in improved agency effectiveness and in ability to downsize by removing redundant positions. The authors also note, however, that decentralization is a "surprisingly sophisticated concept that requires skill and experience to design and manage." Indeed, they add, much of the decentralization of federal departments and agencies in the 1990s was fundamentally flawed.

In chapter 9, "Technocracy: Who Will Bell the Cat?" Barbara Wamsley looks at another design issue: the emergence in government departments and agencies of specialized clusters of professionals who carry out narrow management or administrative functions. These clusters she calls "technocracies."

Technocracies are found in traditional support functions such as personnel, procurement, budget, and finance units. The purpose of technocracy groups is to share information, ideas, and practices within the functional specialty. They also have the ability to influence outcome of specific laws or regulations affecting their specialty area, through both formal and informal processes, both as career service members of the executive branch and as members of professional organizations.

In part technocracies represent the growing professionalism of parts of the federal service. They also represent a form of disaggregation—this time of the management capacity of departments and agencies. Thus, the establishment of chief financial officers, chief information officers, and even inspectors general, all of whom must report to the secretaries of their departments, has led to the creation of fiefdoms that can seriously impede coordination and effective program implementation. The creation of chief human capital officers in 2002 buttresses yet another fiefdom.

Wamsley points out that, instead of seeking comprehensive and integrated management reform, policy makers increasingly rely on technocracies to drive reforms. The "President's Management Agenda for 2002" continues this pattern with its inattention to the need for integrating the strategic plans of the individual technocracies to improve agency-wide performance.

Wamsley relates the disaggregation of departments and agencies into technocratic fiefdoms to the general disaggregation of government and to the loss of management analysis capacity at OMB in particular. She concludes by pointing out that "leadership or reform by committee or interagency groups led by individual technocracies will be piecemeal and fail to improve the overall system of government." She proposes a series of reforms to increase the president's capacity to manage, restore departmental management capability, improve the quality of executive leadership, and expand the curricula of institutions of higher learning so that people who enter technocracies also have a broader understanding of the context in which they perform.

In chapter 10, "Program Design and the Quest for Smaller and More Efficient Government," Thomas Stanton takes issue with the budget-driven and numbers-based approach to downsizing government which has reduced the size of the federal workforce without regard to the impact on program effectiveness. Good program redesign is needed before downsizing is contemplated, to ensure that an agency can maintain or increase its service levels while reducing the number of employees needed for some tasks. Only some agencies and programs can downsize without losing effectiveness.

Program redesign permits government downsizing under three conditions:

- the federal government withdraws completely from a particular activity;
- a government agency adopts new ways of doing business that requires fewer employees to produce the same or greater levels of program performance; or
- a government agency uses selective and intelligent outsourcing to reduce demands upon scarce agency resources.

In theory the first of these approaches, the complete federal withdrawal from an activity, would seem to be the easiest way to reduce the size of the federal government. In practice it is among the most difficult, especially for government activities that employ many federal workers. Efforts to withdraw generally founder for lack of political agreement that the government in fact should withdraw from a particular activity.

With careful planning and political consensus, some privatizations have worked well. These include the sale of the Consolidated Rail Corporation (Conrail) in the 1980s and the sale of the Elk Hills Naval Petroleum Reserve in the 1990s. Other times, privatization has caused problems. Government must disentangle the financial objectives of privatization from questions of public mission. Thus, the government privatized the U.S. Enrichment Corporation in 1998, over the objections of the chairman of the Council of Economic Advisors and members of Congress. It turns out that the processing of uranium is an activity that relates closely to U.S. foreign policy objectives, such as ensuring that radioactive materials from the former Soviet Union do not fall into the wrong hands. Yet there seems no easy way to undo the privatization and restore this critical public function to government hands.

The second approach, adopting new ways of doing business, also can founder because of considerations of interested constituencies. Even when improved work processes make employees redundant, federal agencies may find it difficult to downsize and close unneeded offices. The U.S. Department of Agriculture and the health care system of the Department of Veterans Affairs provide prime examples. On the other hand, if staffing shortages already exist, then adoption of improved work processes sometimes can be more attractive to the interested constituencies.

The use of selective and intelligent outsourcing is another approach that sounds easier in theory than it works in practice. The secret of effective outsourcing is the sound design of a working relationship between the government agency and its private partners. A resource-strapped government agency often focuses on price and takes the lowest bid for contract services. Too often also, government neglects to structure the relationship with its contractors to ensure that they have incentives to perform well. One area in which outsourcing has been done well relates to government sales of loan assets. Building upon the lessons learned from the Resolution Trust Corporation, both the Department of Housing and Urban Development and the Small Business Administration have conducted successful loan sales.

A review of the success stories shows that there are several preconditions for redesigning programs to allow agencies to carry out their functions effectively even under conditions of limited staff and budget resources. These are: (1) effective leadership from the top of the agency, if possible with backing from OMB or even the White House; (2) attention to the concerns of the workforce; and (3) the need for a multiyear commitment of resources to cover the transition costs. All are needed if redesign is to lead to a satisfactory outcome.

This, then, is the message of this book: that the organization of government matters and that there are principles of executive organization and management which can make government departments, agencies, and programs easier to manage. Following the world-changing events of September 11, each of these chapters has become especially important in showing how to improve executive organization and management so that government indeed becomes manageable in its essential functions. We have much work to do; the lesson of this book is that success is possible.

Notes

1. In this regard, see also Amy B. Zegart, *Flawed by Design: The Evolution of the CIA, JCS, and NSC* (Stanford: Stanford University Press, 1999).

2. David Osborne and Ted Gaebler, *Reinventing Government* (Reading, Mass.: Addison-Wesley, 1992), 25.

Part I / The Changing Context of Executive Organization and Management

Citizens into Customers

How America Downsized Citizenship and Privatized Its Public

Matthew A. Crenson and Benjamin Ginsberg

In the nineteenth century America was exceptional for the vitality of its democratic institutions, especially its political parties. The country may have been slow to abolish slavery, but it was first to achieve universal white manhood suffrage, and by midcentury, when European states were taking their first hesitant steps toward mass democracy, America's dynamic party organizations were routinely mobilizing 70 to 80 percent of the electorate in presidential campaigns. Outside the South even midterm congressional contests typically pushed turnout past 60 percent.[1]

American politics is no longer exceptional for its feats of grassroots mobilization. In the midterm elections of 1998, for example, barely a third of the registered voters went to the polls. Candidates are spending more money than ever to turn out their supporters. They are employing mechanisms of mass communications to project their voices and images across a vast electronic electorate. But the citizen response has grown progressively weaker. Behind the receding waves of electoral mobilization, a new kind of American exceptionalism is emerging, marked by rates of voter participation significantly lower than the ones that prevail today in the same European nations that once stood by and watched while America built the world's premier popular democracy.

If further confirmation was needed, the declining importance of the citizen in the American political process was underlined again in the aftermath of the September 11, 2001, terrorist attacks on New York and Washington. President George W. Bush addressed the nation to calm fears, to inform Americans of his plans, and to call upon the citizenry to do its part in the face of the crisis. What exactly was the part the president assigned to ordinary Americans? They were advised to sing patriotic songs, think patriotic thoughts, and, above all, go shopping. In other words, the government had little need for citizens and could think of little for them to do besides buoy up the economy and stay out of the way.

Voting is the most common means of citizen participation, and the contraction of the electorate is the most obvious sign of the diminished role that citizens play in American politics. But the decline of citizen activism extends beyond the voting booth. Although the absence of nineteenth-century opinion polling makes it difficult to trace forms of popular participation other than voting, there are strong indications of a general decline in popular politics since the end of the nineteenth century.[2] The evidence of the last thirty or forty years suggests, at best, a stagnation in political activism. Contributing money to political organizations is the only activity to register an unambiguous gain since the 1950s, and it is unclear whether we should regard such financial donations as a sign of active involvement in politics or as a substitute for it.[3]

American democracy is not dead. It has, however, undergone a transfiguration, and so has American citizenship. These changes are not the results of some vast conspiracy to deprive the general public of its place in politics. In fact, twentieth-century political reforms have given citizens unprecedented access to the political process. The introduction of primary elections, the use of referendum and recall, sunshine laws, legislative mandates requiring agencies to give public notice and hold public hearings before making policy changes—all would seem to have made the government more responsive to citizens than ever before. Through ACTION, Volunteers in Service to America (VISTA), Americorps, and the Peace Corps, the government has sponsored the activism of citizens committed to a vision of the public good, and it has extended the idea of citizenship itself to cover many circumstances of life once regarded as purely private. Gender, race, age, sexual preference, and physical handicap now figure in the claims that we make upon the public. According to Michael Schudson, "a dimension of citizenship has come to cover everything," and he adds that the new political dimensions of life in the United States may compensate for the "slackening of voter turnout."[4]

Yet the new opportunities for citizen involvement have changed the nature of citizenship itself. The proliferation of opportunities for individual access to government has substantially reduced the incentives for collective mobilization. For ordinary Americans this means that it has become standard practice to deal with government as an individual "customer," rather than as a member of a mobilized public. At the same time, Americans of more than ordinary political status find that they can use the market, courts, administrative procedures, and other political channels to achieve their ends without organizing a political constituency to support them and their aims. In short, elites have fewer incentives to mobilize nonelites; nonelites have little incentive to join together with one another. The two circumstances have operated in combination with one another to produce a new politics of individualized access to government and a new era of *personal democracy* for those in a position to take advantage of its possibilities.

Recent trends in popular participation are all the more striking because they seem to run against expectations. The most powerful predictor of political activism, for example, is education, and levels of education have been rising in the United States, but political participation has not.[5] Personal democracy may help to explain why. Increased education, together with the increased accessibility of government, may have equipped Americans to get what they want on their own, without hitching their interests to coalitions of like-minded fellow citizens.

Just as curious as the combination of rising education and declining participation is the conjunction of the so-called advocacy explosion in Washington with quiescence beyond the Beltway. Estimates of the explosion's magnitude vary, but everyone agrees that there has been a dramatic increase in the number of organizations represented in Washington, perhaps as much as a fourfold increase since the late 1960s. Yet the population explosion in organized interest groups has not been accompanied by any comparable increase in organizational activism among the public at large—except for the increase in financial contributions, which may actually represent a retreat from direct involvement.[6] Perhaps the most puzzling anomaly in contemporary democratic politics is the disparity between mass immobility and elite agitation.[7] The coupling of elite conflict with popular quiescence is inconsistent with expectations based on what might be called the neoclassical theory of political democracy. As developed by Robert A. Dahl, Maurice Duverger, V.O. Key, and E.E. Schattschneider, it asserts that high levels of competition or conflict among political elites will increase rates of mass participation as contending leaders and parties engage in rival efforts to mobilize political support.

V.O. Key credited the Jeffersonians with setting the stage for mass mobilization when they built local party organizations to "line up the unwashed in their support." The practice was distasteful to the opposing Federalists, but they were soon forced to do the same or risk exclusion from office and power.[8] Throughout the nineteenth century and well into the twentieth, party leaders and candidates waged political warfare like generals, recruiting and mobilizing regiments of voters whose numbers tended to grow whenever party conflict intensified. But sometime in this century the link between leadership competition and citizen mobilization weakened, then disappeared. Although partisan conflict in Washington has rarely been more rancorous than during the past several years, it does not seem to have been translated into popular mobilization. Voter turnout, for example, once rose and receded with the intensity of partisan division in Congress, but by the late 1960s surges of congressional conflict and tides of electoral activism no longer ebbed and flowed in concert, and voting itself was riding a downward wave that has not yet broken.[9]

Down to the end of the nineteenth century, American elites encouraged popular participation because they needed the active support of nonelites. In its infancy, of course, the United States had to win the allegiance of citizens already attached to states and regions. It was largely for this reason that the framers of the Constitution extended basic rights of participation and representation to common folk in exchange for their consent and support for a new government. Constitutional Convention delegate James Wilson explained that to "raise the federal pyramid to a considerable altitude" it would be necessary to give it "as broad a base as possible."[10] For a century or more after ratification, the federal government remained a small state in a big country. It depended on the support of citizen soldiers, citizen taxpayers, and citizen administrators in order to survive and govern.

The government's need for its people set the terms of political competition. Groups and parties contending for office and influence were virtually compelled to organize and mobilize citizens. Popular support was the currency of power, and in the struggle to acquire it political leaders produced the high rates of participation which persisted until the start of the twentieth century. Left to themselves, many citizens—especially those with lower levels of income and education—would never have taken to politics. Limited political information, limited interest in public affairs, and primitive communications technology would have left many of them on the sidelines of the nation's public life. They became active because vigorously competitive leaders marched them into the public forum.[11]

As they sought popular support, politicians striving for power were compelled to offer concessions and inducements in exchange for the people's allegiance. At first elites offered representation and participation. Later they pledged more concrete benefits. Even today, contending politicians offer voters health benefits, social services, old-age pensions, and job security for their votes. Yet today the promises seem more ritualistic than ever—designed less to mobilize new support than to retain the old and to placate important interest groups. There are fewer promises of new benefits, more pledges to continue old programs while controlling their costs, fewer efforts to galvanize new constituencies, and more fence tending to retain a political base.

This is what happens when elites discover that they can do without the support and service of common folks. Rather than offer concessions, elites suggest that the private marketplace might be a better source than the government for health, welfare, and old-age benefits. Rather than expand the base of the federal pyramid through voter mobilization, elites suggest that representative institutions are so ineffective that their power should be curtailed by such "good government" reforms as term limits and circumvented by privatization, deregulation, and expansion in the role of the judiciary.

The upper classes never relied exclusively upon mass politics to advance their political and economic goals. Facing the rise of popular democracy in the nineteenth century, they tried to ride the majoritarian tide through the astute deployment of campaign contributions and lobbyists.[12] Reformers readily spied the hand of privilege that manipulated these political innovations and railed against the influence of "big money" in elections and interest group lobbying in Congress.[13] But there was no reactionary conspiracy here to reverse the progress of democracy. The money and the lobbyists represented the elite's capitulation to democracy's electoral and representative institutions, and an acknowledgment that they would have to play the democratic game. By contrast, contemporary reforms supposed to democratize government— enhanced access to the courts and to the process of administrative rule making—may actually enable political elites to circumvent the arena of popular politics and exercise power without mobilizing democratic support.

The Making of Modern Citizens

The manifestations of the new era in American politics are subtle and wide-ranging. Consider, for example, the recent transformation of civic education in American public schools. Its purpose is to teach young people a common set of political ideals and beliefs and to habituate them to the rules of conduct that govern public life in a democracy. Promoting good citizenship was one of the purposes for which public schools were originally created in this country.[14] The not-so-hidden curriculum used to concentrate on preparing students for collective political action, especially the electoral process.[15] Students held elections to choose team captains, class officers, and student government representatives. They even held mock elections that paralleled real elections.

Schools have not abandoned all of these rituals. But there is a pronounced shift from these electoral exercises to "student service learning." Maryland was the first state to make it a requirement for high school graduation, but other states are quickly following suit. Elementary and secondary school students are expected to "volunteer" for public service jobs with charitable, civic, and public interest groups. Student service learning is also a growing presence on college campuses, and there have been calls to make it a graduation requirement in the state colleges and universities of California.[16]

Traditional civic education tried to teach students that they could help to govern the country along with their fellow citizens just as they governed their classrooms, teams, and schools with their fellow students. "Service learning" imparts a fundamentally different set of lessons about citizenship. It is no longer about the collective activity of governing. Students are urged to produce the public services that a voting public once demanded from its government, frequently services that government has abandoned or is not prepared to pay for. Lessons in service have supplanted training for sovereignty.

One study finds that over half of all service-learning students report that they have worked in environmental or beautification projects, in which they may not even be providing assistance directly to other human beings. But the principal and intended beneficiaries of these programs may be the students themselves, rather than the service recipients. The service-learning experience is supposed to be personally rewarding and to bolster "self-esteem."[17]

The civic activities of young adults (ages eighteen to twenty-four) reflect a similar shift toward service activities. During the past twenty-five years voter participation among young people has declined by more than 12 percent, while their participation in quasi-public and private volunteer organizations such as Americorps and the Jesuit Volunteer Corps has grown substantially.[18] In a recent study of local activists Nina Eliasoph has found parallel tendencies among adults in general. Activists tended to avoid "politics" in favor of community service projects. Talking about political issues, they believe, is wasteful because such talk seldom arrives at consensus on clearly defined conclusions. Perhaps more important, they were convinced that political issues were unlikely to yield to the efforts of community volunteers such as themselves. They tended to concentrate, instead, on community service projects in which they knew that they could "make a difference"—especially projects aimed at the welfare of children. Not only were such efforts likely to be noncontroversial, says Eliasoph, but the volunteers "took a 'focus on children' to mean 'a focus on private life.' That meant that the only real changes regular citizens could make were changes in feelings."[19] Not least important were the feelings of the activists themselves, whose personal satisfaction depended on the conviction that they were making a difference.

What passes for citizenship today often inverts the feminist dictum that the personal is political. It has transformed the political into the personal. Political activity should feel "empowering." It should enhance self-esteem. It should not engender confusion, ambiguity, or frustration.

An all-too-easy diagnosis of the new, service-oriented citizenship would locate its origins in a more comprehensive feel-good culture of self-gratification and self-esteem. But that would overlook the authentic sacrifices made by volunteers who actually perform tasks useful to their communities. And it would ignore the more authoritative efforts of political elites to recast the meaning of American citizenship: "Ask not what your country can do for you; ask what you can do for your country." President Kennedy's inaugural exhortation bore fruit in the Peace Corps and, later, in VISTA. The National Community Service Act of 1990 would embrace an even wider population of volunteers, and it supplied more than $200 million to fuel President Bush's thousand points of light. President Clinton followed this initiative in 1993 with his half-billion-dollar Americorps program.

These programs unquestionably inspire worthy people to worthy deeds, but they also represent a government-sponsored shift in our conception of citizenship. Rather than make demands of government, we now fulfill them ourselves, and in doing so we gain the personal satisfaction and certainty that we have actually performed a service and made a difference.

The New Science of Public Administration

While citizens have been encouraged to think of themselves as public servants, the more conventional public servants employed by the federal government have also been encouraged to adopt a new perspective on the citizens whom they serve. It emerges in the 1993 Report of the National Performance Review, the manifesto of the Clinton administration's campaign to "reinvent" government. The review is one in a long succession of studies designed to improve the functioning of the federal bureaucracy. Its predecessors emphasized the democratic accountability of public bureaucracy. That was one of the first points made by the first Hoover Commission in 1949: "The President, and under him his chief lieutenants, the department heads, must be held responsible and accountable to the people and the Congress for the conduct of the executive branch." The statement has all the banality of a self-evident truth. But, as James Q. Wilson observes, nothing like it appears in the Report of the National Performance Review overseen by Vice President Al Gore. The subject of democratic accountability is hardly ever mentioned. Nor do citizens figure in the report. They have been transformed into "customers," and the review's explicit objective, declared by the vice president, is "to make the federal government customer friendly."[20]

There is nothing necessarily undemocratic about this aim. The vice president's point is that federal employees should strive to meet the needs of their clients and treat them with respect—in other words, to make the government more responsive to its people. But there are crucial differences between citizens and customers. Citizens were thought to own the government. Customers merely receive services from it. Citizens are members of a political community with a collective existence created for public purposes. Customers are individual purchasers seeking to meet their private needs in a market.

What is missing from the experience of customers is collective mobilization to achieve collective interests, and the omission is not just a matter of changing semantic fashions along the Potomac.

Customer service has also become the focus of training for public administrators in general, a departure from an earlier emphasis on public responsibility. In the 1950s Fritz Morstein Marx summarized the bureaucratic orthodoxy of the time: "Public responsibility . . . asserts the necessity of providing demonstrable public benefits and of meeting public expectations. . . . Public responsibility under popular government further demands the willing subjection of the bureaucracy to the laws as the general instruction of the representatives of the people."[21] But the authors of a more recent text regard the public as a collection of customers to be "managed" rather than a public to be served: "You should work hard to cultivate outside group support for your mission. . . . When you deal with the general public you should expect its members to have a limited understanding of the complexity of most issues. . . . While it is to your advantage to have the public on your side, this may not always be possible. Your organization may have a mission that is in conflict with . . . community groups. . . . Your job is to uphold your organization's mission. . . . Be prepared to suffer through public outcries, insults and demonstrations while supporting your program goals." But suffering can be minimized by effective management of the media, representative institutions, community groups, and the public at large.[22] Citizens have been demoted to customers, public administration to customer relations.

Who Needs Citizens?

The narrowing political role of American citizens has done nothing to diminish the ethical elevation of citizenship itself. Citizenship, in fact, seems to have become an embodiment of the virtues and values in which American society is alleged to be deficient—civic consciousness, the sense of community, and responsibility to others. Among academics a recent "explosion of interest in the concept of citizenship" is partly a response to a perceived deterioration in the practice of citizenship.[23] The new requirements for community service in public school systems are introduced to reinvigorate a sense of public-mindedness weakened by a market-driven society that inspires the avarice of its consumers rather than the spirit of its citizens. One of the more recent eulogies for the lost virtues of citizenship comes from a representative of the television industry, an institution often blamed for the erosion of America's civic community. Anchorman Tom Brokaw's best-selling book honors an entire generation of citizens who endured the hardships of the Depression and the hazards of World War II.[24] They are the measure of what we have lost and the model of what we should have become. In a sense they are modern America's counterparts for the fallen soldiers glorified in Pericles' famous funeral oration, the citizen-heroes who sacrificed themselves for the sake of Athens.

We are witnessing a radical divergence between the moral conception of citizenship and the political conduct of citizens. The mismatch is widely acknowledged and conventionally attributed to deficiencies in the moral, cultural, or social resources of today's citizens, which prevent them from acting on behalf of interests larger than their own.[25] The general diagnosis is that America has amassed money and power at the expense of its "social capital"—the interpersonal connections and mutual trust that used to sustain collective enterprises. In a book and a series of articles Robert D. Putnam documents a general decline in civic engagement since the 1960s which has transformed us into a nation of increasingly solitary and mutually mistrustful citizens.[26] Even in our services to others, we have become more likely to act alone. Putnam finds an increase in "volunteering" since the mid-1970s, but it is accompanied by a decline of participation in community service projects.[27] Altruism itself has been privatized.

Although Putnam attributes an array of social and cultural ills to the erosion of social capital, its political consequences must weigh most heavily in any assessment of American democracy and citizenship. They strike at the sources of political engagement. Formal associations and informal socializing once instilled habits of cooperation and elevated private interest into public spirit, but the social ties that sustained the practice of democratic citizenship have weakened or dissolved. This depletion of social capital has impoverished grassroots democracy, depopulated the public forum, and undermined the effectiveness of popular government, which the people have come to regard with growing mistrust.

By Putnam's account three-quarters of the decline in civic engagement can be attributed to just two factors—television and generational change. Television has turned the private home into a place of private entertainment. The diversions of an older America—visiting with neighbors, lodge meetings, church socials—must compete with a calculated campaign of amusement designed to capture an audience for commercials. Americans, long known as a rootless people, have become a nation of stay-at-homes.

But self-interestedness, as Peter Riesenberg points out, has been the constant companion of citizenship.[28] Even Pericles recognized the intimate connection between the public sacrifices of citizens and their private interests. Political communities had to offer inducements to inspire good citizenship: "For where the prize is highest, there, too, are the best citizens to contend for it."[29]

States offer "prizes" for citizenship because they have need of citizens. In classical antiquity the extension of citizenship rights often followed from an escalation in the need for military manpower, especially foot soldiers. At the beginning of this century Otto Hintze noted that in modern states there had been a similar connection between dependence on citizen-soldiers and the extension of suffrage. The existence of militia forces was associated with the early onset of democracy, and even in more centralized and authoritarian systems, Hintze argued, universal military service eventually led to universal suffrage, if only after several generations.[30]

Armies, of course, had to be equipped, provisioned, paid, and pensioned—all of which enlarged the state's need for taxpayers—and the need for taxpayers gave states another incentive to extend the rights of citizenship. Long before American colonists demanded that representation accompany taxation, England had begun to recognize taxpayers as citizens. The step was taken not just to part taxpayers more peacefully from their money but also to increase the wealth available to be taxed. Property rights, the right to practice a trade or engage in commerce, and the right to secure those rights through the courts all helped to enhance the prosperity of taxpayers and expand the state's revenue base.[31] In absolutist France the transformation of taxpayers into citizens occurred later, but more suddenly, when a revenue crisis forced Louis XVI to summon the estates-general for the first time in centuries.[32] Within a few years almost everybody in Paris was addressing everybody else as "citizen."

The modern states of Europe invented modern citizenship, not just because they needed standing armies and the money to pay for them but also because the very existence of the state defined the conditions for citizenship. The modern state was a membership organization to which people belonged directly as individuals, not indirectly through their membership in families, clans, tribes, guilds, or status orders, and the state itself replaced this jumble of premodern political jurisdictions as the single, paramount object of political allegiance.[33]

Understood in this way, the connection between the modern state and modern citizenship is tautological. The definition of *citizenship* is implicit in our definition of *state*. But citizenship was more than a vertical relationship between subject and state; it also implied a relationship among fellow citizens, a common tie of blood, belief, or culture which united them into a political community. Beyond that citizenship also has behavioral implications—a role in governing the state and the support of state authority. These were the activities denoted by Aristotle's definition of the citizen as one who rules and is ruled. The benefits of rulership were the prizes that citizens won for being of service to the state, and, as Pericles observed, the more valuable the prizes, the higher the standards of citizenship were likely to be. His ancient observation, as well as the modern state's cultivation of citizen-soldiers and taxpayers, suggests an alternative to the view that the recent decline in the role of American citizenship is a product of the citizens' personal characteristics, their cultural values, or their access to "social capital."

Citizens become politically engaged because states and political elites need them and mobilize them. If they remain passive, politically indifferent, or preoccupied with private concerns, the reason may be that our political order no longer provides incentives for collective participation in politics. The state may no longer need citizens as much as it once did, or perhaps citizens have become a nuisance to political elites, or it may be that citizen "prizes" have gotten too expensive for the state to bear.

Citizens, of course, do not disappear simply because they have become institutionally inconvenient. A political system engaged in the collective demobilization of citizens fashions other arrangements for the political management of its population. In general, American institutions operate increasingly to disaggregate and depoliticize the demands of citizens. The reinvention of American government has reinvented citizens as customers. It has offered "stakeholders" easy access to the decision-making process as a low-energy alternative to collective mobilization. It emphasizes private rights at the expense of collective action. It is promoting arrangements for policy implementation which encourage individual choice rather than the articulation of public interests. It has reduced the occasions for citizens to congregate around "opinion leaders," and it has weakened the incentives for political entrepreneurs to organize public constituencies. It has begun to privatize not only many of its own functions but also the public itself. American politics has entered the era of personal democracy.

A Short History of Personal Democracy

The routine operations of American government once relied on the large-scale mobilization of the public to a far greater extent than they do today. Conceptions of political democracy which focus on parties, elections, and pressure groups tend to overlook this fading dimension of popular sovereignty. But the complete citizen, as Aristotle observed, plays two roles—ruling and being ruled—and they have been bound to each other. The more government rule depended upon citizen cooperation, the more government submitted to the rule of citizens. As government has learned to manage the public business without the public, it has also diminished the occasions for the kind of popular mobilization that demands the reshaping of public policy or changing political institutions.

Some of the first steps toward the demobilization of American citizens date to the Progressive era, when reformers sought to eliminate waste and incompetence from government by abolishing patronage and crippling the political party organizations that mobilized working-class, immigrant voters who offended the Progressives' "public-regarding" conception of citizenship.[34] The Progressives' conception of an autonomous citizen independently evaluating candidates and policies was an early anticipation of personal democracy. But some of the most significant discouragements to the collective mobilization of citizens followed the end of World War II, perhaps the last and greatest summons to citizen duty in the nation's history.

These discouraging developments were expressions of the postwar conservative reaction against the New Deal. The Administrative Procedure Act of 1946 and the Taft-Hartley Act of 1947 were both intended to curb the authority of New Deal regulatory agencies by holding them to formal standards of rule making and adjudication. The ostensible purpose of these enactments was to prevent the interest groups under regulation from "capturing" the agencies that were supposed to regulate them. The chief concern of congressional conservatives at the time was the privileged status of labor unions with respect to the National Labor Relations Board. To counter such interest group influence in the regulatory process, Congress tried to open the administrative rule making to the public at large by means of requirements for public notice and comment. To avoid bias in particular cases, the Administrative Procedure Act attempted to construct a firewall between the agency's rule makers and its administrative law judges. And, finally, Congress decreed that an agency's decisions could be appealed to the courts.[35]

In the effort to eliminate factional bias from the regulatory process, Congress also reduced the incentives for citizens to mobilize and form interest groups. After the Administrative Procedure Act, pressure successfully exerted on an agency's rule makers did not necessarily extend to its adjudicators, and, since the rule-making process was now open to the public at large, there was not so much need to organize groups and mobilize constituencies in order to gain access to it, especially since unfavorable decisions could be appealed from regulatory agencies to the courts. The postwar regulatory reforms were eminently democratic, at least in a formal sense.[36] It could be argued, in fact, that they opened government more fully to the participation of its citizens because of their notice and comment provisions and the opportunity to appeal agency decisions to the courts. The Taft-Hartley Act was explicitly justified as a measure that would protect individual workers from undemocratic labor unions as well as from the unfair labor practices of their employers. But, since the new regulatory regime facilitated individual access to policy making, it reduced the value of collective mobilization.

The legalistic mode of administration imposed by the postwar conservative reaction was extended, in the 1960s and 1970s, to types of policies that the conservatives could hardly have anticipated—civil rights, occupational health and safety, environmental protection, and consumer protection.[37] A further step in the progress of legalistic policy making was the use of public interest lawsuits as instruments of regulation. The civil rights movement had used litigation to advance its aims since the 1940s—but it did so, in part, because the denial of voting rights to African Americans and their minority status meant that blacks were seriously handicapped in the usual arenas of democratic decision making. Litigation was, like the resort to civil disobedience, a way to overcome their electoral disabilities. In the 1970s, however, public interest groups emerged whose chief democratic disability was not minority status but the very breadth and diffuseness of the disorganized constituencies that they claimed to represent. They devoted less energy to mobilizing their potential supporters than to litigation. Aided by responsive federal judges, these new public interest groups employed lawsuits against federal agencies—such as the Environmental Protection Agency—to establish regulatory standards that the agencies were then required to enforce.[38]

What ensued was an "advocacy explosion." Groups claiming to represent

diffuse population groups such as consumers, children, the disabled, the elderly, or the public in general opened Washington offices, not just to conduct
traditional lobbying activities aimed at Congress or the federal bureaucracy
but to litigate on behalf of their constituents. The relationship between the
constituencies and the organizations claiming to speak for them, however, was
often quite tenuous. Litigation required money, research, and expertise but
not the political mobilization of a popular following. The "membership" of
these groups sometimes amounted to nothing more than a mailing list of face-
less contributors who had never met with one another to discuss the group's
political objectives or strategies. A few highly influential groups, in fact, were
actually supported by foundation grants and legal fees won in court cases, and
some received funding from the federal government itself.[39]

The legalization of national policy making accentuated an emphasis on individual rights which has always been inherent in American ideas about citizenship. Public interest lawsuits aimed not only to assert those rights but also
to invent new ones, and in the process they changed the character of national
political discourse. Mary Ann Glendon argues that the language of rights is a
conversation stopper. It "puts a damper on the processes of public justification, communication, and deliberation upon which the continuing vitality of a
democratic regime depends."[40] The successful assertion of a right trumps all
other arguments. In some instances, of course, political argument can actually
be stimulated by the contest between competing rights or the attempt to extend a recognized right to a new situation. Once established, however, a right
can be invoked without engaging in the collective action that awakens and re-
news the common ties of citizenship.

The vast increase in interest group litigation since 1970 and the rights-based
politics that followed from it may help to explain a contemporary curiosity of
American politics.[41] By all accounts the population of Washington lobbyists
and interest groups has grown rapidly since 1970, to unprecedented levels, but
there has been no corresponding increase in group membership among
Americans at large. One possible reason for this disparity may be that some of
the newest interest groups have begun to target ever narrower interests.[42] But
an explanation with even longer reach is that contemporary interest groups
tend to concentrate more on litigation, research, polling, fund raising, and
media relations and less on mobilizing popular support. The handful of
Washington-based interest groups which actually have extensive grassroots
memberships, such as the National Rifle Association (NRA) and AARP (for-

merly known as the American Association of Retired Persons), are connected with the vast majority of their constituents only by mail.[43] The interest group struggle in Washington, like the clash of party elites in Congress, becomes increasingly disconnected from the mobilization of citizens, and the scope of citizenship itself narrows.

While Washington interest groups floated free from the constituencies that they claimed to represent, the federal government seemed to fasten itself more firmly to the grassroots. *Maximum feasible participation* were the controversial watchwords of federal policy.[44] Requirements for citizen participation spread from one national program to another. Public bureaucracies and private interest groups seemed to be moving in opposite directions, but they were both dancing to the same music. Like the conservative reforms of the postwar era, they were opening the administrative processes of regulation and policy implementation to outside forces—to citizens—and, like their conservative precursors, they accomplished almost exactly the opposite. "Maximum feasible participation" usually achieved only minimal mobilization of the public. In the Community Action Program, the Model Cities Program, and other antipoverty ventures of the federal government, the chief effect of participatory administration was to absorb and dissipate the political pressures generated by urban protest movements, often by co-opting the actual or incipient leaders of these movements.[45] The participatory programs also lacked substance. In order to allow for policy making by the people, after all, official policy makers had to refrain from issuing precisely designed programs with clearly articulated objectives. The immediate result, as Theodore Lowi pointed out, was that "the absence of central direction and guidance simply deprives the disappointed of something to shoot against. This is a paternalism that demoralizes.[46]

It was also a formula for policies that would be difficult to justify and defend when under attack, precisely because the policies and their purposes were not clearly or compellingly defined. When the Reagan tax cuts made deficit reduction the organizing purpose of federal politics in the 1980s, the last vestiges of community action were swept away, along with the revenue-sharing and block grant programs of the 1970s.[47] They suffered from the same political disabilities as their participatory predecessors—vaguely defined objectives and weak or politically diffuse clienteles.

What replaced them was a new conservative policy regime that preached the virtues of the market, not just as a substitute for big government but as an instrument of big government. Privatization and vouchers were supposed to free the public sector of bureaucratic inefficiency and unresponsiveness. But they also represented a new stage in the erosion of citizenship. Vouchers and programs of "choice" were designed so that public policies could be disaggregated into private decisions. Under a school voucher system, for example, parents dissatisfied with the kind of education their children receive need never complain or join with other parents to protest. They can simply choose to send their children to a different and more satisfactory school.

There is an undercurrent in twentieth-century American politics that flows through movements and measures strikingly at odds with one another. The postwar conservatives who backed the Administrative Procedure Act and the Great Society liberals who launched the War on Poverty will never be mistaken for ideological soul mates. They are connected, however, by a shared political sensibility that ties them not only to one another but also to the Progressives who preceded them and the Reagan-Bush conservatives who followed. It is a tendency to individualize democracy—an inclination to provide citizens with personal access to politics, policy making, and administration and, by so doing, to reduce the frequency and the need for collective action.

Personal democracy lowers the political barriers that citizens used to breach only by collective assault. Freedom of information policies, sunshine laws, mandatory public hearings, public notice and comment requirements, quotas for "citizen" representation on boards and committees, public agency "hotlines," and policies of choice—all these and other arrangements permit citizens to play politics alone. Yet the principal effect of these apparently benign arrangements for personal democracy is to shrink the role of citizens in American politics. Organizational entrepreneurs and elites who once mobilized followers in order to earn a place among the government's power holders and policy makers now discover that they can achieve similar or better results through litigation or that, by claiming to speak on behalf of a diffuse and otherwise voiceless constituency, they can qualify as "stakeholders" whose presence is essential to the legitimacy of federal policy.

When popular mobilization ceases to be a favored strategy among leaders, citizens are left to their own devices—of which there is no shortage these days. But they generally lend themselves only to an attenuated kind of citizenship. It seldom results in political mobilization for collective ends; more frequently, the outcome is individual action for improved service or personalized treatment. One alternative for citizens is community activism designed not to raise political issues or reshape public policy but to produce public goods and ser-vices directly—cleaning up the environment, for example, or serving meals in a homeless shelter. This dimension of personal democracy may be personally rewarding and certainly helpful to needy people or the local community at large, but it does not represent an exercise of political democracy. A nation of citizens, once illuminated by democratic purpose, has disintegrated into a thousand points of light.

CHAPTER TWO

Governance Principles

The Neglected Basis of Federal Management

Ronald C. Moe

Informed political discussion does not require that on each and every occasion the fundamental theoretical bases of the American polity be revisited and resolved. Most political discussions properly take these theoretical values, or governance principles, as givens and move rapidly to policy and political issues. It is important, however, to reassess periodically the governance principles that instruct the American polity. Governance is concerned with political theory, institutions, laws, and fundamental rights of participants in the political system. Management of the government is necessarily a derivative and dependent element of the system of governance. With these thoughts in mind, this chapter has as its purpose a current assessment of the governance principles that inform and direct the management of the federal government. Attention will be paid to the challenges facing these governance principles especially as they relate to the growth of hybrid organizations that commingle the governmental and private sectors.

American Political Theory

The United States is unusual, if not unique, in the extent to which the national government, and state governments for that matter, is based on a comprehensive and coherent political theory. Unlike most nations, the national government did not simply evolve over time with organizations being established as part of ad hoc accommodations to changing political circumstances. It emerged full-blown, albeit on a small scale, at the outset of the republic. The organization of the government and of the executive branch was intended to reflect the fact that the United States was being established as a democratic republic.[1] The framers spelled out their theories and intentions at the Constitutional Convention, many of which were discussed in greater detail and insight by James Madison and Alexander Hamilton in their *Federalist Papers.*[2]

It is interesting to note that the United States government was established at the close of the Age of Reason with its realistic, yet ultimately optimistic, view of the role of individual reason in political deliberations. Just a few years later, in 1789, the French Revolution began and ushered in the Age of Revolution, in which reason was largely rejected as a value to be replaced by mass politics, class warfare, and various forms of absolutism. If the United States had been established after 1789, rather than before, there is little doubt that it would have been organized much differently, reflecting the social revolutionary values of the new period.

Legal Authority

The source of authority respecting the organization and governance of the federal (national) government of the United States is the Constitution of 1787. While questions regarding how best to organize the executive branch were raised at the Constitutional Convention, the Constitution itself is nearly silent on organizational matters.[3] The document does reflect, however, the clear intent of the framers to organize a government based on theoretical principles, its three premier political principles being:

1. The institutions of government shall be divided among three co-equal branches, the legislative, executive, and judicial, and these branches shall be at once institutionally separate and interdependent.

2. All administrative functions are to be located within the executive branch and responsible to the president and through the latter accountable to Congress.

3. There shall be a governmental sector (agents of the sovereign) and a private sector and they shall be kept separate and function under distinctive theories of jurisprudence.

Lest these principles sound commonplace to the American ear, its needs to be recognized that, collectively, they are not to be found operative in any other nation. Indeed, if there is an international trend evident in governance, it is a movement farther away from these principles. The popular international trend is to deny the legal distinctiveness of the sectors and to move government management away from its constitutional and legal basis and toward the preeminence of generic management principles most closely associated with the private corporate sector. Organizational autonomy is now the magic elixir of international public management.[4] The United States has undergone its own pressures to move in the direction of generic management[5] and governmental disaggregation, and today we face emerging challenges in political accountability having to do with the management of federal agencies and programs.

The Congress

The key to understanding governance in the United States is to recognize the centrality of Congress to the political system. The powers of Congress are defined and listed in Article I, a location selected intentionally. It is Congress that establishes departments and agencies and, to whatever degree it chooses, the internal organization of agencies, personnel systems, confirmation of executive officials, funding systems, and ultimately determines whether the agency shall continue in existence. No agency or office of the United States may be created or dissolved except by explicit approval of Congress. The missions and priorities of agencies are determined by law, not by the president or by department heads, either collectively or separately. While comity and cooperation among Congress, the president, and the agencies are the bases for most relations between the branches, the authoritative element in the relationship is clear. Management of the executive branch, both in terms of process and behavior, is ultimately dependent upon Congress and the law.[6]

Under the Constitution, Congress is a bicameral body consisting of two equally powerful chambers. Every bill sent to the president must be passed in identical form by both Houses. Congress has developed a powerful support apparatus to fulfill its constitutional obligations. Each member has a large office staff; each committee has staff; and there are support agencies, including the General Accounting Office, Congressional Budget Office, and Congressional Research Service, to serve in a nonpartisan capacity. A major function of Congress is to oversee administrative agencies and their programs. All programs must have authorizing legislation, and all agency heads must respond to congressional committees and to investigations by the General Accounting Office. Every top official in the executive branch can be assured that a major portion of his or her time will spent either testifying before committees, meeting with members and staff, writing reports, or simply preparing for the these activities. In every respect Congress was intended to become, and has become, an active comanager with the president of the administrative branch of government.[7]

The President and Executive Officers

Article II of the Constitution provides, in part, that "the executive power shall be vested in a President of the United States." Various specific powers (e.g., president as commander-in-chief of the armed services) are listed, but the term *executive power* as it might apply to the organization and management of the executive branch is not elaborated upon. In general, when Congress passes a law the responsibility for its implementation rests with the president, or department head, who in turn manages this responsibility through delegation to subordinate officers. It is generally considered unwise to assign a program directly to a subordinate agency and officer because it results in a break in the hierarchy of accountability critical to effective management by the president.

In this review of governance principles it is understandable that legally based, formalistic analysis will tend to take precedence over the informal political elements of power currently emphasized in political science literature. The presidency, both institutionally and personally, is generally viewed as having come to dominate the political culture in the twentieth century.[8] The writings of Richard Neustadt support the dominant presidency view and have influenced several generations of scholars. In 1960 Neustadt's *Presidential Power* appeared and launched a broadside against the institutionalist/legalist view of the presidency. While never fully rejecting the role of law in the armory of presidential powers (no one would be that foolish), Neustadt's thrust was clearly in the opposite direction, toward enhancement of the president's political role. "Laws and customs," Neustadt averred, "tell us little about leadership in fact."[9] The message was for scholars and practitioners to study the techniques of influence and persuasion rather than public law and organizational management if they wanted to understand how decisions were really made. The nub of Neustadt's thesis was to be found in the aphorism: "Presidential power is the power to persuade."[10] Forsake rigorous study of laws and governance theory, the implicit argument went; concentrate, instead, on processes and personalities.

It is undoubtedly correct that in the last century the institutional presidency gained in political influence relative to the other branches. This shift has been caused in part by the pervasive growth in the types of media communications and its omnipresence in contemporary life. It is easy, however, to attribute more importance to this phenomenon than is warranted. The fact remains that our political system is still governed by law, and it is incumbent upon a president, both as an individual and institution, to be a major player in determining the rules that influence the implementation of our governance principles.

Agency

The term *agency* of the United States is critical to understanding how the federal government is organized and managed. *Agency* is a term and concept defined and employed generically to refer to all executive branch entities. The precise nomenclature used to designate an entity has no bearing upon its legal status. Thus, the Department of the Treasury, Peace Corps, Federal Bureau of Investigation, Office of Comptroller of the Currency, U.S. Agency for International Development, Pension Benefit Guaranty Corporation, and Tennessee Valley Authority are all agencies of the United States. In Title 5 of the U.S. Code, it is indicated that the entire code applies to all agencies of the United States. This is critical because it means that all laws and relevant regulations apply to all agencies unless specifically exempted as a category of organization or exempted in the enabling legislation of an agency. There are presently many exemptions to this generalization, but those seeking exemption have been forced to accept the burden of proof to overcome the presumption of general applicability.

General Management Laws

The principal tools by which Congress and the president comanage the executive branch are the management laws of general applicability. *General management law*, as used here, refers to those crosscutting laws regulating the activities, procedures, and administration of all agencies of the federal government, except where exempted by category of organization or by a provision in their enabling statute.[11]

General management laws are intended to provide appropriate uniformity and standardization for government organization and governance processes. Uniformity and standardization by themselves, however, are not the objective of general management laws. Such an objective would stultify government as "one size does not fit all." What these laws do reflect, therefore, are the conceptual and legal agreements between the branches with respect to the management of the executive branch. In functional terms general management laws are statements of presumption guiding governmental behavior; that is, certain doctrinal provisions reflected in legal language stand until and unless an exemption is permitted. Exemptions may be assigned by a general statute to a category of agency (e.g., government corporations), or they may be present in provisions of the agency's enabling statute. Exemptions from general management laws may be mandatory or discretionary.

General management laws come in various guises and may be dramatic in their coverage and impact—as is the case with the Administrative Procedure Act, Budget and Accounting, Ethics in Government, and Freedom of Information Acts—or they may be of relatively low visibility (although visibility is not necessarily equitable with importance), such as the Federal Advisory Committee Act and the User Fee Act of 1951. In recent years two somewhat contradictory trends have been evident. First, many new general management laws have been enacted (e.g., the Inspectors General Act and the Chief Financial Officers Act), each supported and justified on its supporters' definition of a problem but often with what some observers believe to be little consideration of its probable impact upon other related general management laws.

(Barbara Wamsley provides a list of such laws and discusses some of their consequences in chap. 9.) Second, increasingly agencies and interest groups have been successful in gaining exemption from the coverage of these acts, especially exemptions in the fields of personnel, compensation, and intragovernmental regulations.

Three Branches: Separate and Interdependent

The framers of the Constitution, well aware that prior attempts at popular government had universally failed, sought to create a regime that was at once energetic and limited. Although common interpretation has it that the separation of powers doctrine was intended to thwart tyranny, even at the expense of government efficiency,[12] this interpretation is only partially correct and is thus misleading. In point of fact the framers sought government efficiency and viewed a separate executive as the necessary means to that end.[13] George Washington was especially concerned to separate the executive from the legislature, having suffered throughout the Revolutionary War and later the Confederation from the incompetence of a single-chamber Congress. In concentrated institutional authority Washington and the other principal framers saw a formula for both debilitative inaction and possible majoritarian tyranny. Thus, the separation of powers concept, meaning in this instance an independent executive, was seen as the engine of administrative efficiency, while the checks and balances between the branches were viewed as the means to protect liberties.

The decision to establish a unitary administrative structure under the president, an innovation at the time, was intended by the framers to complement their more comprehensive theory of government. They believed that efficient administration was more likely to occur with an integrated executive branch under a president elected independently of the legislature. Congress, however, was to retain significant administrative oversight powers, as has been previously noted. While the concept of a unitary executive would be violated on occasion,[14] it was generally viewed as a critical precondition for workable lines of political accountability, the latter being the highest value in the system.

The appeal of an integrated executive branch under the president retained its persuasiveness throughout the nineteenth century. It would be misleading to assume, however, that a unitary executive branch necessarily meant that presidents were strong managers during this period. In point of fact, presidents lacked the institutional capacity, budgetary tools, and inclination to be active managers.[15] For the most part, it was Congress that provided whatever executive branch oversight was forthcoming.[16] Departmentalism retained its hold until Congress approved the creation of the Civil Service Commission in 1883 and Interstate Commerce Commission in 1887. This break with departmentalism and the single administrator–headed agency was associated in many respects with the triumphant civil service reform movement that sought to cleanse administration of partisan politics by introducing the merit system.

Presidents as Chief Managers

In the twentieth century the concept of a strong president emerged as the driving force in government organization and management.[17] Various landmark commissions issued reports calling for presidents to exert more managerial leadership, the creation of central managerial agencies, and the reintegration of executive agencies in departments reportable to the president. The view that all government activities should be accountable in some manner to politically responsible officials received its most forceful iteration in the twentieth century, in the Hoover Commission report of 1949: "[We] must reorganize the executive branch to give it simplicity of structure, the unity of purpose, and the clear lines of executive authority originally intended. . . . [The] organization and administration of the Government . . . must establish a clear line of control from the President to the department and agency heads and from them to their subordinates with correlative responsibility from those officials to the President, cutting through barriers which in many cases made bureaus and agencies partially independent of the Chief Executive."[18]

Through the mid-1970s the organization and management of the executive branch generally followed some basic rules. If an entity was established by Congress to accomplish a public purpose, it would be considered an agency of the United States operating under the general management laws enforced by the president and the central management agencies. These values, originating with the framers and reinterpreted by successive generations of reformers, featured the centrality of public law, departmental integration, and political accountability. The purpose of federal management was to implement the laws passed by Congress.[19] The president was charged with responsibility for management of the executive branch. The governmental and private sectors cooperated but were kept legally separate and distinct in the interest of protecting citizens' rights against a potentially arbitrary government. This public law, or constitutionalist, paradigm of governance prevailed largely unchallenged up until the late 1970s.

Organizational Disaggregation

Since the 1970s the constitutionalist paradigm of governance has been under pressure to permit exceptions, both of a general and particular nature. The pressures come from within as well as without. Within the executive branch it is a seemingly innate characteristic for agencies and their chiefs to seek autonomy from central direction in both policy and operations.[20] In this quest for autonomy the internal forces are often reinforced by outside support organizations. It takes considerable skill and resources by the president and central management agencies to counter the prevailing centrifugal forces. Unfortunately, presidents have retreated from many of their responsibilities in the management field, a retreat with consequences for their immediate institutional family. For one thing, the capacity of the central management agencies has been permitted to atrophy.[21] No longer is there a cadre of top professionals in the Office of Management and Budget (OMB) who understand or enforce the principles of governance defined earlier. The executive branch today is, in many respects, hollow,[22] forced to rely on an ever-expanding army of contractors, as Dan Guttman discusses in chapter 3. The cumulative effect of misguided personnel "reforms" and management process exercises, such as those associated with "reinventing government," have depleted the capital of the executive branch to meet the rapidly expanding duties assigned to executive agencies. Recent presidents have worked to extend their influence to more subject fields but in the process have lost some of their capacity to influence in depth those responsibilities historically associated with their office.[23]

Disaggregation in the executive branch (not to be confused with decentralization) has taken several forms; legal, organizational, financial, and personnel. There are more agency-specific management laws today than in the mid-1970s. Agencies (e.g., the Social Security Administration) are being split away from departments and assigned independent agency status. More agencies are being given control over their funding systems and revenues, and the number of separate personnel systems has increased.[24] Philosophically, the federal government is often out of favor with the public; hence, there is pressure to create new, hybrid organizations that appear less bureaucratic. Financially, budget constraints encourage agencies to develop new sources of revenue,[25] and with this revenue come renewed efforts to shift functions either out of the government entirely (i.e., privatization) or to contractors. This gives the impression, if not necessarily the reality, of reducing the size of government.

Coupled with this trend toward disaggregation has been the popularization of new management principles. A New Public Management (NPM) paradigm emerged in the early 1990s and rapidly gained international currency through its promotion by the Organization for Economic Cooperation and Development (OECD).[26] The underlying premise of the NPM is that the governmental and private sectors are alike in their essentials and subject to generic management principles based on economic premises. Promoters of NPM ("entrepreneurs") rely on literature, propositions, and practices that strive toward convergence of the governmental and private sectors. The acceptance of the convergence model of public management worldwide has been both rapid and in some instances disrupting.[27] In New Zealand the transformation from a traditional public law model that tended to keep governmental and private sectors relatively separate to an entrepreneurial model in which the sectors have become largely indistinguishable is well developed, if not fully settled.[28]

New Public Management

Beginning in the immediate post–World War II period, several strands of economic literature emerged arguing a case for the superiority of the market over governmentally planned and managed economies. One strand consciously assumed the mantle of "public choice" theory. At its heart public choice theory rests on the premise that political as well as economic behavior is based on the rational, self-serving maximization of material income or the satisfaction derived therefrom. In the words of scholar Dennis Mueller: "Public choice can be defined as the economic study of nonmarket decision making, or simply application of economics to political science. The subject matter of public choice is the same as that of political science: The theory of the state, voting rules, voting behavior, party policies, the bureaucracy, and so on. The methodology of public choice is that of economics, however. The basic behavioral postulate of public choice, as for economics, is that man is an egoistic, rational, utility maximizer."[29]

The political impact of this premise has been extraordinary. By the mid-1980s it had swept many nations to varying degrees, including the United States, and contributed its share to the collapse of the communist world and to centralized government planning and management generally. Planned economies fell from favor. Free market advocates pushed a variety of related concepts internationally, many with profound implications for government management. The American variation on the New Public Management was the "reinventing government" exercise by the National Performance Review (NPR),[30] led principally by Vice President Al Gore.[31] The reinventors largely rejected the language of public choice, however, preferring instead the language of business schools. In the new "entrepreneurial management paradigm" the four new principles of government management were to be: (1) cast aside red tape; (2) put customers first; (3) decentralize authority; and (4) work better and cost less.[32]

The entrepreneurs view the legal distinctions between the government and private sectors as largely artificial, serving to hinder the implementation of contemporary business management practices. To their mind the future should be one of government-private partnerships functioning in almost all fields. The partnerships, ideally, will be largely autonomous bodies run by managers under contract to meet negotiated performance standards. Managers of the future will be risk takers who are willing to ignore the "unnecessary" rules, regulations, and control systems to get the job done right—and less expensively. There will be little need to change the laws, the goal being to change attitudes and behavior. The role of Congress, under the entrepreneurial model, will be minimized.[33] Empirical results, however defined, will be what counts, not legal processes and political accountability. The precedence of economically based values over legally based values is evident throughout the NPM literature.[34]

Emerging Quasi-Government

In recent years both Congress and the president have increasingly turned to hybrid organizations (e.g., Fannie Mae, the National Park Foundation, the Polish-American Enterprise Fund) to implement public policy and functions traditionally assigned to executive departments and agencies. There are today, associated with the federal government alone, literally hundreds of hybrid entities that have collectively come to be called the "quasi government."[35] The relationship of this burgeoning quasi-government to elected and appointed officials is of growing interest, and some concern, as it touches the heart of democratic governance: To whom are these hybrids accountable? How is the public interest being protected against the interest of private parties?

The truth is that the *quasi-government,* virtually by its name and the intentional blurring of its boundaries, is not definable in any precise way. In general the term describes those entities that have some legal relation or association, however tenuous, to the federal government. The one common aspect to this mélange of entities is that they are not agencies of the United States as that term is used in Title 5 of the U.S. Code. This distinction turns out to be critical because it determines which system of jurisprudence shall prevail in the governance of organizations. If an entity is an agency of the United States, it comes under public law. If the entity is not an agency of the United States, it comes under private law. The first task is to break down the many hybrid entities in the quasi-government into manageable categories about which legal and behavioral generalizations may be made. This taxonomy has been conducted elsewhere.[36]

The distinguishing element of the several organizational categories of the quasi-government is the commingling of the legal characteristics of the governmental and private sectors. It may be an implicit guarantee by the federal government of debt instruments or simply permission to use a logo implying governmental approval. In any case, to some degree the attributes of the sovereign are assigned to an otherwise private party.[37] The decision to create a quasi-governmental body is not politically neutral. Presumably, the private parties receive advantages not available to others. On the other hand, the private beneficiaries then become liable for reporting and supervision of their activities by the sovereign to protect it and the citizenry against abuse.

Even in situations in which abuse seems unlikely, it may still exist in subtle forms. Perception can become reality in the political world. The interests of the private and governmental sectors may appear at one level to be congruent or complementary while at another level to be in direct conflict. At the very least they are generally different interests. For instance, the federal government's interest in national security against espionage is likely to be greater than that of any one of its contractors engaged in operations. The federal government's concern for protecting the interest of taxpayers may be in conflict with the private shareholder interests in a government-sponsored enterprise (GSE), such as the Federal Home Loan Mortgage Corporation (Freddie Mac). Even in the most tenuous element of the quasi-government, congressionally chartered nonprofit organizations, the government's interests may be at odds with the interests of, say, the American Legion or the U.S. Olympic Committee.[38]

Government-Sponsored Enterprises Highlighted

Distinctions between the governmental and private sectors are especially blurred with respect to the category of organization known as government-sponsored enterprises.[39] For our purposes a GSE "is a privately owned, federally chartered financial institution with nationwide scope and spending powers that benefits from an implicit guarantee to enhance its ability to borrow money."[40] Congress created GSEs generally to help make credit more readily available to sectors of the economy believed to be disadvantaged in the credit markets.[41] Contemporary GSEs are part of a tradition of mercantilist financial institutions in that the government assigns them benefits and privileges in their charters not available to fully private corporations. In return the government is able to limit their activities and lines of business and require them to promote selected public policy objectives.

GSEs are highly controversial.[42] Defenders argue that GSEs meet national needs that would be met poorly or not at all by private corporations. They contend that the current GSEs are well managed, financially sound, and assist less-advantaged mortgage borrowers. They maintain that the subsidy that flows from the federally implied guarantee of GSE obligations is largely passed on to consumers in the form of lower mortgage rates. Critics contend, on the other hand, that the GSE concept is fundamentally flawed. With GSEs private parties are assigned attributes normally reserved to the sovereign, such as exemption from state taxation. Federal regulatory oversight is less stringent than that applied to similar private sector entities while the GSEs accumulate massive unfunded liabilities. GSEs, with their privileged and legally protected status, tend to develop into sector dominating enterprises with advantages to the corporate investor, especially since the GSEs are assumed to be protected from the risk of bankruptcy.[43] In 1996 the Congressional Budget Office conducted a study of GSEs and concluded: "The conduct of GSEs . . . is not scandalous or even anomalous. Rather it is entirely consistent with the management's obligation to protect the interest of the shareholders. The lawful, but unbridled, advance of shareholders interests at the expense of taxpayers, however, is an essential and inescapable consequence of the choice of GSEs as a means of delivering a federal subsidy to borrowers. It is part of the price of using GSEs as an instrument of public policy. Not least, it is a fact to be weighed in any decision to continue the practice or to end by privatizing Fannie Mae and Freddie Mac."[44]

There have been instances in which law provides that the president shall appoint members to the boards of otherwise private corporations, such as Fannie Mae and ComSat. The issue has been raised: To whom are these governmentally appointed board members accountable? Should they represent the administration that appointed them; the so-called public interest, however defined, even when it may be in conflict with the financial interests of the GSE shareholders; or the shareholders exclusively? It is worth noting that, even though the president may appoint such directors, they are not considered to be officers of the United States. As for the competing purposes of government directors, to represent the public interest, as distinguished from the corporation's private interests, clearly the latter choice has been persuasive. GSEs work to increase the identification of the government directors with the interests of the shareholders, rather than the public. In general, the practice of appointing governmental directors to private corporations has been viewed as unsuccessful.[45]

The accountability issue for GSEs, and for much of the quasi-government, involves the allocation of benefits and risks between private parties and the federal government and taxpayer. One observer, Harold Seidman, has remarked: "Intermingling of public and private purposes in a profit making corporation almost inevitably means subordination of public responsibilities to corporate goals. We run the danger of creating a system in which we privatize profits and socialize losses."[46]

Hybrid Organizations: Problem or Solution?

The number and variety of hybrid organizations commingling government and private sector characteristics is growing. Does this constitute a positive or negative factor in the performance of effective democratic governance? Should growth in the number be encouraged, benignly recognized, or actively resisted? The answers will be largely influenced by the inquirer's philosophy of public management.

There are two principal paradigms of government management, as previously noted, competing for the allegiance of the public management community. It is useful to refer to them as the *constitutionalist management paradigm* and the *entrepreneurial management paradigm.* Constitutionalists generally view the government and private sectors as distinct in character with the distinctions founded in law. The distinguishing characteristic of governmental management, contrasted with private management, is that government actions must have their basis in public law, not in the financial interests of private entrepreneurs or in the fiduciary concerns of nonprofit corporate managers. The hierarchical structure found in the executive branch is designed more to ensure accountability for managerial action; promoting control over employees is secondary. The value of accountability to political leadership and the importance of due process in decision making trumps the premium placed on performance and results. It is less a question of pursuing one value at the expense of the other, however, than it is a matter of precedence in the event of conflict.

Entrepreneurs, on the other hand, have as their underlying premise that the government and private sectors are fundamentally alike and subject to most of the same economically derived behavioral norms.[47] In the private sector the principal, if not exclusive, objective is results in the form of profits. Entrepreneurial management advocates argue that this standard should be applied to the government sector as well.

This shift toward results over legal process as the primary value in government management is a statement about political power as well as administrative management. Vice President Gore indicated as much in 1993 when he stated, "Chief Executive Officers—from the White House to agency heads—must ensure that everyone understands that power will never flow through the old channels again. That's how GE [General Electric] did it; that's how we must do it as well."[48]

Under the entrepreneurial management paradigm the vision is to create a society of government/private partnerships based on pragmatic application of performance-oriented objectives, or what Harlan Cleveland approvingly refers to as the "nobody-in-charge society."[49] Carried to its logical end, entrepreneurial management results in some remarkably anomalous situations. In 1998, for instance, the Central Intelligence Agency (CIA) established, without statutory authority, a domestic venture capital fund, "In-Q-Tel." The purpose of In-Q-Tel is to permit the CIA to invest in, and thereby encourage, corporations producing technology the agency will need to perform its mission in the future. Capitalized by $150 million in government funds, this nonprofit corporation is expected to be self-sufficient. On the board of directors are private corporate executives from firms such as Lockheed Martin and Xerox. In the words of Gilman Louis, In-Q-Tel's CEO: "The best thing about In-Q-It [*sic*], to me, is that it's risky. The CIA and the rest of the government need to catch the entrepreneurial, risk-taking spirit that's driving the Silicon Valley technology revolution. The CIA's new venture may fall flat, but so what. Washington has been a zero-defect culture too long. If we want a CIA that performs better, we'll need to take more risks—and give our government freedom to fail."[50]

A parallel set of entrepreneurial ideas, involving behavioral modification by federal government officers more than creating hybrid organizations, enjoys wide approval. The principal purpose of this behavioral modification strategy is to alter the management philosophy and reward/punishment mind-set of federal management and move it toward practices followed in the private sector. One reporter, in an article on "bureaucrats as businesspeople," notes: "Unbeknownst to most American taxpayers and to many federal employees, the government is growing its own businesses. Entrepreneurial outposts are taking root inside the federal agencies in the fertile soil of management reform, new purchasing rules, downsizing, and performance pressure. Government business people are shaking off the shackles of limited congressional appropriations and staving off job threats using money they earn selling services within their own and other agencies."[51]

A typical instance of the "business mind-set" being promoted by entrepreneurs involves the naval command at Patuxent Naval Air Station in Maryland. In the name of "profit" the command has contracted out its high-tech planes and personnel to the State of Maine to hunt for healthy blueberry patches. "With the defense budgets shrinking and more cuts threatened, military research labs and testing bases in the Washington area are aggressively seeking such business deals to help pay the bills and keep expensive facilities and equipment operating. Consultants are even training government program managers and engineers to think like copier salesmen and 'sell' their products."[52]

There can be a legitimate clash of opinion over whether it is wise, creative, or even legal for Patuxent to go entrepreneurial. Whether this initiative, like so many others, results, if not immediately then soon, in a perversion of the mission and character of government management should concern all who seek a healthy public sector. What may appear initially as a rather simple operational decision may, in fact, be a decision with considerable policy and legal implications.

Skeptics of the entrepreneurial vision of government management tend to see something disquieting emerging—a society in which the centrality of public law is being unwisely displaced by business axioms. The focus of management, once the citizen, is now the "customer." Departmental integration as the norm is being replaced by organizational dispersion, with managers institutionally insulated from credible political accountability. Under the entrepreneurial paradigm critics believe that the protective wall between the government and private sectors is being breached, not merely as a managerial convenience but as a philosophy of governance. Constitutionalists believe they see an antidemocratic bias in this new entrepreneurial society, unintended but inevitable.[53]

Governance Principles Retain Validity

The opening lines of this chapter asserted that the United States is unusual, if not unique, in the extent to which our national government is based upon a comprehensive and coherent political theory. The Constitution of 1787 is the source of legal authority for the organization and management of the federal government. The Constitution provides for, among other points, that ours shall be a government of separated and interdependent branches; that administrative functions shall be located within the executive branch and responsible to the president and through the latter accountable to Congress; and that the governmental and private sectors shall be kept separate and function under distinctive theories of jurisprudence.

These three main principles of governance have been neglected in recent years. This is especially true for the third and least understood, that the governmental and private sectors be kept separate and legally distinctive. It is very much in vogue, internationally even more so than in the United States, to dismiss the legally distinctive character of the governmental and private sectors as a dated concept that impedes the achievement of performance-based public management.

The author argues that the framers' intention that the governmental and private sectors be kept separate and subject to distinctive theories of jurisprudence retains its validity and persuasiveness. It makes a difference where a function cloaked with a public purpose is assigned. Notwithstanding an apparent public preference for the delivery of government services by private sector contractors, common understanding has it (and "official" policy agrees, as Dan Guttman explores in chap. 3) that the *core* functions of government should be carried out by government officials. There is a collective sense, generally, that such functions as the making of law binding on citizens, authoritative adjudication of disputes, control over elections for government office, the taking of private property without consent, the exercise of coercive force over others, and the denial of private rights on behalf of the state are, peculiarly, those that ought to be exercised solely by the state.[54]

The most fundamental difference between public and private law jurisprudence lies in the realm of presumptions. In the governmental sector the presumption is that the actions of an agency or officer must have their basis in public law. Silence in law is not permission to act. In the private sector, on the other hand, the reverse presumption holds sway. That is, private persons may act as they please unless there is a law prohibiting their actions. Officers operating under public law are held to a higher standard of behavior (e.g., they must follow constitutional due process) in their dealings with the public. The function performed by an agency, such as operating a railroad, does not determine to what sector it may be assigned. Nor can Congress provide in law that the constitutional basis of a federal agency be altered so that it becomes private.[55] The history of hybrid organizations in the United States attests to the soundness of maintaining legal distinctions between the sectors as a bedrock principle to protect the rights of citizens.

It is the view of the constitutionalists that the federal government is not (nor should it become) a loose collection of several hundred semiautonomous entities, officers, and quasi-private proxies, all seeking to establish their own missions, designating their own favorite customers (aka citizens), following their own management rules ("no red tape"), and defining their own standards of success. The problem is not that the public law governance principles have failed, thereby justifying their abandonment, but that they have succeeded so well that the crucial protections and advantages they provide are taken for granted and neglected. The principles of governance articulated here work, but the price for having them work well is high. New generations of public managers must be trained in the fundamentals of their field and not simply taught glib aphorisms from another and very different field to serve as ersatz theory.

Rather than continue the contemporary drift toward an ever deeper misunderstanding and active confusion of critical differences between governmental and private sector management, a far better course would be to recognize the particular strengths and responsibilities of each sector. The critical distinction between the sectors has been, and will continue to be, their relationship to the power of the sovereign. Federal government institutions are agents of the sovereign and function under public law. Private institutions are not agents of the sovereign and function under private law. Law-based principles of governance are not quaint proverbs, nor are they impediments to sound government management practices. To the contrary, they provide the necessary foundation for a growing and evolving administrative system within a democratic context.

CHAPTER THREE

Inherently Governmental Functions and the New Millennium

The Legacy of Twentieth-Century Reform

Dan Guttman

In his famous farewell address to the American public President Dwight D. Eisenhower warned of the damage to constitutional checks and balances wrought by the post–World War II emergence of the "military-industrial complex." In fact, the president's Bureau of the Budget had already taken notice that the federal government's Cold War reliance on third parties to perform the work of government called into question the ability of the civil service and political appointees to hold the work of government to account. In a long forgotten budget bureau circular (A-49), the bureau wrote the contemporary concept of "inherently governmental function" into governing policy—the notion that certain governmental activities must be performed by agencies and officials and cannot be delegated to nongovernmental actors.

The bureau's concerns, as explained years later by Harold Seidman, the bureau official who authored the circular, were not those of Platonists contemplating the ideal republic, nor were they those of antiquarians bent on preserving the perceived tradition of a golden age or scholastics intent on elevating taxonomic nitpicking to a cardinal principle of government. Rather, in the tradition of American pragmatism, bureau officials saw the practical import of the distinction between governmental and nongovernmental activities. "In the exercise of its sovereign powers," Seidman later observed, "the state is subject to a different body of law than that applicable to private individuals and, in a democratic society, held to different standards of behavior."[1] Where the people enacted rules to protect themselves against abuses by "Big Government," as, most saliently, in the United States Constitution, they enacted rules that deter or govern (mis)conduct by public agencies and officials.[2]

In 1992 the Office of Federal Procurement Policy (OFPP) issued a "policy letter" that restated the proposition that only officials can perform "inherently governmental" activities. In 1998 Congress placed the OFPP's restatement into law in the Federal Activity Inventory Reform (FAIR) Act.

At first blush these executive branch and congressional declarations might appear to represent the slow but steady transformation of midcentury Eisenhower administration concerns into sound and effective national policy. But the story is much more interesting, and its conclusion remains to be written.

The codification of the principle of inherently governmental functions into "public law" is coincident with its negation in practice. Since World War II bipartisan limits on the numbers of federal employees have, like a hydraulic force, caused the government to fuel its growth through reliance on third parties, often with limited regard for the inherently governmental principle.

The limits on federal personnel represented the bipartisan aspiration that Big Government could be tolerably grown through increased reliance on the private sector, bipartisan appreciation that third parties possess the political clout to help make Big Government grow, and bipartisan belief that the polity would indulge in the fiction that Big Government does not grow if the civil service does not. Today, as the Brookings Institution estimated in the late 1990s, the "shadow of government"—those employed under grants and contracts—is many times the size of the federal employee workforce.[3]

Paradoxically, just as it appears to have lost its last teeth, the concept of inherently governmental functions has taken on new life. Most fundamentally, the concept's reassertion as governing principle by Congress and the executive branch provides them with fig leaf to cloak, and permit these branches to avoid discussion of, the fundamental change in the structure of government.

At the turn of the millennium, however, the concept took on renewed meaning. On coming to office, the Bush administration announced that it would put out for "competitive outsourcing" civil service work—estimated at 850,000 jobs—which is "commercial" and not "inherently governmental" in nature. This pillar of the administration's management agenda has turned the definition of *inherently governmental* into a battleground for debate between contractors and federal employee advocates on the limits, if any, for the continued contracting out of the work of government.[4] Largely missing from the debate has been the essential practical concern long expressed in the initial budget bureau circular—that the value of the concept of "inherently governmental function" lies, to paraphrase Oliver Wendell Holmes, in the consequences of its use (or nonuse), and not in the concept's logic in the abstract or in the historical archives (though these may be relevant). The terrorist attacks of September 11, however, which sparked a renewed focus on the broad public interest in the operation of government programs, has again brought these practical questions to the fore.

Shaded by bipartisan and scholarly neglect, the laws and rules by which the new means of government can be held to account could hardly have been, and have not been, the subject of adequate public debate. The deficiency in scholarship and oversight does not mean, however, that the world does not go on. With or without public debate, the laws and rules to govern the "diffusion of sovereignty" are evolving.[5] By default they are developing on an ad hoc basis, often driven by third parties themselves—and with inadequate attention to the public interest at large. The question in the new millennium is whether they will continue to evolve by default or, consistent with the founding vision, benefit from "reflection and choice."[6]

The Emergence of the Inherently Governmental Concept

The mid-twentieth-century development of government by third party was not an accident but reflected a bipartisan design by reformers to grow the federal government while avoiding the perceived perils of enlarging the official bureaucracy.[7] Today's network of federal grant and contract relationships is based on a template established in the early twentieth century, when private philanthropists (such as Robert Brookings and the Rockefeller Foundation) created private research institutions (such as the Institute for Government Research, the Brookings Institution's progenitor) to serve as levers for the reform of the federal government (such as the 1921 passage of the Budgeting and Accounting Act, which created the modern budget bureau and congressional accounting offices).

The informal network of early-twentieth-century relationships—among private money and private expertise and public agency—was mobilized for the World War II effort. The research and development required for the war was, of course, immensely expensive, and private philanthropy could not foot the whole bill. Thus, what had begun as an informal set of relationships in which money flowed from the private sector to private experts, was transformed into a set of relationships defined, in primary part, by the government contract and grant. The success of the wartime grant- and contract-based relationships among government, industry, and university led to the determination to make them a permanent fixture of postwar America. When demobilized government researchers returned to the private sector, they continued to work on the taxpayer dollar, under contract and grant.[8] The postwar network in turn spawned new institutions: "independent nonprofits "(with RAND and Aerospace the prototypes) created to manage Cold War military research and development.

The military's postwar contracting out of weapons R&D and production was not mandated by law; indeed, the seminal text on postwar weapons contracting explained that "the preference for private enterprise conduct of U.S. weapons development and production work . . . is essentially an unwritten law, and, indeed, statutory references seem to contradict it."[9]

The Manhattan Engineer District, progenitor to today's Department of Energy, established the template for government by third party as the essential means of government, and not a mere adjunct to render services on a "temporary and intermittent basis." Following the core of the Manhattan Project's 1947 reconstitution as the Atomic Energy Commission, the weapons complex continued to perform its work fundamentally relying on contractors. Bureau of the Budget Circular A-49, which Seidman drafted in the 1950s, responded to the problems of official control posed by the sweeping delegation to "management and operating (M&O) contractors" of the management of the "government-owned contractor-operated" (GOCO) nuclear weapons facilities at Oak Ridge, Los Alamos, Hanford, and other weapons complex sites.

In 1980 Senator David Pryor's subcommittee on federal services sought to take the measure of decades of contracting out and found that the Department of Energy's 20,000 federal employees were a small fraction of the 100,000 to 200,000 employed on contract. The subcommittee found that "the reliance on contractors is so extreme that if the terms of its contracts, the resumes of its contractors and their employees, and the contractor work the department adopts as its own are to be believed, it is hard to understand what, if anything, is left for officials to do."[10]

In 1997 S. S. Hecker, director of the Los Alamos National Laboratory, expressed the reality of fidelity to the inherently governmental principle: "The development, construction, and life-cycle support of the nuclear weapons required during the Cold War were inherently governmental functions. However, the government realized that it could not enlist the necessary talent to do the job with its own civil-service employees. Instead, it enlisted contractors to perform the government's work on government land, in government facilities, using the specialized procurement vehicle of the management and operating (M&O) contract."[11]

If there were a public imprimatur for the new governing principle, it was the creation of the National Aeronautics and Space Administration (NASA), which marked the halfway house—the transfer of the military model to a quasi-civilian agency. NASA, created overnight through the transformation of the National Advisory Committee for Aeronautics (NACA), a small in-house research agency, was designed to depend on contractors for the bulk of its workforce. A court decision stemming from a reduction in force (RIF) of federal employees at the Marshall Space Center embodies the transition. The federal workers complained that "NASA was employing many technical service workers at Marshall supposedly as independent contractors, but actually with a degree of control by NASA and with other characteristics that made them functionally employees of the United States." The use of contractors, instead of federal employees, they complained, violated civil service laws, the NASA enabling act, and the union collective bargaining agreement.[12]

Indeed, there was apparent conflict within the NASA Enabling Act, which provided that federal employees would perform NASA's basic work, but capped their number and then broadly provided for the deployment of contractors. The Court of Appeals explained: "At the same time that Congress enacted the enabling act that compelled NASA to produce a mammoth research effort, 'the number of civil service personnel that could be hired was limited due to personnel ceilings imposed within the Federal Civil Service.' Thus, it is not surprising that support service contracts [were] a way of life at Marshall."

NASA, the court observed, "resorted to support service contracts as the alternative means of overcoming the civil service personnel ceilings." The court concluded that the enabling act's provision for contractors provided a "separate means, independent of [the federal employee provision] for performing NASA's functions."

The Reformers' Design

The writings of the public servants, businessmen, and scholars present at the creation show that the post–World War II growth of the contract bureaucracy was the product of design, not bureaucratic happenstance. At the dawn of the Cold War reformers believed that the harnessing of private enterprise to public purpose would serve two complementary purposes. First, the private sector would provide both technical expertise and powerful political support for increased federal commitment to national defense and public welfare tasks. Second, the private bureaucracy would countervail against the dead hand of the official bureaucracy and alleviate concern that a growing government meant a centralized Big Government. The officials, consultants, and scholars saw themselves as engaged in reforms of profound, even constitutional, dimensions.

In his 1965 classic *The Scientific Estate* public policy scholar Don Price, first dean of Harvard's John F. Kennedy School of Government, described the transformational import of the "fusion of economic and social power" and the "diffusion of sovereignty": "the general effect of this new system is clear; the fusion of economic and political power has been accompanied by the diffusion of sovereignty. This has destroyed the notion that the future growth of the functions and expenditures of governments . . . would necessarily take the form of a vast bureaucracy."[13]

This basic and benign reconstitution of government, marveled John Corson, a New Deal civil servant who, in the mid-twentieth century, opened the blue chip management consulting firm McKinsey's Washington office, took place with "little awareness." Corson began his 1971 book *Business in the Humane Society:* "There is little awareness of the extent to which traditional institutions, business, government, and universities and others, have been adapted and knit together in a politico-economic system which differs conspicuously from the conventional pattern of our past."[14] Postwar contracting, Corson proclaimed, was a "new form of federalism" under which the federal government gets its work done by private enterprise.[15]

It was left to President Dwight D. Eisenhower, in his famed farewell address, to provide another portrait of the implications of developments: "The conjunction of an immense military establishment and a large arms industry is new in the American experience. The total influence, economic, political, and even spiritual, is felt in every city, every state house, every office of the Federal government. We recognize the imperative of this development. Yet we must not fail to comprehend its implications. . . . In the councils of government, we must guard against the acquisition of unwarranted influence . . . by the military-industrial complex."[16]

The Bell Report

The high-water mark of the dialogue between those who viewed the basic changes in the structure of government with alarm and those who applauded them lies in the 1962 report of a cabinet-level panel convened by President John F. Kennedy, directed by budget bureau director David Bell and staffed by Harold Seidman. The panel was to consider the contracting out of military research and development.[17]

The "Bell report" addressed the "highly complex partnership among various kinds of public and private agencies related in large part by contractual arrangements." The panel found that "the developments of recent years have inevitably blurred the traditional dividing lines between the public and private sectors of our Nation."

The panel put its finger on the two characteristics of the new developments which were most troubling then—and are even more so today. First, the rules enacted to protect citizens against abuse by public servants did not, in important respects, apply to contractors or their employees. In particular, the Bell report noted that pay caps on federal employees did not apply to contractors and that conflict of interest rules that governed federal employees did not apply to contractors or their employees.[18] The conflict of interest rules applicable to federal employees did not apply to contractors and their employees on the presumption that they will be overseen by competent officials, who themselves are conflict free.[19]

Second, the panel neatly laid out the seductive psychology that undergirded the new system—-short-term rationality but possibly long-term irrationality. From the vantage of politicians and officials the choice of contractors to perform new missions made sense; they could be deployed quickly, brought new political support to programs, and, in theory, could be disposed of when no longer needed. In the short run the employment of contractors to serve vital

Cold War needs seemed undeniably reasonable. The panel perceived, however, that the "cumulative" effects of contracting could be debilitating. The salaries of contractor employees were not capped, and their work was increasingly more interesting than that performed in-house. Because differing rules applied to federal employees and contractors, there would be, over time, a tendency for the intelligence of government to migrate from the official workforce into the third-party workforce—thus further eroding the capability of the official workforce to control the third-party workforce. Over the long run the intelligence of government needed to control contractors might only be found within the contractors themselves. The danger was compounded because of the qualitative difference in the interests of contractors as well as the rules governing those interests.

The report portentously declared the emergence of "profound questions affecting the structure of our society [due to] our inability to apply the classical distinctions between what is public and what is private." Most pointedly, the panel expressed concern that officials would lose control to contractors, particularly where contractors were performing "the type of management functions which the government itself should perform."

The Bell panel deemed it "axiomatic" that certain "functions" can only be performed by officials:

> There are certain [research and development] functions which should under no circumstances be contracted out. The management and control of the Federal research and development effort must be firmly in the hands of full-time government officials clearly responsible to the President and the Congress. We regard it as axiomatic that policy decisions . . . must be made by full-time Government officials clearly responsible to the President and the Congress. Furthermore, such officials must be in a position to supervise the execution of work undertaken, and to evaluate the results. These are basic functions of management which cannot be transferred to any contractor if we are to have proper accountability for performance of public functions and for the use of public funds.

The Bell panel emphasized that the test for government control is one of substance, not form. "There must be sufficient technical competence within the Government so that outside technical advice does not become defacto technical decisionmaking." In the end, however, even as the report described the problematic nature of the "blurring of public and private" with acuity, it begged the "philosophical" questions this situation raised. Having laid out the problems and their import, the Bell report backed away from the abyss. The Cold War was no time to address such fundamental issues of governance. Instead, the task was to learn the best uses of the panoply of new institutional tools—profits, independent nonprofits, universities, and in-house research groups—at hand.

The 1960s and 1970s: Government by Third Party on Automatic Pilot

Following the Bell report's go-ahead, third-party government grew as if on automatic pilot. The contracting out of military, atomic energy, and space programs was, of course, hardly a secret. The growth of third-party bureaucracies as appendages to new "civilian agencies" (such as the Departments of Transportation, Housing and Urban Development, the Office of Economic Opportunity, and the U.S. Environmental Protection Agency [EPA]) was less visible but no less pervasive. Driven by the force of bipartisan limits on the number of federal employees ("personnel ceilings"), those directing new agencies and programs had no recourse but to call on third parties to do the work of government. As in the case of the Cold War agencies, the promoters of third-party government viewed third parties as purveyors of new management techniques but also as tools in the politics of bureaucratic reform. The reformers claimed that social problems could be solved if "institutional obstacles" to change were overcome.[20]

From another perspective, however, government by third party was not a benign reform effort to control Big Government bureaucracies but a veneer for politics as usual. The "Nixon Personnel Manual," unearthed by Congress during the Watergate hearings, mused:

> In 1966, Johnson offered legislation, which Congress passed, [which] required the Executive Branch . . . to reduce itself in size to the level of employment in fact existing in 1964. The cosmetic public theory . . . was that . . . a personnel ceiling for the Executive Branch would first cut, and then stabilize, Federal expenditures connected with personnel costs. . . . What the Johnson Administration did after passage . . . was to see to it that "friendly" consulting firms began to spring up, founded and staffed by many former Johnson and Kennedy Administration

employees. They then received fat contracts to perform functions previously performed within the Government by the federal employees. The commercial costs, naturally, exceeded the personnel costs they replaced.[21]

Privatizers, Downsizers, and Reinventors

In the 1980s and 1990s smaller government gained popular support around the globe. Citizens, however, generally wanted no diminution in governmental functions. To address this inconsistency, strategies for the reform of governance took hold: reinventing government, public-private partnerships, devolution, privatization, deregulation, the third way, to name a few. These strategies sought to make government more responsive and efficient by engaging nongovernmental actors in its functions.

At the level of the federal government of the United States, the reforms were forwarded with passing regard, if any, for the fact that what they proposed had, in fact, long since taken place. Thus, after identifying the "new" mechanisms for delivery of social services that form the core of "Reinventing Government" (REGO), David Osborne and Ted Gaebler note that, "surprisingly," the federal government had already deployed many of these innovations.[22]

Advocates of new governance strategies acknowledged, even boasted, that application of their regimen would "blur" conventional boundaries. Counseling that officials "steer" and nongovernmental actors "row," the authors of *Reinventing Government* (1992) further urged that innovation not be held back by "outdated mindsets." "We could do well," they quoted public administration scholar Harlan Cleveland approvingly, "to glory in the blurring of public and private and not keep trying to draw a disappearing line in the water."[23] Upon taking office, the Clinton administration brought REGO front and center, declaring that the initial commitment of the reinvention effort would be the reduction of the federal workforce by 300,000 employees.

In the new millennium globalization provides another new frontier for third-party governance—foreign policy. In 1998 the United States contracted out the administration of the nuclear nonproliferation agreement under which the United States purchases Russia's nuclear weapons–grade uranium—placing national security in the hands of a private entity whose legitimate profit-making interests are in obvious potential conflict with those declared by the Congress of the United States in providing for the privatization.

The Clinton administration also called on a nongovernmental entity (Harvard's Institute for International Development) to manage U.S. funds for the restructuring of the Russian state and economy. The now well-publicized failings of these efforts showcased the discrepancy between American readiness to deploy third parties as agents of foreign policy and American ability to deploy the means of accounting for them.[24]

The Bush Administration Stays the Course

Whatever its differences with the Clinton administration, the Bush administration quickly and decisively chose to follow it in pursuing the bipartisan reform tradition as centerpiece of its public management agenda. It did so through the "outsourcing" component of its "Management Agenda" and also through its "Faith-Based Initiative." On assuming office, the administration announced that it would call on religious organizations to provide social welfare services, under contract or grant. The Faith-Based Initiative was immediately controversial, with opponents arguing that the provision of public funds to religious organizations would violate constitutional traditions requiring "separation of church and state." While the church versus state controversy has been the primary focus of public attention, less attention has been paid to the perspective that, when viewed from the vantage of the story told here—the effort to grow government through the use of third parties—the Bush proposal is true to a bipartisan reform tradition. Contractors and grantees had long since been deployed by federal and local agencies to provide social welfare. The Bush proposal was nothing new in this regard; rather, the administration explained, it was seeking to deploy the kind of third party that, in the administration's view, could best perform the tasks at hand.

Even as it has focused on church versus state questions, the debate over the Faith-Based Initiative highlights the continuing tensions underlying the bipartisan tradition of reform through third-party government. Supporters of the initiative state that the use of religious organizations will bring better management and better results to the program; in doing so, however, they have strongly questioned the historic accountability of third parties' performance of these services.[25] Opponents of the initiative, for their part, have argued that the initiative should not be seen as a reform but, rather, as another form of political patronage (i.e., it will provide grants and contracts to a favored [Republican] party constituency). This skeptical perspective on third-party government as a reform, as we have seen, may have been first voiced by a Republican administration.

The Bush administration's Management Agenda, directed by the Office of Management and Budget (OMB), "grades" agencies annually on their performance of "management objectives" set by the administration. A central objective is the requirement that agencies provide for "competitive outsourcing" of civil service jobs that are not "inherently governmental"—that is, which are appropriately performed by nongovernmental sources.[26]

In contrast to Reinventing Government—which began with a promise to cut hundreds of thousands of civil service jobs—the Bush administration refrained from declaring that civil service jobs must be eliminated. Rather, the Management Agenda provides that civil servants may themselves compete with third parties to win contracts, with "the best man to win." Management Agenda proponents explain that their goal will be met if the incumbent workforce (i.e., the civil service) is subjected to the discipline of competition.

The Bush administration's determination to avoid calling for "cuts" in the civil service may reflect learning from the bipartisan criticism of "arbitrary" civil service cuts announced at the onset of the Clinton administration's Reinventing Government plan. Nonetheless, the Management Agenda's approach does not confront the actuality that, even in national security areas, civil service oversight capability may already be inadequate to oversee the contractor workforce.

For example, the nuclear weapons complex, the core of the Department of Energy, has always been managed and operated by contractors. Congress and the executive branch have long recognized that the Department of Energy (DOE) lacks the in-house workforce needed to supervise and control the contractors. At the beginning of the Clinton administration Energy Secretary Hazel O'Leary told Congress that the department lacked the capacity to control its contractors and promised "contract reform." By the end of the administration two generations of contract reform had proven unsuccessful. Nonetheless, in this key national security area the Bush Management Agenda may further cut into an official workforce that has long been deemed inadequate to oversee the contractor workforce.[27]

In 2001 DOE reported that it had 14,700 employees (civil servants and officials), and over 100,000 contractor employees; 44 percent of the official workforce was over fifty, and nearing retirement. Under the FAIR Act requirements (i.e., that each agency identify "commercial" jobs that may be contracted out), 9,889 official jobs have been deemed eligible for outsourcing. In brief an agency that could not manage the (100,000-plus) contractor workforce with 15,000 officials may soon be called on to manage an even greater number of contractor employees with a less experienced workforce of perhaps 10,000 employees or less.[28]

Similarly, in October 2002 the secretary of the army announced that the army will permit private contractors to compete for "noncore" positions, including those now held by 154,910 civilian workers—more than half of the army's civilian workforce—and 58,727 military personnel.[29] Not surprisingly, this effort comes on top of years of "downsizing" and "outsourcing," the consequences of which, by the army's own admission, remain unexamined. In a March 2002 memo to the defense department management hierarchy, Army Secretary White explained: "In the past eleven years, the Army has significantly reduced its civilian and military work force. These reductions were accomplished by an expanded reliance on contractor support without a comparable analysis of whether contractor support services should also be downsized. Currently, Army planners and programmers lack visibility at the Departmental level into the labor and costs associated with the contractor workforce and of the organizations and missions supported by them."[30]

In sum, the Bush initiatives, like the Clinton era reforms, further highlighted tensions and fault lines within the long-standing bipartisan design to grow government through third parties without assurance that the remaining official workforce retains oversight capability.

Homeland Security and the New Nation Building

Particularly when coupled with the Bush administration's November 2002 (postelection) reassertion of its outsourcing goals,[31] post–September 11 developments provide a critical occasion for refocusing on the unanswered questions that are a legacy of past reform.

First, post-9–11 developments have highlighted the practical importance of the differing sets of rules governing officials and third parties who perform the work of government. When airport baggage checkers are officials, their conduct is limited by the Constitution; when they were contract employees, this was not, or at least was less likely to be, the case.

Second, as the baggage checker example illustrates, recent developments also underscore that the notion of inherently governmental function does not fully capture the questions we want to answer when we ask, "Who should do the work of government?" Baggage checking is not an inherently governmental function; indeed, prior to September 11 airport baggage checking was routinely not performed by officials. Nonetheless, from the vantage of constitutional protections, it makes a difference whether the individuals performing that work are officials or third parties. In short, post–September 11 public concerns suggest that the question is not simply "What functions are inherently governmental?" but, also "What other functions do we wish to see performed by officials because, for example, they will then be governed by the body of laws that apply to officials?"

Third, new homeland security activities raise novel questions about the protection of citizens where third parties are relied on to perform work that, if performed by officials, would be the subject of long-standing constitutional and statutory limitations. In late 2002, for example, public controversy developed about the defense department's "Total Information Awareness" program, a high-technology effort to mine and organize personal data. The controversy focused on the potential role of the government as "Big Brother." In fact, it appears that the bulk of the program's activities are not being performed by government at all but by contractors deployed by a small official oversight team. While the activities of the officials would be limited by constitutional and statutory requirements, relevant limitations—-such as those in the Bill of Rights—are not likely applicable to contractors. Moreover, from available public information it was not clear how, if at all, the government had restricted the contractors' use (e.g., for commercial and/or foreign clients) of the surveillance techniques and methods developed under the auspices of the official antiterrorism program.[32]

Fourth, and on what might be called the other side of the coin, the increasing role of third parties in homeland security and "nation building" raises questions about the legal status of third parties when their own interests or rights are at issue. The mid-twentieth-century reform chronicled here included fundamental reliance on third parties to serve as the workforce for foreign aid programs. The U.S. Agency for International Development (USAID), for example, has always depended on third parties to administer its programs abroad. At the end of the Cold War, as noted earlier, contractors were deployed to restructure Russia and other former Soviet bloc countries. Nonetheless, recent military interventions and subsequent peacekeeping and nation building—as has taken place in the Balkans and Afghanistan and may take place elsewhere—raise questions that, if not unprecedented, remain to be addressed. For example, are third parties engaged in these efforts entitled to the public law protections given "state actors" (including officials and members of the military), or is their legal status solely or primarily that of private actors? There has been little public examination of the increasing practical import of third-party status and the way in which answers to such questions might or should effect deployment of third parties.[33]

Finally, and perhaps hardest to assess, is the effect of September 11 on catalyzing and accelerating changes in the rules governing the civil service which may render it more like the third-party workforce. These changes include both the increase in the number of specialized sets of rules to govern particular workforces, such as those governing the status of the thousands of newly hired federal baggage inspectors, and wholesale changes in civil services rules in the name of efficiency, performance, and/or national security, as may be undertaken in the Department of Homeland Security.

In sum, post–September 11 developments suggest that the blurring of the boundaries between the official and third-party workforces will continue apace, punctuating the continued relevance of the questions of official control and public accountability which are implicit in the notion of inherently governmental function.

The Inherently Governmental Concept Redux

The program of blurring of the boundary between public and private was, as has been discussed, aided by the absence of clarity about just where the boundary lies. In the abstract the definition of *inherently governmental* can be cast in terms of subject matter (e.g., national defense, taxation) or function (e.g., budgeting, rule writing, without regard to the sanctity of the subject). In either case there is the further question about whether the test is one of substance or form—is the public interest satisfied if an official signs a contractor drafted rule, without regard to whether he or she read it prior to blessing it with the imprimatur of officialdom?

The Constitution is a constitution and not a tax code, and it cannot be expected to provide a comprehensive taxonomy of inherently governmental functions. It might be supposed that two centuries of Supreme Court jurisprudence would provide some explication of the concept. But this is not the case.

In its 1978 decision in *Flagg Bros. v. Brooks,* a Supreme Court majority found that in all of our history only two activities—elections and the police activities of company towns—could be termed "exclusive public functions."[34] The majority noted that "the Court has never considered the private exercise of police functions."[35] (A more recent decision, discussed later, finds, however, that the enforcement of the "public interest" is an exclusively governmental function.)

The inherently governmental concept was, for practical purposes, either dead or in hibernation when, in 1989, Senator David Pryor, following upon his investigations into the role of contractors in the performance of the work of government, sought to test its vital signs. The senator asked the comptroller general whether the inherently governmental principle was violated in cases in which: (1) the Department of Energy (DOE) relies on contract hearing examiners to review security clearance determinations; (2) DOE relies on a contractor to prepare congressional testimony (including that given by the secretary of energy); (3) EPA contracts out its "Superfund Hot-line," through which members of the public can learn how to comply with the law.

The uses of contractors identified by the senator sharply raised the question of whether the inherently governmental test (when viewed as a test related to the exercise of governmental authority without necessary regard to the subject area) was one of form or substance. If a cabinet secretary signs a document he or she has not read, does it make a difference whether officials or third parties drafted the document?

In a December 1989 response to the senator, the General Accounting Office (GAO) declared the test to be one of substance, not form. It is not enough for an official to rubberstamp contractor work product. "Our decisions and the policy established by OMB Circulars," the comptroller general stated, "are based on the degree of discretion and value judgment exercised in the process of making a decision for the government." DOE's argument that the secretary could review the decisions of the (contractor) hearing examiner was not persuasive, nor was the fact that the secretary of energy, and not the contractor, appeared before Congress to read the secretary's testimony.[36]

Shortly thereafter, again in response to the senator's inquiries, the GAO undertook to define the concept of inherently governmental function, surveying precedent and expertise. Following a survey of experts, literature, and precedent, the GAO brought forth a mouse. In 1991 the comptroller general reported that "GAO's review of historical documents, relevant books and articles, prior GAO work, applicable laws, government policy, and federal court cases showed that the concept of inherently governmental functions is difficult to define."[37] Following the GAO report, in 1992 the Office of Federal Procurement Policy (OFPP) issued a policy letter to explicate the concept (OFPP 92–1). The policy letter was, in turn, reinforced by its inclusion in the Federal Activities Inventory Reform Act of 1998.[38] In May 2003 the Office of Management and Budget issued a revision of Circular A-76 (which has long provided for contracting out of "commercial" activities) which reaffirmed the inherently governmental principle, while modifying its particulars.[39]

Reconstituting the Federal Government: Meshing Public Law and Public Reality

In today's America it is probable that any nongovernmental entity that performs the work of government will, in some manner, be the object of laws and rules generally applicable to those that serve or deal with the public. The question posed by the reconstitution of the federal government is whether, and to what extent, these nongovernmental entities should also be subject to rules enacted to constrain those who had been presumed to perform inherently governmental functions—that is, agencies and officials.

In chapter 2 of this book and elsewhere, Ronald C. Moe points out that an important failure of the late-twentieth-century federal government is the failure to recognize the continued relevance of the public law tradition and the substitution of the illusion that the modern managerial tradition renders the public law tradition irrelevant. The story sketched here suggests that the situation may be described not so much as the abandonment of the public law tradition but as the failure to recognize that today's governing process is not that which the tradition contemplated. The question is how the tradition can be put to use to address today's reality. This question, as discussed, has been the subject of scant congressional and/or executive branch consideration, much less informed public discussion.

There are several alternative paths of development, which are not mutually exclusive. It would be useful to lay them out briefly.

The Default Option: Muddling Through

In the absence of congressional and executive branch attention, new rules have, in fact, been evolving to govern the diffusion of sovereignty.[40] The default system has virtues—it works sporadically, and the new rules can be discerned through diligent inquiry. But it is suboptimal—it favors "accident and force" over "reflection and choice."

The Salient Characteristics of the Default System

The salient characteristics of the new rule-making process are:

1. Third-party governance rules are developed on an ad hoc basis; third parties themselves drive rule making, with courts playing an important default role.
2. The rules do not preclude private actors from performing governmental functions but oblige those who do so to follow selected rules of the kind that impose constraints on officials in similar settings.
3. The new rules reflect the interests of the third parties that call for them but not necessarily the interest of the public at large. There is no assurance that the larger public interest will be served.
4. There is a tension inherent in the reliance on third parties; the design to call on private actors runs the risk of governmentalizing them and thereby negating the initial logic behind their deployment. Third parties are employed because they are said to differ qualitatively from civil servants (e.g., they are entrepreneurial and flexible, whereas civil servants are risk averse and hidebound). Rules that render private parties accountable to public purposes may alter the qualities that made them desirable. (By the same token, the drive to make the civil service more "entrepreneurial," "customer responsive," and "businesslike" may dilute or negate the qualities valued in the civil service *ab initio*.)

The Default System's Suboptimization of the Public Interest

The vices and virtues of the default rule making can be seen at work in the application of notions of conflict of interest and openness to the third-party bureaucracy. The concept of "organizational conflict of interest" (the term for the conflict of interest rules applied to contractors) emerged at midcentury when aerospace manufacturers complained that the location of the initial Project RAND contract within a competitor (Douglas Aircraft) was unfair, arguing that RAND might recommend hardware projects that Douglas would bid on. To resolve the conflict of interest concerns, the RAND contract was spun out of Douglas into a new nonprofit organization.[41] Following a similar episode in the management of the intercontinental ballistic missile (ICBM) program (which resulted in the creation of Aerospace, another nonprofit company, to manage the program), the organizational conflict of interest concept crystallized in the notion of the "hardware ban"—"think" contractors could not be affiliated with entities in the running for the lucrative hardware contracts that flowed from their thoughts.[42] The essential problem with the organizational conflict of interest concept was that it protected the interests of competing contractors but did little to protect the interest of the public at large. To the contrary, as the Bell report noted, the governing boards of the new nonprofits made them intellectual holding companies for the contractor establishment at large. It was not until the late 1970s that the notion of a public interest—an interest independent of that of the contractor establishment at large—came into being.[43]

In the case of public access to contractor-maintained data, courts have repeatedly held that the Freedom of Information Act (FOIA) does not apply to (taxpayer-funded) records maintained by contractors, because they are not agencies (as required by the act). In doing so, the courts acknowledge that nongovernmental entities are, in fact, making governmental decisions.[44] It was not until 1998, following protest by powerful components of American industry that they lacked access to data underlying proposed EPA rules, that FOIA was amended to provide for access to grantee-produced data underlying proposed regulations.[45] Even so, the rule applies to some kinds of third parties but not others.

A similar suboptimization is evident where rule making requires intervention by the courts. Federal courts necessarily proceed based on the cases before them, but in setting rules for the diffused sovereignty they are further handicapped because prevailing official fictions (e.g., the presumption that only officials perform inherently governmental functions) precludes the realistic testing of the precedential implications of the decision at hand.

The landmark decision in *Lebron v. National Railroad Passengers Corporation*, 513 U.S. 374 (1995), illustrates the vices and virtues of the default judicial role. Whereas *Flagg Brothers* showed that the Court is loathe to find many "exclusively public" functions, *Lebron* showed that the Court will look beyond form to substance where the applicability of the Constitution to a twilight zone entity is at issue.[46]

The good news is that the *Lebron* decision shows a Court willing to look beyond form to the substantial location of governmental responsibility. The more troubling news is that ad hoc judicial enactment of the rules to govern third parties who perform governmental functions may yield an incoherent set of rules. Thus, in 1996 the Supreme Court majority found that contractors are functionally identical to officials and, therefore, should be entitled to the same First Amendment protections as officials; in 1997, however, the majority found that contractors are subject to market discipline and are therefore qualitatively different from officials and should not be the beneficiaries of limited official immunity from suit.[47]

Finally, there is the question of whether the ad hoc development of rules will provide adequate attention to the possibility that such rules will dilute or negate the distinct organizational qualities for which third parties are valued. Thus, in denying citizens Freedom of Information Act access to admittedly decisional data maintained by universities and other nonprofits, courts repeatedly cited the congressional determination that the imposition of these constraints on such institutions would dilute the autonomous qualities that made them desirable sources of expertise.[48] Following the enactment of the Shelby amendment, hundreds, perhaps thousands, of nonprofits complained to OMB that this would be the effect of the law. The current debate on federal funding of faith-based organizations has raised similar concerns about the "governmentalization" of these organizations.

The periodic *ad hoc* debates that attend propositions such as that embodied in the Shelby amendment and in the current discussion of funding of faith-based groups are necessary, but not sufficient, to address the common recurring questions they raise.

The Truth in Government Option: Viewing the Workforce as a Whole

The most immediate alternative to the current "default" rule-making process is self-evident; the executive branch and Congress should view the federal workforce as a whole. This would require abandonment of the fiction that government equates to the official workforce. While the outcome of this effort cannot, and should not, be predicted, the initial steps seem clear:

1. Periodic reviews of federal personnel and procurement policy can no longer be "stovepiped," as if there were no relationship between the integrity of the federal workforce and the utility of the contractor

workforce. The recent congressionally mandated blue-ribbon review of A-76 Policy provided opportunity for a breakthrough on this count but, unfortunately, resulted in a reaffirmation of the inherently governmental principle without examining the discrepancy between rhetoric and reality.[49]

2. The third-party workforce must be rendered visible—to Congress, officials, and the public. Federal budgets, organization charts, and agency directories provide details on the federal workforce; there is no such detail on the third-party workforce, even where it works in federal buildings and even where it outnumbers officials. Inside agencies, as well as in transmissions to Congress and the public, third party–prepared materials are presented as if they were the handiwork of officials.

3. There must be public review and comparison of the differing rules that apply to federal employees and to nongovernmental actors in the performance of the government's work. The rules to be reviewed would include those governing ethics, pay, political activity, and transparency.

A Revived Public Law Tradition

Whether the country continues to muddle through or steps back to look at the big picture, the legal fiction of "government regularity" has inhibited the deployment of traditional legal principles to order the performance of public purposes by private actors. If it is assumed that third parties do not exist and/or do not have de facto responsibility for public purposes, there is little reason to invoke the tradition.

Our legal tradition has long recognized that private actors may perform public purposes. This, for example, is the common law premise of modern public utility regulation.[50] This tradition includes concepts such as the (non)delegation doctrine, government instrumentality, and "business affected with a public interest." It also includes experience in translating publicly derived obligations to private actors.

(Non)Delegation and Government Instrumentality Concepts

A priori, the (non)delegation doctrine would seem to lend itself to application to government by a third party. Analytically, there appear to be three relevant strands of the doctrine. As a manifestation of the constitutional separation of powers principle, the application of the doctrine to nongovernmental actors should be a direct derivative of its application to their official clients. (If an agency cannot perform an activity, then the agency's contractor cannot perform the activity.) As a manifestation of the principle that the sovereign cannot alienate authority outside of itself,[51] delegations of authority to private parties have been upheld—at least in the absence to a challenge to the presumption of regularity concerning official oversight.[52] When viewed as a due process doctrine, however, the attenuation of accountability involved in third-party government may render third parties subject to distinct treatment.[53]

In contrast to the delegation doctrine, the concept of government instrumentality (and that of business affected with a public interest) provides for the attribution of sovereign status to nongovernmental entities. The concept is used in many statutes and has been the subject of numerous court decisions. Historically, government contractors have not been deemed "government instrumentalities." As the Supreme Court's decision in *Lebron* indicates, however, where fact patterns merit it, the courts may be prepared to find effective instrumentality status.[54]

The Common Law Translation of Publicly Derived Obligations to Private Actors

The common law tradition has provided for the vindication of public rights against private actors where such rights would exist against creatures of government. The Supreme Court's 1876 decision in *Munn v. Illinois,* the fount of twentieth-century public utility regulation, is an elemental example of this translation. Both the Court majority and minority agreed that the common law tradition provided for state regulation of monopolies. The question that divided the Court was whether the state could regulate a monopoly in cases in which, as the Munn brothers' grain warehouse, it grew without benefit of charter from the king. Both majority and minority searched the (preconstitutional) British common law for the answer to the question. The majority found that the tradition provided that the police power could, indeed, be exercised to constrain businesses affected with a public interest—even where the business did not owe its monopoly to state charter.[55]

The Court's seminal explication of the "rule of reason," in Section 2 of the

Sherman Act,[56] provides a bookend to *Munn*. "Monopoly" law, Justice Edward Douglas White explained, was initially directed at injuries from abuse of power engaged in by king-chartered grants of exclusive right (e.g., to operate the only inn on the king's highway). But there came to be recognition that the injurious consequences of monopoly could arise no less where monopoly developed absent state charter. "In other words," White observed, "practical commonsense caused attention to be concentrated not upon the theoretically correct name to be given the condition or acts which gave rise to the harmful result, but to the result itself, and to the remedying of the evils which it produced." The method applied by the Court in *Munn* and *Standard Oil* resonates with the Seidman perspective on inherently governmental functions— the question is not that of defining an actor as public (or governmental) or private but that of focusing on the consequences of the definition in view of the actor's role and the constraints on that role.

Third-Party Enforcement of the Public Interest: A Special Case of Translation

In public utility regulation it is the government that regulates the nongovernmental actor, on the premise that the private actor is, as the *Munn* decision provided, a "business affected with a public interest." In antitrust law private actors may act to enforce the law, but they act on their own behalf and interests. Under a further tradition, "*qui tam*," private actors may act in the name of the sovereign to vindicate the sovereign's interest. Recent Supreme Court treatment of the Federal False Claims Act shows the Court employing what might be called the translation process in its effort to provide rationale for this centuries-old tradition.

In *Lujan v. Defenders of Wildlife*, 504 U.S. 555 (1992), Justice Antonin Scalia (for the majority) found that, in the absence of the constitutionally required injury to individual interest, Congress did not have the authority to give private citizens the right (i.e., "standing") to vindicate the public interest. In deciding the case, Justice Scalia essentially found: (1) that there is such a thing as the public interest; and (2) that its enforcement is an exclusively, or inherently, governmental function. At the same time, however, Justice Scalia explained how the performance of this inherently governmental function can be effectively transferred into private hands.

Scalia explained that "vindicating the public interest (including the public interest in Government observance of the Constitution and its laws) is the function of Congress and the Chief Executive—and not private parties." How, then, account for the constitutionality of "bounty hunter" laws? In permitting private actors to sue in the name of the United States under a bounty hunter statute, such as the Federal False Claims Act, Justice Scalia explained, "Congress has created a concrete private interest in the outcome of a suit against a private party for the government's benefit, by providing a cash bounty for the victorious plaintiff."

In May 2000, in *Vermont Agency of Natural Resources v. United States*, the Supreme Court upheld the constitutionality of the False Claims Act against a renewed challenge. Justice Scalia, again for the majority, noting centuries of experience with such laws, explained that whistleblowers have standing as assignees of the government's claims. Thus, it appears that even as the Court concluded (through Justice Scalia in *Lujan*) that "the vindication of the public interest" is what might be called "an inherently governmental function," this function can be translated through the device of the contract to a private party. The Court left for another day an explication of the permissible bounds of third-party law enforcement in the name of the public interest.

Finally, the common law of contract may provide further means for translation of public obligations to private actors. The common law provides for the enforcement of contracts by third parties (i.e., nonsignators) who are beneficiaries to the contract (e.g., the beneficiary of a trust agreement). The application of this principle to government contracts has been limited by courts on the reasonable premise that, since the public at large (or some substantial portion of it) is the beneficiary of public contracts, the deployment of contractors could be ground to a halt if suits were freely permitted.[57] The traditional hesitance to permit third-party suits may depend, however, on the validity of the presumption of regularity—that is, the presumption that government officials can and do protect the interest of the public at large in the administration of the contract. Where the facts show that this presumption is inappropriate, courts may be more ready to permit third-party beneficiary claims. Thus, in *Oil, Chemical and Atomic Workers International Union v. Richardson*,[58] the U.S. Court of Appeals suggested that a third-party claimant lacking standing to make a claim under a statute or the Administrative Procedure Act may nonetheless have a day in court under claim that it is a

third-party beneficiary of a contract entered into by the government to effec-
tuate the statute.

Conclusion: Due Diligence on the Legacy of Twentieth-Century Reform Is in Order

As we proceed with the post–September 11 reexamination of government, it
is time to address the difficult questions raised, but not answered, by
mid-twentieth-century reform. Components of due diligence include:

— Truth in Government: Who's Doing the Work of Government? In reviewing and authorizing programs, who is the workforce, and how will
  we make sure it is visible to citizens and officials?
— What Rule(s) of Law Will Apply to Those Who Do the Work of Government? Will we continue to have two sets of rules—one applicable to
  officials and the other to nongovernmental actors who perform the
  work of government? Will nongovernmental actors be subject to some
  or all constitutional and statutory provisions we apply to officials? Are
  new principles of law needed to govern nongovernmental actors who
  perform governmental functions?
— What Are Our Accountability Mechanisms, and How Well Do They
  Work? Do we still presume that officials must and do have the skills
  and resources to control government? If so, how do we know this is the
  case? Or do we believe that alternative accountability mechanisms—
  such as performance measures and competitor and stakeholder/inter-
  est group vigilance—are enough to do the job in the absence of capable
  official oversight? If so, how do we know this is the case? What is our
  fallback if third-party government does not work?
— If We Continue to Blur Boundaries between Officials and Private
  Workforces, Is There Danger We May Lose the Very Qualities We
  Most Value in Both? Can we constrain nongovernmental actors (be
  they corporations, universities, or other nonprofits) without diluting
  the qualities of autonomy and independence for which we relied on
  them in the first instance? By the same token, as we seek to reinvigorate
  the civil service by making it more entrepreneurial and incentive
  driven, will we lose the qualities that rendered the civil service of value
  in the first place?

In sum, the concept of inherently governmental function has long been a placeholder for a host of basic and unanswered questions raised by the legacy of mid-twentieth-century federal government reform. As both pre– and post– September 11 developments show, a renewed appreciation of the concept is necessary, but not sufficient, to address the basic questions of control and accountability posed by this legacy.

Part II / The Impact of Organization and Program Design on Management of the Executive Branch

The Cabinet Officer as Juggler

The Accountability World of the Secretary of Health
and Human Services

Beryl A. Radin

Public organizations that are in operation at the beginning of the twenty-first century exhibit characteristics that are quite different from those that were found during most of the twentieth century. A snapshot of such organizations—particularly those operating at the federal government level—provides a picture that is without a clear visual focus. It is often difficult to ascertain which aspects of the organization are in the foreground of the picture and which are in the background.

This creates a real challenge for a new secretary of a cabinet department. Not only are these organizations extremely complex, but also they are increasingly charged with the implementation of a variety of policies and programs, employing a range of instruments to carry them out. In more and more circumstances federal organizations do not actually carry out the service delivery function themselves but, rather, rely on others (both actors in other levels of the public sector as well as those in the private and nonprofit sectors) to carry out the mission of the organization. The combination of complexity and involvement of others creates a sense of increased uncertainty for top managers, who must respond to constantly changing circumstances. While many of these elements were in place individually during the second half of the twentieth century, the aggregation of the elements has created a new sense of complexity as the new century has begun.

The changes that have taken place in the federal bureaucracy include:

- an appreciation of the close interrelationship between management decisions and policy outcomes;
- increased public expectations about the performance of government agencies;
- a movement away from the norm of centralized organizations to various forms of decentralized systems;
- a movement away from the "one best way" attitude toward management decisions and an appreciation of the use of multiple strategies that are appropriate for different agencies;
- diminution of the role of the federal agency as deliverer of services;
- an increase in the devolution of authority to states and localities;
- a dramatic increase in the contracting out of services outside the public sector;
- an increase in the level of controversy surrounding many issues, particularly involving domestic programs;
- a shift in the boundaries of issues and growing expectations of interagency and crosscutting efforts; and
- changes in technology and communication mechanisms.

These elements are played out in the context of specific organizations dealing with the programmatic and historical realities of the organizations at hand. The combination of these issues has changed not only the internal dynamics of federal agencies but also the external expectations about the way that they operate. The role of the cabinet secretary has always been complex and difficult. As Harold Seidman has noted, cabinet officials "rarely bring to their jobs the unique combination of political insight, administrative skill, leadership, intelligence, and creativity required for the successful management of heterogeneous institutions with multiple and sometimes conflicting purposes."[1]

It is important to acknowledge that the combination of both internal and external shifts has created a new set of accountability expectations for federal departments and those who lead them. One of the major consequences of these changes involves an acknowledgment that politics and policy making interpenetrate public administration. While this acknowledgment is not new, it has become more obvious in the contemporary situation. Separation of politics and administration—while discredited in the academic literature for some years—seems to be even more inappropriate as the society enters the new millennium. An observation made by Paul Appleby more than fifty years ago is worth accentuating: "Arguments about the application of policy are essentially arguments about policy. Actual operations are conducted in a field across which mighty forces contend; the forces constitute policy situations. Administration is constantly engaged in a reconciliation of these forces, while leadership exerts itself in that process of reconciliation and through the interstices of the interlacing power lines that cut across the field."[2]

The traditional ways of thinking about accountability do not capture the breadth of the term, especially when viewed as a part of an ever changing environment. As Garry Wills has noted, the U.S. system of government and the values that undergird it uphold very different directions, moving back and forth between liberal and conservative positions. When government is opposed, we believe "that government, as a necessary evil, should be kept at a minimum; and that legitimate social activity should be provincial, amateur, authentic, spontaneous, candid, homogeneous, traditional, popular, organic, rights-oriented, religious, voluntary, participatory, and rotational."[3] At the same time, we believe "that government is sometimes a positive good, and that it should be cosmopolitan, expert, authoritative, efficient, confidential, articulated in its parts, progressive, elite, mechanical, duties-oriented, secular, regulatory, and delegative."[4]

Given these conflicting values, the American political system—with its fundamental cultural norm of distrust of concentrated governmental power—has always made the accountability task of governance extremely complex. Recent skepticism about government has increased this sense of distrust. Martha Derthick's study of the Social Security Administration points to the consequences for management of federal agencies of both the multiple values within the society and the results of shared power: "It is at the oversight stage that an agency feels the full impact of the separation of powers. Under the system of separated powers, although the agency has several sources of command, it has no reliable source of protection when things go wrong. . . . Because no single institution is preeminently in charge of agency conduct, none must accept responsibility when it falters. In distress, it is isolated, a naked object of blame."[5]

Further, she notes that a number of changes that have occurred in the relationship between the agency and its environment have complicated the administrative task. These include federalism, the propensity of the president to sponsor policy initiatives, as well as interbranch and interparty differences.[6]

Accountability as a Juggling Process

Several decades ago Herbert Kaufman characterized the demands on top federal officials as a process requiring "a juggler's disposition":[7]

> Some people do not function well when they have to shift their minds back and forth among different, widely disparate matters in rapid-fire order. They are at their best if they can stay within a single, coherent set of tasks until they complete it and then move to another.
>
> There are some, on the other hand, for whom dealing with many things simultaneously is more congenial. They find it stimulating and exciting to keep many balls in the air at once. Doing one thing at a time bores them. . . . They may go from an issue of national policy to the problem of a single employee, from an intense struggle over substance to a light-hearted ceremony, from giving testimony at a legislative hearing to receiving a presentation by an interest group or staff. The most constant characteristics of their work are its diversity, fragmentation, and velocity.[8]

Accountability in the federal government in the twenty-first century requires public sector leaders who are able to keep multiple pressures, actors, and processes in the air at once. There are three types of accountability expectations at play in this process of juggling: policy, politics, and processes.

The Policy Expectations

The traditional approaches to accountability have tended to ignore the policy dimensions of the process. This is important because accountability relationships are defined within the contours of program design and the traditions of different policy cultures. Accountability is quite different for a block grant program that provides funds to third parties (often state or local government) than for a program that provides services directly to the public through federal staff. Similarly, the historical relationships that have been developed in some policy areas exhibit a high degree of agreement on program goals, objectives, and implementation technologies, while other policy areas are characterized by contentiousness and conflict.

The Political Expectations

This set of expectations flows from the complex set of relationships that are attached to the U.S. decision-making system as well as other aspects of fragmented authority. Shared powers—particularly those between the White House and the Congress—have created pressures for administrative agencies as they deal with top-level appointments, the budget, program authority, and relationships with those who are concerned about the business of governance. Political expectations come from the White House, from the multiple committees and subcommittees of the Congress involved in both appropriations and authorizing process, and—of no small account—the expectations of interest groups and others who may be involved in the implementation of programs. This set of expectations varies from program to program, reflecting the relationships between the various players. In many instances the set of expectations also contains conflicting demands by these players.

Management And Internal Process Expectations

Managing the internal operations of a federal department involves a number of classic management issues. It relates to leadership style, questions of centralization and decentralization (both in terms of program autonomy as well as the role of regional offices), the role of the office of the secretary, development of the budget, legislation and regulations, and dealing with other federal agencies in areas in which program operations and goals overlap. It also involves relationships between career staff and political appointees.

These three areas define the world of a cabinet secretary in the twenty-first century. They create pressures and demands that push and pull an individual in multiple directions. They provide the framework to anticipate the sources of, if not the substance of, such pressures and demands. These areas help a cabinet official define the space in which he or she operates. The definition of these three forces allows this individual to think about accountability expectations in a way that is integral to how he or she behaves in a day-to-day fashion. A new cabinet secretary is required to find a way to scope the landscape in which he or she operates, always keeping the various elements in motion. These three forces define the world of the cabinet secretary—the accountable juggler.

The Cabinet Secretary as a Leader

Much of what has been written about leadership in both public and private sector organizations suggests behavior that verges on the heroic. These writers have noted that it was important for a cabinet officer to come to the cabinet position with a vision of what is important, what that person can do to imprint his or her personality on that organization, and making sure that his or her vision is central and clearly articulated to others in the organization. Former Navy Secretary Richard Danzig characterized this heroic approach: "Think of three things that the organization wouldn't otherwise be doing, make them as radical as you think you can realistically achieve, and go for it. This idea has a lot of appeal. It is an intuitive sense of your own significance in the scheme of things, and if you're coming in as an outsider, as most political appointees are, to your organization, that you would bring to it something, which rationalized, in effect, your characteristics as an outsider."[9]

Danzig notes that this view of leadership in a public organization has roots in the private sector models drawn from the business community and from what he views as the biblical concept of leadership: "It is a Moses-like notion. Preach a new vision. Go up on the mountain and see it. Then lead the chosen people, if necessary, through 40 years in the wilderness to the Promised Land."[10] For Danzig, however, this approach to leadership is wrong, misleading, and, in many situations, dangerous. "You have only to look at how many visions are, in fact, fundamentally wrong to appreciate how potentially misguided this notion of operation is."

What, then, is an alternative approach to leadership which allows a public sector leader to think about ways to approach accountability? Richard Danzig challenges a new appointee to listen to what the organization is saying about what it cares about and what it values. "Many of these propositions have the ring of gospel and an elegant and uplifting character but, in fact, in many respects some of the most interesting and important things that the organization says about itself it says in the form of its clichés." Danzig felt that the propositions he found within the Department of the Navy were not translated into the day-to-day life of the organization: "The most crucial question for the organization after you listen to it is to look hard at these propositions and see what they mean in practice. When we began to mind that, we started to come up with all kinds of propositions that could fairly be described as radical. Indeed, in the end, in many dimensions revolutionary, but this had the enormous advantage that these were all derived from premises that everyone accepted and that were in no way personal to me or to the idiosyncrasies of my vision, and in themselves got beyond controversy."[11]

Managing the Department of Health and Human Services

Health and Human Services (HHS) is one of the most complex and largest federal agencies, with a FY 2003 budget of $460 billion and a workforce of sixty-five thousand people. It is an organization that is extremely diverse, containing almost a dozen separate program units that administer more than three hundred federal health and social programs. Created in 1953, the department has experienced major changes in a number of areas since the early 1990s. Its structure has changed in terms of both the program areas and agencies that are included within its borders. In the recent past the approach to management and accountability found within the department has emphasized the decentralized nature of the department. Unlike earlier HHS secretaries, Donna Shalala, secretary from 1993 to 2001, focused on management approaches that did not attempt to devise processes based on command and control or centralized techniques.[12]

Historically, HHS has relied on others (state and local governments and third-party providers) to deliver the services that are supported by federal dollars. Today, in an age of devolution, its programs have been increasingly implemented by others—particularly state agencies. As such, accountability is much more complex than it would be if federal staff actually implemented the programs. And many of its issues involve very controversial societal issues in which there is significant division of opinion within the broader society.

Despite efforts at centralization in the past, that strategy did not appear to be an effective way of dealing with external and internal realities surrounding the department.[13] These realities included:

Diversity and size of operating programs. The large number of programs contained within the HHS umbrella represents a very diverse array of objectives, cultures, and approaches. Each of the components within the department has its own history, needs, and approaches. Attempting to homogenize them within a centralized unit, even for planning purposes, dilutes their strengths and their unique values.

Vague, difficult goals. The department's programs embody goals that are often contradictory, vague, not unified, and difficult to measure. Efforts to find goals and objectives that link separate programs too often result in situations in which controversies embodied in the programs are ignored or posed in highly abstract forms.

Fragmented accountability structures. The accountability structures that frame the programs within the department mirror the fragmented nature of the American policy-making system. Units within the department are responsible to a number of separate budget, oversight, and authorizing congressional committees that represent different perspectives on programs. Some of these committees and subcommittees have established very detailed expectations for the implementation of programs under their control. They are also subject to the expectations that are defined by the Executive Office of the President, particularly the Office of Management and Budget and the domestic policy staff, which often differ from congressional expectations.

Fragmented program authority. Some of the programs within the department have more in common with programs found in other departments or agencies than they do with other HHS programs. The congressional predilection to fragment program authority has created a crazy quilt array of program responsibilities across the federal government.

Different program responsibilities. HHS has responsibility for programs that contain a wide range of administrative and policy mechanisms. Some of the programs that are implemented by HHS actually require department staff to perform the work or deliver the services. Others involve providing funds (either as block grants, discretionary grants, or other forms) to others, particularly states and communities, which deliver the services.

Controversial issues. Many of the policy issues that are contained within the HHS portfolio represent some of the most controversial domestic policy issues in the society. Issues such as government expenditures for abortion, welfare reform, and financing of health services evoke a variety of views and reflect very different perspectives on politics and policies. While the department may seek to take a clear position on such issues, the external forces work in different directions. In addition, the department's role involving these issues may be as a funder of programs that are delivered by other levels of governments, not as the actual deliverer itself.

Diverse constituencies. The diversity of programs within the department is paralleled by an even more diverse set of constituencies that follow the details of decisions involving their concerns. Constituency or interest groups focused on a specific set of programs often represent very different approaches to those programs. The department attempts to deal with multiple perspectives on a program area. In such a situation ambiguity rather than clarity often serves the department well.

Multiple policy perspectives. The controversies found within the society sometimes have been reflected within the department itself. In the past individuals appointed to top political roles represented diverse policy and political agendas. It was not uncommon to have a secretary committed to one perspective on an issue and a deputy secretary or assistant secretary to a very different approach. When this occurred, it was difficult to reach agreement on policy directions, and loyalty to a single agenda defined by the secretary was difficult to achieve.

Conflicting policy approaches. At times the diverse program components within the department represent different approaches to the same policy problem. When there is not agreement on the most effective way to address policy issues, various program elements may be charged with quite different (indeed, sometimes conflicting) approaches. For example, health research agencies may develop effective treatment forms that are not reimbursed by the agencies charged with financing services. This evokes conflict among the units for the preeminent role on the issue.

Staff-Line Competition

The growth of an active and large office of the secretary staff, with its various components, led to competition between the program units and the office of the secretary for influence and the secretary's ear. Program units sometimes perceived that the role of the office of the secretary was to second-guess the decisions of the operating components and to overturn their recommendations. As the office of the secretary grew larger in size, the various staff units had increased ability to monitor the program unit decisions more closely and to substitute their own technical judgment for that of the operating unit staff. This led to practices in which program units sought ways to avoid interacting with the staff components and, instead, learned how to minimize their impact on the program.

The roles that are currently found within the office of the secretary have remained fairly consistent over time. Staff offices in the office of the secretary include management, budget, planning and evaluation, legislation, public affairs, the general counsel's office, the office for civil rights, the inspector general, regional and intergovernmental offices. While the names of the units have remained much the same over the years, the size of these units and the extent of their responsibilities have increased and then decreased over time.

Gaming filtering units. The creation of filtering units (i.e., units that are established to filter information and package decision memos before they reach the secretary) did not guarantee that decisions would be more effective or provide a way to represent varying perspectives within the department.[14] At times the program units found ways to bypass these efforts or bring such filtering units into the process very late in the game.

Given these realities, it is a challenge for a new secretary of HHS to find a way to identify what that department cares about and what it values. This combination of values and premises sets the backdrop for any effort to respond to the constantly changing and conflicting set of accountability expectations that are found in this very large and diverse department.[15]

What are the premises embedded within the cultures of the Department of Health and Human Services which a new secretary can describe and classify? There are at least five such premises that become a new secretary's point of departure: (1) the life-or-death nature of many HHS issues; (2) the acknowledgment that a significant number of programs and policies live with controversy and conflicting values; (3) the recognition that most of the HHS programs call on the federal government to be partners, not controllers, in achieving the goals of programs; (4) the importance of and reality of a range of well-honed professional identities within the department; and (5) the fragmentation of approaches which stems from the diversity of programs and client groups found within HHS.

The Life or Death Nature of Many HHS Issues and Programs

Many of the programs found within the department's portfolio involve issues that directly affect the life chances of many Americans. Programs that deal with health and illness are obvious examples of this reality. Whether focused on research dealing with treatment of HIV/AIDS, causes of breast cancer, or mapping the genome to create protocols to deal with differences between individuals, HHS programs are understood to lead to real consequences for the nation's citizens. Similarly, efforts to regulate food and drugs are put in place to ensure that the products purchased by consumers are safe and actually achieve the results that are promised. Still other HHS health programs actually provide services to those who do not have alternative forms of treatment available to them (such as health services to Native Americans, rural citizens, and individuals who cannot afford or have access to other health services). Since September 11 HHS has become the locus of national efforts to respond to potential bioterrorism threats.

Beyond the health programs, other HHS efforts actually provide life chances and protect those who otherwise would be left without any sources of support. Financial assistance to those without other support is made available through the welfare block grant. Funds are made available to those who have high energy bills and inadequate income to pay for them through the Low-Income Home Energy Assistance Program (LIHEAP) program. Resources are provided to help parents pay for adequate childcare and for programs that provide food for the elderly who do not have the physical or financial means to arrange meals for themselves.

Whether or not the federal government intervenes directly in providing these services (or, instead, provides financial support to others who actually provide the service), one of the important values in the department is to acknowledge the role that it plays in assisting others.

The Controversial Nature of HHS Programs and Policies

Some federal departments operate with relatively clear support from the general public in terms of the goals of their programs and policies. Perhaps few departments match the Department of Transportation's general support within the society; highways and transportation safety are clearly "motherhood and apple pie" values within the society. Other departments have some level of controversy attached to their programs; for example, the Environmental Protection Agency (EPA) and the U.S. Departments of Interior and Agriculture need to balance the value of environmental protection with that of economic development.

It is almost impossible to find a program area within HHS which does not need to deal with controversy and conflicting values within the society. In a number of areas there is strong conflict within the citizenry about the appropriate role of the federal government or, indeed, whether any government should be involved at all. Over the years there has been a constant movement back and forth between responsibilities assumed by the federal government and responsibilities and funds devolved to state or local governments or other entities. For example, should the federal government attempt to establish standards as a bottom line in programs such as day care or for medical care for the needy? Should the federal government be responsible for ensuring that individuals without other sources of support receive cash assistance? Is it appropriate for the federal government to regulate industries such as pharmaceuticals or, conversely, to find ways to encourage the private sector to develop products that meet social needs? Should the federal government support programs that serve as a basic safety net in areas such as health insurance for children when the private sector does not provide that service?

In other areas some HHS programs actually represent strategies that are in conflict with other program areas. These conflicts sometimes occur because there is not agreement within the society about the most effective or most appropriate mode of intervention. There are times when funds that are used for research to develop new treatment procedures produce treatment forms that will not be reimbursed by other federal health programs. Similarly, attempts to develop drug prevention efforts may collide with other efforts (such as needle exchange) to protect the health of drug users.

Prohibitions against the use of human embryos in research protocols may inhibit the research that would lead to new understanding of treatment potentials in other areas. In still other cases the federal government supports programs that seek to improve the training and quality of those who provide services, setting quality standards that may have the impact of rationing or limiting the provision of services. Yet, at the same time, other programs are designed to increase the access and thus the demand for services, increasing the numbers of people who need services without focusing on the availability of its providers.

The Federal Government as a Partner

Unlike the social programs of many other countries, a number of the programs found within the Department of Health and Human Services have depended on others to ensure that services are provided to the nation's citizens. At the same time that social programs were expanded during the New Deal, greatly increasing the federal role in those efforts, this expansion did not simply extend the authority in Washington. Several of the programs created as a result of the 1935 Social Security Act and its amendments, for example, provided federal dollars but called on states and localities to deliver the actual services (and, in some instances, also contribute funds to match the federal dollars). Yet there were some services that were actually provided by federal staff, such as the programs of the Indian Health Services and other services of the Public Health Service. In yet other instances, even when the federal government was dependent on others for the operation of the programs, it assumed its role was preeminent and that the other actors who were involved should defer to the federal controls.

By the end of the twentieth century, however, the changes that took place in the design of programs such as the Temporary Assistance for Needy Families (TANF) and the Maternal and Child Health programs (moving them into block grant constructs) diminished the levers that federal agencies could use to evoke change. Devolution of authority away from Washington meant that it was more difficult to defend a sense that Washington always knows best. As the structural changes occurred, others were becoming more aware that the reality of implementation of federal programs was much less that of a controller than it was a facilitator. Also, in many instances federal agencies were unable to pull the political and fiscal strings required to change state or local practices. Despite the rhetoric of control, federal agency behavior was likely to call on bluffing strategies rather than sanctions that might have been legally available.

By the beginning of the Clinton administration the concept of partnership was used to describe the emergent federal role. HHS no longer defined its position as that of a controller but pointed to changes in the way that programs looked at their relationships with state and local government. The language of the reinvention movement was used to give state and local governments more control over programs and their own ability to produce results. The idea of partnership—acknowledging that the federal government shares responsibility for the achievement of program goals—replaced earlier descriptions of the federal role. Partners were defined to include not only state and local governments but also Native American tribes and a wide range of nongovernmental actors, particularly groups from the not-for-profit sector. Opening the door to the array of groups with which the program units in the department do business created a real challenge. The department was called on to devise approaches that allow it to carry out its policy responsibilities and to operate within the existing framework of program structure and design. Yet, concurrently, HHS had to work effectively with those outside the department to carry out its responsibilities. The need for bipartisanship naturally flowed from this set of changes since the partners involved in programs were likely to be drawn from all sides of the political spectrum.

Although the partnership concept became a part of the rhetoric within HHS, it was not always easy to put it into operation. The partnership approach required federal officials to acknowledge that their role was much more variegated than it had been in the past. In most instances relying on the traditional process of issuing regulations and guidelines was no longer available. Federal officials were challenged to learn how to be facilitators, brokers, and often behind-the-scenes actors in the implementation process. New policy instruments were emphasized which made more sense in the altered environment (such as support of peer-to-peer technical assistance efforts, allowing grantees to find ways to learn from one another).

Having a Range of Well-Honed Professionals within HHS

In some respects one could describe the staff of HHS as a variation on Noah's ark—there seem to be two of most living staff species found within its organizational borders. While most contemporary public organizations do contain personnel drawn from many fields of expertise, the HHS reality is compounded in complexity because many of the staff members come from multiple professional areas that are well defined and known for their expert knowledge. The federal personnel system is sometimes defended as a generic arrangement in which career public servants are subject to legal and administrative controls. But many of the tasks that are required in HHS to implement policies and programs call for individuals who are trained and evaluated by a set of standards defined by other members of a particular profession.[16]

The range of professions found in HHS varies in terms of the status of the group within the society, the ability of the government agency to compete with the private sector for staff, and the relationship between those in the public sector and those outside. The individuals who work in the National Institutes of Health (NIH), for example, include the nation's top researchers in specific fields of study, a number of whom continue to work as bench scientists and have been responsible for major scientific discoveries. High-status professionals are also found in the Centers for Disease Control (CDC) and the Food and Drug Administration (FDA), both of which employ individuals with expert training in their fields. CDC involvement in identifying and treating health epidemics across the globe has made staff experience the basis for Hollywood films. Research and investigation of problems that have been undertaken by FDA staff members are responsible for tracking down unsafe products and removing them from consumer purchase.

There are other professions found within HHS which are less visible. NIH includes staff members who specialize in the management of research and development programs. While they are less obvious to the general public, they are also people who are known within a narrower field of specialization. Staff attorneys within the department often develop a field of specialization in the law and are active in their professional organizations. Although it is difficult for HHS to attract state-of-the-art computer staff because of competition from the private sector, there are a number of individuals with computer training who have attempted to keep up with developments in the field. Other department staff are trained in child development, social work, gerontology, research and evaluation, public health, and other related professions and value their identity within those fields of practice.

These externally defined relationships provide a point of departure for many HHS staff members. They give career staffers the ability to stay up-to-date with developments in their field. They establish standards and quality measures that define objectives for staffers. But these external relationships also make it more difficult for agency leaders to treat their staffs in traditional bureaucratic ways, relying on legal and administrative controls to elicit behavior.

The fragmentation of approaches stems from the institutional structure, the diversity of programs as well as their conflicting approaches, and the range of client groups found within HHS. When viewing HHS as a single unit, it is very difficult to see it as a unified entity. Rather, it seems much more accurate to characterize it as a fragmented organization. The fragmentation present in the department stems from the cumulative effects of shared powers between various institutions of government, the large number of programs within HHS, the conflicts between approaches, and multiple groups that are affected by its programs. Although there are subsystems (or, more likely, sub-subsystems) within HHS which can be described as policy communities, even those entities often contain aspects of fragmentation. They are not always able to describe others with interest in a particular policy area or find ways to develop relationships with them which reflect common features, shared orientations, and similar ways of thinking.[17]

There are a number of consequences of fragmentation. Policy fragmentation emerges when, as John Kingdon noted, the right hand does not know what the left hand is doing.[18] In addition, fragmentation generates policy instability—that is, situations in which policy design moves and shifts when various aspects of the policy community are predominant over others.

No matter where one looks, it becomes clear that the American fragmented structure of government actually prohibits any institution or actor from viewing the department as a whole. Despite the illusion that the president's budget can be viewed as a single entity, in reality that budget is developed through a process in which specific parts of the HHS budget emerge from different parts of OMB. The scale and scope of HHS programs make it almost impossible for any single individual to focus on detailed crosscuts or interrelationships between elements. Similarly, the fragmented nature of congressional authority also reinforces the tendency for members to look at specific programs individually, disaggregating the maze of programs and policies into small bits that make the system more comprehensible.

The multiple nodes of this variegated system provide a range of entry points for groups and individuals who seek to influence the development of policy. It creates a set of possibilities that resemble the contemporary department store—an array of individual boutiques organized not by the product for sale but by the producer of that product.

Living in a Web of Accountability Expectations

It is this fluidity and turbulence that make the task of managing the Department of Health and Human Services challenging, at the least. The secretary of the department has been described as an accountable juggler—someone who must balance multiple actors and pressures. Dropping one of those elements not only has political consequences, but it also has substantive consequences for those individuals who are affected by HHS programs as well as the thousands of career public servants and others who make these programs come alive.

One could view the world that the HHS secretary inhabits as a random world in which processes are unpredictable and results emerge strictly out of luck. But, as Kingdon argued, the fluidity of the policy process does not mean that structure is absent from the process. The attributes of the agenda-setting process that he describes are also found in the world of a cabinet secretary attempting to manage policy, politics, and processes. His model is both structured and flexible enough to contain what he calls "residual randomness." He calls on theories of complexity, chaos theory, and the garbage can model to help understand a system with several properties: pattern and structure in complicated, fluid, and seemingly unpredictable phenomena; residual randomness; and historically contingent behavior.[19]

The ability to respond to these attributes calls for leaders who are highly skilled, able to listen to the cacophony of voices around them, and capable of adapting to constantly changing circumstances. The task of leading the Department of Health and Human Services is incredibly challenging. But there are few other public organizations which allow an individual to make a measurable difference in the lives of American citizens.

The Post–September 11 Experience

Almost no federal agency was untouched by the tragic events of September 11, 2001. While many of the responses to these events took a policy focus, management strategies were also involved. The management approaches by the Department of Health and Human Services in the post–September 11 environment actually reinforced the efforts by Secretary Tommy Thompson to centralize activities within the office of the secretary.

The annual federal budget submitted by the president often contains important but seemingly obscure information about management approaches within the executive branch. While most of the public attention after the State of the Union focuses on the proposed allocation of funds to specific programs, the budget provides important clues to the ways that federal agencies expect to carry out their functions.

Such is the case in the budget submission offered by the Department of Health and Human Services for FY 2003. Tucked within an overview statement entitled "Ensuring a Safe and Healthy America," the department called for a management approach called "One Department"—a centralized strategy that moves authority from the program components to the office of the secretary. It sought to consolidate administrative functions in a number of areas, including personnel, public affairs, legislative affairs, construction funding, leasing, and other facilities management activities.

This strategy follows a reorganization that had occurred in early November 2001, creating two offices within the office of the secretary from a single unit. These offices provide the infrastructure for an increased role for the office of the secretary, moving away from the decentralized approach that had characterized the Clinton-Shalala administration. One office has been named the office of the assistant secretary for administration and management and the other the office of the assistant secretary for budget, technology, and finance.

In some agencies these organizational structural changes could be viewed as the normal swing back and forth between management strategies when administrations change. But both the post–September 11 experience and history make the current HHS drive for centralization problematic.

As has often been noted in the press, Secretary Thompson's attempt to speak for HHS during the 2001 anthrax scare led to inaccurate and misleading information reaching the public. It took him some time before he recognized that the experts—the heads of the program units—were the individuals who ought to appear before the press. They were the ones who were able to answer the technical questions at a time when the public was anxious and wanted as much information as possible in a highly uncertain environment. The proposed strategy for centralization of public affairs functions would continue Thompson's tendency to offer a general, not an expert, view on future issues.

The experience of the past also raises questions about Thompson's strategy. Over the years various secretaries of HHS (and earlier the Department of Health, Education, and Welfare [HEW]) tried to employ a command and control strategy, seeking to deal with the department as if it were a relatively homogeneous and unified entity. Yet this is not the case. Efforts at centralization were not able to deal with the predictable realities of the department's external environment. These are forces that any secretary must confront.

When past HHS secretaries have tried the Thompson approach, they have been frustrated. That strategy just doesn't fit into the department's reality. HHS operated during the Clinton administration employing a very different strategy. The secretary was comfortable serving as an advocate for the program units, supporting their agendas, and relying on personal relationships and policy discussions instead of formal bureaucratic processes to arrive at decisions. The secretary, Donna Shalala, was not interested in establishing an office of the secretary that defined its role as second-guessing or micromanaging the program components.

The system that has been put in place was flexible enough to build into itself the ability to respond to demands for centralization as well as decentralization when issues emerge from public concerns or crises, articulated by the Congress, the White House, and the press. It also was robust enough to respond to the different perspectives that emerge when individual actors look at issues through a political rather than a programmatic lens. That experience of managing HHS as a largely decentralized department attests to the possibility of adopting a management strategy that provides an alternative to a traditional centralized, command and control mode.

The effort by Thompson to centralize authority has several problematic consequences. It creates multiple layers of review, providing increased opportunities for individuals who do not have specialized knowledge of issues to play a more important role. As in the anthrax case, the political spin on issues without attention to the technical realities can lead to misleading statements and policies. In addition, the centralized strategy elicits a response from the career bureaucracy (particularly those in the line agencies) which is characterized by cynicism and negativity and may lead to an increased exodus of officials whose knowledge is important to running the government.

Making government manageable in the contemporary setting requires that cabinet officials devise strategies and principles of management which are appropriate to the unique realities and demands of a particular agency. One hopes that Secretary Thompson and those who follow him will modify his current centralized, command and control mode and, instead, devise a management strategy that fits the HHS reality.

CHAPTER FIVE

The Future of the Postal Service

Murray Comarow

The future of the U.S. Postal Service (USPS) is so bleak that the General Accounting Office has placed the USPS on its "high-risk" list, asserting that it may not be able to continue to provide universal service at reasonable rates. Congress insists that the Postal Service be run like a business, but its organizing statute gives it little control over wages and prices. Postal reform legislation has been stalled since 1992.

The Kappel Commission

In June 1967 I had been executive director of the Federal Power Commission for a year, still trying to get my arms around that talent-rich but change-resistant agency. Lee C. White, my friend and chairman of the commission, walked into my office and said that Joseph A. Califano Jr., President Lyndon B. Johnson's domestic advisor, told him that the president had established a Post Office commission headed by AT&T's chairman, Frederick R. Kappel,[1] and that Kappel wanted me as its executive director.

I had never heard of Kappel, knew nothing about the Post Office Department, and told Lee to tell Joe Califano—whom I knew from our Pentagon days—that I was not interested. It didn't work. Kappel persisted, LBJ insisted, and they prevailed. I assembled a team and went to work for a remarkable group, the President's Commission on Postal Organization, charged to "determine whether the postal system as presently organized is capable of meeting the demands of our growing economy and our expanding population."

The commission consisted of ten men. Kappel and five others headed corporations such as General Electric, Bank of America, and Federated Department Stores. The seventh was George Baker, dean of the Harvard Business School. There were two prominent Democrats, David Ginsburg and David Bell, and, finally, AFL-CIO president, George Meany. Meany never attended a meeting but sometimes sent an aide as an observer. President Johnson wanted him on the commission so that we could brief him, which we did, and he was not an obstacle. Meany aside, there was full attendance at almost every meeting. The commissioners agreed that their substitutes could only observe, not participate.

Their principal finding after a year's study was that the Post Office Department was "not capable of meeting the demands of our growing economy and our expanding population." The primary problem was political management, and they asserted, with the exception of a mild, two-sentence comment by Meany,[2] that political management had to go. Allow me to describe "political management."

How the Post Office Department Was Managed

The postmaster general (PMG) was appointed by the president. By custom he was the chairman of the political party that had won the previous election. His top executives were frequently chosen from the party faithful. Well over sixty thousand postmasters and rural carriers were selected by the members of Congress, openly and legally. Many more were subject to behind-the-scenes influence.

True story: A speaker of the House of Representatives called the postmaster general and asked that a constituent be hired as an accountant. The PMG said that he would have his legislative assistant, D. Jamison Cain, look into it. As I recall Cain's account, he learned that the man was an automobile mechanic, so he called the speaker. "Mr. Speaker," he said, "give us a break. This guy is an automobile mechanic!" The speaker answered: "Now, Jamie, I know that, but this is a *good* young man. I know the family. It's a *fine* family. Tell the General that this man should have the job." He was hired.

Congress set postal rates, so its members were lobbied hard by mailers. Congress set postal wages, so its members were lobbied hard by the unions. Congress heavily influenced contract awards, so its members were lobbied hard by contractors. Congress influenced the location of post offices and even of individual mailboxes. Postmasters were responsive to those who appointed them, an endemic problem for their putative managers.

The Post Office ran at a loss for 131 of the 160 years before postal reform. Congress appropriated funds to make up for the money the department lost most years, typically running a deficit of 18 percent. In 1967, when the Kappel Commission was created, the Post Office Department collected $4.96 billion and spent over $6.13 billion. The $1.17 billion deficit—nearly 24 percent—was made up by the federal treasury (i.e., by taxpayers, who had the illusion that their stamps paid for the mail). That same year the first-class stamp said "six cents," but not one American in a thousand knew that customers were paying six cents and taxpayers almost two cents more. Most mail, then and now, is generated by business. In 1967 letters from one person to another constituted 14 percent of the mail stream. Today it is 4 percent. Newspapers and magazines, for example, whose subscribers are generally more affluent than average citizens, were highly subsidized by taxpayers, including many non-subscribers.

In 1984 journalist David Whitman prepared a two-part case study for Harvard's Kennedy School of Government called "Selling the Reorganization of the Post Office."[3] In it he wrote: "No department of the Federal government was so shackled by vested interests, by stultifying personnel practices, by archaic regulations and equipment, by an absence of elementary management practices, and last but not least, nowhere was the sauce of political patronage thicker than at the heart of the lavish office of the Postmaster General."

The Commission's Recommendations

Against that background the Kappel Commission recommended:

- a self-supporting government corporation;
- elimination of patronage, which controlled all top jobs, 33,000 postmaster jobs, 30,000 rural carrier jobs, and, less visibly, many other positions;
- that rates be set by a board of directors after due process hearings by a judicial panel;

- that labor-management impasses over contracts or pay be referred to the president, who "would be free to establish whatever *ad hoc* methods he chooses to resolve the matter."

These recommendations were described by *Business Week* (March 28, 1970) as "the most comprehensive overhaul of a U.S. public institution ever considered." Supported by President Richard M. Nixon, Congress enacted the commission's recommendations in the 1970 Postal Reorganization Act,[4] but with a number of changes. Of these two were critical: binding arbitration to settle wage disputes; and a politically appointed, full-time Postal Rate Commission. Postmaster General Winton R. Blount, the Nixon administration's point man for the overhaul effort, said that these regrettable provisions "were the price we paid for postal reform." The vote in the House was 359 to 24 and in the Senate 76 to 10, a great surprise to the pundits and insiders who had assured me that the commission was wasting its time, since Congress would never give up its precious patronage.

With one exception, which I will discuss later, Nixon kept his word to Blount to support postal reform. Republican leadership in Congress hammered Blount hard to give them patronage opportunities before shutting the door, but he stood firm, and Nixon backed him. In fact, Section 1002 of the 1970 Postal Reorganization Act prohibits members of Congress and other public and party officials from intervening in an appointment or promotion. If they do, the law requires that the Postal Service send it back appropriately marked as "in violation of this section."

The Postal Unions Strike

Blount had developed a reform legislative package that included pay increases. The unions regarded reform with horror—and the pay increases as inadequate. When he went forward, there was a furious union reaction. Letter Carriers Branch 36, which covered Manhattan and the Bronx, took a strike vote on St. Patrick's Day of 1970 and walked out. Other unions followed. By March 21 one-third of the workforce was on strike, the first major strike by federal workers since the founding of the republic. They shut down 671 post offices, including all but one of the ten largest. The impact was immediate and crushing; huge parts of the business sector ground to a halt. Administration lawyers got back-to-work court orders, which were ineffective. Postal inspectors went to the homes of union leaders, telling them they were in violation of the no-strike law and might be subject to arrest and prosecution. The union leaders claimed that they had lost control of their members.

Blount demanded that troops be called out. Secretary of Labor George P. Schultz strongly disagreed. Faced with Blount's threat to resign if the president didn't support him, Nixon declared an emergency and on March 23 announced that he would send the National Guard into New York City to move the mail. The strike was over in two days.

There's a superficially appealing linkage between the strike and postal reform. Some argue that the strike brought about postal reform and a better deal for postal workers. That is the view of recently retired National Association of Letter Carriers (NALC) president, Vincent R. Sombrotto, who headed Branch 36 in 1970. In his "President's Message" in the NALC's *Postal Record* of October 2002, he minced no words, claiming that "The quality of life *you* enjoy— the wages you earn, the home you live in, the education your children have received—is a direct result of the courage and even recklessness of a relatively small band of letter carriers more than 32 years ago."

He is surely right about "recklessness," since strikes by federal employees violate the law (Title 5 U.S. Code 7311) and subject such employees to fines and imprisonment for up to one year and a day (Title 18 U.S. Code 1918). The Nixon administration lacked the political will to "faithfully execute the laws" by prosecuting violators, but one may wonder what the result would have been if it had at least targeted strike leaders. President Reagan's swift firing of the striking air controllers seems to have dampened strike talk among federal workers.

It is not possible to weigh the strike's effects with precision, but "correlation is not causation," as the axiom goes. The strike may have been a contributing factor to reform, but some believe that it may even have been a setback. On March 25, when the strike ended, George Meany said: "We are not even going to talk about postal reform. We're back at work, but all we want to bargain about is wages. We intend to get a lot more money."[5] Labor was feeling its oats at that point. It had pulled off the biggest strike of federal workers in history and gotten away with it.

Blount would not back off, which set the stage for a White House end run, offsetting Nixon's support of Blount. Charles Colson, often termed one of Nixon's hatchet men, called James Rademacher, president of the National Association of Letter Carriers, who, like other union presidents, had militantly attacked postal reform. Still, Rademacher was one of the few union presidents in the country to support the Nixon campaign and the only postal union president to do so. Colson and Rademacher drafted new provisions that would give postal workers binding arbitration, a 6 percent increase retroactive to December 27, 1969, plus an 8 percent increase when the bill became law. Rademacher then publicly reversed his position on reform and was picketed by his own members, who called him a traitor. It is a great irony that his deal on wage arbitration has been a boon for the unions and a burden to customers. There is no precedent in American history for arbitrating federal employees' wages.

The Origins of the Postal Rate Commission

The Postal Rate Commission (PRC) also came about in a convoluted way. The Kappel Commission's concept was to have judges recommend rates that would be subject to review by presidentially appointed directors. Judicial review would also be available, and, of course, the Congress could step in if the system produced a bizarre outcome.

The 1984 Harvard study referred to earlier had concluded, in this connection, that "the House presented relatively few problems . . . but several special interest groups, particularly the airlines, managed to work provisions into the Senate bill that modestly diminished the rate-making autonomy of the postal corporation. . . . About the only major concession Blount was forced to make by Senator McGee was the addition of an independent Postal Rate Commission." Senator Gale McGee (D-WY) was chairman of the Senate Committee on the Post Office and Civil Service. This change, which was far from "modest," was cast in terms of protecting the public interest. Public administration scholars and practitioners may not agree that the public interest is protected by creating a bureaucracy to set prices and otherwise supervise the actions of another bureaucracy. Since the Postal Rate Commission has been around for over thirty years, many assume that's the way government works. It is not. It is a unique and dysfunctional arrangement.

It takes the Postal Service about five months to prepare a rate case, usually followed by ten months of hearings in which anywhere from 60 to 120 parties are represented by counsel, economists, accountants, and assorted experts. Three more months are needed to set up the procedures for the new rates. In eighteen months market conditions may have changed considerably. The PRC's five presidential appointees, with a permanent staff of about sixty, are full-time second-guessers of nine presidentially appointed part-time postal governors. PRC's chairmen have sought even broader authority, not unusual for regulatory agencies, and the draft bills in the House would have done just that. The nine postal governors may override the PRC only if they are unanimous, which has happened only two or three times in thirty years. There is a simpler way.

Three retired judges could be retained or administrative law judges borrowed from regulatory agencies to hear rate cases, with full due process procedures. Experienced judges should be able to compress the present ten-month process. Their initial decision should be reviewed by the postal governors, who should be authorized, based upon the hearing record, to accept, reject, or modify it by a two-thirds vote, with appeal to the federal courts, as at present. Restructuring the board along the lines suggested later in this chapter will be necessary to accommodate its more demanding role.

The Effects of the 1970 Postal Reform

The results of the 1970 statutory reform have been impressive, and the Postal Service has much to its credit. It is 99.5 percent self-supporting, service is good, and the thirty-seven-cent stamp in 2003 costs the same in real dollars as did the six-cent stamp in 1968, which, as noted earlier, covered less than 80 percent of postal costs. Further, patronage is long gone. These are no small accomplishments.

Management miscalculations, however, have exacerbated statutory weaknesses, and a serious and embedded blunder came to pass in the first collective bargaining agreement after postal reform. The statute, in Section 101(c), speaks of compensation for postal employees "comparable to . . . compensation paid in the private sector." This was intended to refer to compensation for similar work, but then Postmaster General Elmer T. Klassen, pressed by mailers who feared strikes, agreed to interpret the phrase to mean compensation comparable to wages in highly unionized industries, even if unrelated to mail processing and delivery.

That agreement also made concessions on cost-of-living adjustment (COLA), layoffs, and employment of part-timers. On top of binding arbitration, it laid a foundation for subsequent arbitrators' awards. Today postal clerks average $52,000 a year (including health and retirement benefits). The average for letter carriers is $55,000. New postal employees receive, on average, a 28.4 percent wage increase over their old jobs.

Management of the Postal Service

Postal executives function within a system of constraints which make effective management impossible. If the nation's best executives occupied every top postal position, they could not comply with the statute's mandate for efficiency, since the statute itself precludes efficiency. They would run an organization that has only marginal influence over how much it pays its people and how much it charges its customers. They would have great difficulties in closing unprofitable post offices, combining processing centers, or making service changes that might make sense. These are core management responsibilities.

Labor issues are at the heart of effective reform and create more tensions than any other. When Republicans gained control of the Congress in 1994, there was some loose talk about "smashing the unions." Democrats circled the wagons, the postal unions flexed their muscles, and Republicans not only backed off but became as leery of taking on labor issues as the Democrats. On both sides of the aisle, true reform has taken a back seat.

Binding arbitration, as noted earlier, has been a boon for postal unions and a burden for postal customers. After billions of dollars invested in research and automation, 79 percent of postal costs still go to wages and benefits, of which 19 percent are benefits. In 1968 the figure was 83 percent, of which 8 percent were benefits. Some have argued that this is because postal work is "labor intensive." United Parcel Service (UPS) and FedEx are also labor intensive, but their comparable labor percentages are much lower. FedEx's labor costs are 42 percent of its total costs; the UPS figure is 56 percent. Public employees' wages should be set by public officials under congressional guidelines, not by private arbitrators who have no management responsibilities.

The effects of binding arbitration are not well understood, even by some observers of the Postal Service. Rick Merritt, executive director of Postal Watch, stated: "The USPS self-admittedly pays its workforce 30 percent more than its private sector counterparts. This is Congress' fault?"[6] Well, yes, to a substantial degree.

An example of an arbitrator's impact: The National Association of Letter Carriers and the American Postal Workers Union (APWU) clerks had been at "level 5" parity since 1907. On September 19, 2000, neutral arbitrator George Fleischli fractured that pattern, promoting NALC carriers to level 6. There was virtually no possibility of appeal from Fleischli's award; the 1970 Postal Reorganization Act provides that such awards are final. Arbitrators are not driven by the same values or the same dynamics that drive top managers. It may not be "fair," for example, to deny a wage increase, but a financial crunch and responsibilities to customers may be compelling, as in the case of some airlines. Although it was not a legally binding precedent, Fleischli's award seriously affected later negotiations and arbitrations with other unions. Its last paragraph virtually challenged other unions to press for identical wage levels. While noting that the agreement put negotiations with the NALC "out of sync" with APWU clerks and mail handlers, Fleischli asserted that it ought not prevent the USPS from pursing its goal of negotiating identical and moderate wage increases with its major unions.

Within hours after the award was announced, the clerks, the rural carriers, and the mail handlers were gearing up. APWU president Moe Biller said: "APWU will accept nothing less than full equality. We will leave no stone unturned and no tactic overlooked—whether lawful or otherwise—to secure economic justice for our members."

Sure enough, APWU-USPS collective bargaining failed, and the APWU went to arbitration. Stephen B. Goldberg, the neutral arbitrator, perhaps influenced by the Postal Service's dire straits, awarded the union relatively modest increases on December 18, 2001. On January 11, 2002, he issued a supplemental opinion, which stated flatly that there is "powerful support" for the argument that "the Postal Service provides a wage and benefits package to APWU represented employees that is better than that available for comparable work in the private sector." Goldberg also noted that "Postal Service jobs are highly sought after, and once obtained, are held onto. Applicant queues are long, and the quit rate is all but non-existent. Employees represented by APWU have total job security, an extraordinary benefit package, and wages that have fully kept up with inflation."

Some Costs Are Uncontrollable

The Postal Service is required to offer universal service (an undefined concept in the statute) and to break even, but it lost $1.7 billion in FY 2001, and for the fiscal year that ended September 30, 2002, it may lose close to $1 billion. Mail volume growth averaged 4.5 percent in the 1980s and half that in the 1990s. Some costs are uncontrollable. About 5,600 new delivery points are added every day, 1.7 million new delivery points a year. That requires not only

4,800 new workers but 80 new facilities as well. The Postal Service has over 215,000 vehicles. A ten cent a gallon increase in gasoline prices comes to $55 million a year, and the Postal Service can't simply raise prices as UPS and FedEx can.

Retirement costs are similarly uncontrollable. In 1971 the Postal Service was stuck with a generous Civil Service Retirement System (CSRS). In the 1980s Congress decided that the Postal Service should fund the cost of COLAs paid to CSRS retirees and directed the Office of Personnel Management (OPM) to bill the USPS for these costs back to 1971, plus retroactive interest. The FY 2001 payment for this and other CSRS deferred liabilities was $3.75 billion, which includes $1.6 billion in interest. The General Accounting Office (GAO) reported in December 2001 that the unfunded retirement and post-retirement health care costs were $9.3 billion a year, growing to $16 billion by 2010, an unsustainable situation. On September 12, 2002, Comptroller General Walker recommended that the Postal Service figure out how best to account for and disclose its pension and health care obligations. To stay afloat, the Postal Service borrows from the Treasury. It owes the Treasury more than $12 billion.

A large part of these costs was incurred before postal reform; they were imposed, willy-nilly, on an organization designed to be self-supporting (i.e., costs are passed on to postal customers). In FY 2001, if not for the $1.6 billion interest on pension liability, the Postal Service would have had a net income instead of a deficit. Postal customers bear huge costs, which do not flow from the service they are receiving.

On November 5, 2002, this part of the picture changed dramatically. Postmaster General Potter announced that the Postal Service had overpaid its pension obligations for thirty years, based on billings from the U.S. Office of Personnel Management. Instead of being $32 billion in the red on pensions, the funding gap was "only" $5 billion.[7] The Office of Management and Budget, the Treasury Department, and the General Accounting Office confirmed OPM's recalculation. Two bills, S.380 and H.R. 735, were introduced to get this done,[8] and with some changes, have been enacted. The result will be to postpone rate increases for a few years, but the fundamental structural problems remain.

The Postal Service has tried valiantly to cope by freezing capital expenditures and cutting staff. There are about 800,000 workers, down over 50,000 from 1999. It has also raised rates. On March 22, 2002, the Postal Rate Commission approved an increase in the price of a first-class stamp from thirty-four cents to thirty-seven cents, plus similar increases for other types of mail. If not carefully calibrated, rate increases will further reduce volume and revenues and exacerbate the fiscal shortfall. The Postal Service's suggestion that five-day delivery might be considered drew howls of protest from Congress and many mailers, as do suggestions to remove some of the 323,000 collection boxes or to close postal facilities. On March 2, 2001, the nine governors signed a letter to President George W. Bush asking for his "leadership . . . to modernize the Nation's postal laws."

Having criticized the Postal Service for its failure to grasp the nettle, it is fair to examine what its associated industries and unions propose.[9] After all, a healthy Postal Service is essential to their success and, for some, their survival. In April 2001 a coalition was formed "to preserve the nation's universal mail service." Its members include the Direct Marketing Association, Magazine Publishers of America, Association for Postal Commerce, Alliance of Nonprofit Mailers, Parcel Shippers Association, National Association of Letter Carriers, National Rural Letter Carriers Association, National Association of Postmasters of the United States, National Postal Mailhandlers Union, and other heavyweights.

These groups opposed reducing service, closing post offices, diminishing collective bargaining rights, and increasing rates. They recommended eliminating the "break-even" requirement, improving "core products and services," and increasing borrowing and rate-making authority, within narrow limits. They also favored eliminating inefficiency and improving productivity. So much for real reform. Some stakeholders, such as the Envelope Manufacturers Association, were more realistic. Many major mailers, including most of those mentioned, have since shifted their positions, however, and have asked the president to intervene.

The Governing Structure of the USPS

Directing the affairs of a $70 billion enterprise is not just a matter of common sense. Some postal governors have been highly qualified, but many, while successful in their various endeavors, lack the experience gained from running large companies or institutions or serving on their boards. For over three decades the finger has pointed at the singularly inattentive White House. The organizing principle of postal reform was to get rid of political management and permit the Postal Service to operate "efficiently and economically." That requires the appointment of governors and PMGs who know how to do this. The president might well look to an outside panel to advise on prospective nominees, and the statute should require that appointees have the requisite high-level experience.

The Congress should reconsider the original Kappel Commission proposal: Six part-time governors would select a postmaster general, who would be chairman of the board. These seven would select two more top postal officials, who would also be members of the board. The nine-member board would make rate decisions, after full due process hearings, subject to appeal to the U. S. Court of Appeals for the Federal Circuit.

Postal Service Problems Are Not New

The Postal Service's difficulties long predated the 2001 anthrax attack on its Washington, D.C., facilities. In 1996 David Ginsburg, Robert Hardesty, David Harris, and I coauthored an op-ed piece in the *Washington Post*. (Ginsburg was a member of the Kappel Commission; Hardesty had chaired the Board of Governors; and Harris had been the board's long-standing secretary.) The first sentence of that article stated, "The U.S. Postal Service is in deep trouble." We had no inside information, nor were we prescient. We knew what everyone knew, that the competitive world in which the Postal Service is a major player was not standing still. The lethal combination of statutory constraints on setting wages and prices and the impact of competitive technology, we said, may reduce the Postal Service to a shell. If the USPS fails, can companies such as UPS and FedEx do the job? Consider: One week's Postal Service volume equals one year's UPS volume; two days' Postal Service volume equals one year's FedEx volume.

It was also clear to us that the legislative process would fail to achieve genuine reform. Competitors such as United Parcel Service (which has 78 percent of the package market) have a stake in a tightly regulated Postal Service and lobby effectively to maintain their advantages. In the last national election UPS and FedEx political action committees (PACs) donated almost $3 million, plus $2.4 million in soft money. The postal unions were not about to give up their unique arbitration rights. And many mailers hold fast to the illusion that a Postal Rate Commission is the only way to get a fair shake. In a June 12, 2001, press release PMG John E. (Jack) Potter said correctly that the "current statute no longer provides tools to manage the organization effectively," and in an April 5, 2002, speech at the National Press Club he said, "We now need legislative change that preserves mail delivery for the next 30 years and beyond." Understandably, he is trying to reach consensus, but consensus will not give the Postal Service a handle on wages and prices.

In 1967 a colloquy took place between the chairman of the House Appropriations Postal Subcommittee and Postmaster General Larry O'Brien:

> *Mr. Steed:* General . . . would this be a fair summary: that at the present time, as the manager of the Post Office Department, you have no control over the pay rates of the employees that you employ, you have very little control over the conditions of the service of these employees, you have virtually no control, by the nature of it, of your physical facilities, and you have only a limited control, at best, over the transportation facilities that you are compelled to use—all of which adds up to a staggering amount of "no control" in terms of the duties you have to perform. . . .
>
> *Mr. O'Brien:* Mr. Chairman, I would have to generally agree with your premise . . . that is a staggering list of "no control." I don't know [whether] it has ever been put that succinctly to me. If it had been at an appropriate time, perhaps I wouldn't be sitting here.[10]

A Presidential Commission Is Needed

If the legislative process will not deal effectively with the Postal Service's problems, a reasonable alternative is to appoint a commission. I so testified on November 15, 1995, before the House Subcommittee on the Postal Service. If properly designed, it would have a fair chance of success.

It is a fact, of course, that most commissions fail. In April 1977, for example, a congressional commission's report on the Postal Service sank with scarcely a ripple; its very existence will be news to many well-informed members of the postal community. The appointing authorities of that commission committed the cardinal sin of selecting stakeholders, including representatives of the two biggest postal unions, major mailers, and, ex officio, PMG Benjamin F. Bailar and PRC Chairman Clyde S. DuPont. The commission was doomed from day one. Its seven members produced two separate dissents, one signed by one commissioner, the other by two commissioners. There were separate "Views" of three commissioners, two of whom had signed dissents, "Supplemental Views" of one commissioner, and "Additional Views" of another. Compare that to the Kappel Commission, whose bipartisan unanimity gave its report political and moral authority.

Some believe that a commission representing opposing interests will of necessity compromise, thereby producing balanced recommendations. What usually happens is quite different. In such a body there is a struggle for the hearts and minds of the uncommitted neutrals, if any. Analysis of past commissions by a National Academy of Public Administration group has identified the characteristics of effective commissions:

1. The commission should be composed of objective, highly respected people with no close ties to the affected groups.
2. Its mandate should involve a fairly specific social, economic, or political issue that the legislative process apparently cannot handle. Too sweeping a charge generally results in failure.
3. The commission should have real support from the president and key members of Congress, from a fair number of affected interest groups, and from the media.
4. Members should be prepared to support their recommendations personally; they and their supporters should play active roles to persuade decision makers.
5. The commission should be supported by a high-quality professional staff. The notion of ten wise individuals brainstorming their way to a solution is illusory.
6. The commission should have a reasonable deadline.

Commission Reports Are Not Self-Executing

Point number 4 deserves particular attention, since experience demonstrates that commission reports, however credible and persuasive, are not self-executing. This was well known, of course, to Red Blount and Larry O'Brien, but the first lobby formed to achieve reform, Citizens for a Postal Corporation (CIPCO), didn't have the resources or the clout.

In October 1968 I wrote to Kappel: "What we need is a sustained, well-organized and well-financed effort to bring to bear the weight of public opinion upon the Congress. . . . The opposition from the postal unions is sustained, well-organized, and well-financed. It cannot be effectively countered by a part-time [staffer] working out of a post office box in Dallas."

I was hardly the only one to realize this. CIPCO was dissolved, and a new group, the Citizens Committee for Postal Reform (CCPR), cochaired by Larry O'Brien and Thurston Morton, grasped the laboring oars. Each had been chairman of his political party; both were highly respected. Getting O'Brien was a real coup for Blount. In addition, an experienced lobbyist, Claude Desautels, was CCPR's executive director. Desautels had worked for O'Brien in the Kennedy and Johnson administrations and was his legislative aide in the Post Office Department. The result was a broad-based "marketing plan" developed by William D. Dunlap (on free loan from Procter and Gamble) which reached every relevant sector and interest group: the Congress, the media, labor, business, the public, and postal employees.

A brief examination of a few other commissions may offer further perspective.

Internal Revenue Commission

The 1995 National Commission on Restructuring the Internal Revenue Service (IRS) and the 1998 statute that it spawned were, on balance, failures. This has yet to be widely acknowledged, notwithstanding the resultant steep drop in tax collections. Cochaired by Senator Bob Kerrey (D-NE) and Congressman Rob Portman (R-OH), the commission's seventeen members included stakeholders of every stripe: four members of Congress, three federal officials, a state official, two members of anti-tax interest groups, the president of the Treasury employees union, and accountants and lawyers with IRS practices.

In focusing on alleged excesses of IRS staff, the commission gave short shrift to conflicting evidence and rode the antibureaucrat wave. Although some IRS agents may have been culpable as charged, the statutory remedy was flawed and the assumption that many IRS agents routinely and egregiously abused large numbers of taxpayers could not be corroborated by General Accounting Office investigators. The GAO's April 24, 2000, report exonerated the IRS on charges of personal vendettas and other misconduct, charges that drove the commission's recommendations. (A panel headed by William Webster, former FBI and CIA director, had reached the same conclusion in April 1999.)

The GAO works for Congress and has every incentive to support its masters' views. It was therefore a shock to many on the Hill to read a GAO report that said it could find "no corroborating evidence" that criminal investigations were "retaliatory." Nor could it "independently substantiate" that IRS employees had conducted "vendettas." It could "not find any evidence" that IRS employees had improperly dropped large tax assessments to curry favor with potential private employers.

Kudos to the GAO's integrity, but the sharp drop in tax revenues was widely predicted. The *Washington Post*, whose supine position on tax reform earned it no credit, finally editorialized, on February 7, 2000: "The message to agency employees was that if they leaned on resisting taxpayers, they risked being fired. They and the resisters both reacted to that about as you would expect." And the *New York Times* asserted on August 19, 2000: "Congress's assault on the agency has been needlessly damaging. . . . Audits of large corporations have fallen by almost 40 percent since 1992. Seizures of property of delinquent taxpayers are down 98 percent."

In 1996, 1.9 million individual tax returns were audited (1.6 percent). In 2001, 732,000 were audited (0.49 percent). Even for taxpayers earning more than $100,000 a year, the audit rate was less than 0.8 percent. If the chances of an audit are less than one in a hundred, count on it, some will play the odds.

Internet Sales Taxes Commission

The Advisory Commission on Electronic Commerce (ACEC) was another preordained disaster. Consisting of "business commissioners" who didn't want to be taxed and "government commissioners" (state, local, and federal) who wanted to tax goods sold over the Internet, it dissolved without consensus on March 21, 2000. Retailers charged that most business members represented high-tech companies. Government members abstained on every vote. The report was signed only by the "business commissioners."

The Two Hoover Commissions

The first Hoover Commission was created by the Congress in 1947, at President Harry S. Truman's behest. The twelve-member body focused primarily on organizational structure and simplification. Of its 273 recommendations, 116 were fully adopted and 80 partially adopted, an astonishing accomplishment.

Among its major recommendations were the creation of a Department of Welfare to run Social Security, welfare, and Indian affairs; cutting the number of federal agencies from sixty-five to twenty-three; giving department heads central authority, including the transfer of hiring from the Civil Service Commission; establishing an Office of General Services for buildings and supplies;

giving the secretary of defense real authority over the military services; and consolidating all housing activities in one agency.

In 1953 President Dwight D. Eisenhower initiated the second Hoover Commission. Its charter encompassed the elimination of government programs if they were not essential or if they competed with private business. Among its recommendations were terminating the college housing loan program; ending Commodity Credit Corporation loans to farmers; ending the Export-Import Bank's short-term loans; closing some Veterans Administration hospitals, stopping building new ones, and making veterans pay for treating nonservice disabilities; negotiating Defense Department food and clothing procurements rather than soliciting bids; and selling off federal power facilities. Its reach was too broad, and its 1955 report achieved little.

Other commissions that support the principles set forth in this chapter are the Brownlow Commission (Roosevelt, 1937); the Heineman Task Force (Johnson, 1967); and the Ash Council (Nixon, 1969).

The Postal Service's Minimalist Approach

The USPS is a treasured part of our culture and is essential to our economy. Far more than the 800,000 Postal Service jobs are at stake. The mailing industry employs nine million workers and constitutes about 8 percent of our gross domestic product. Its situation is deeply troubling and calls for strong and clear leadership.

For years postal officials have refused to speak plainly and specifically about the contradiction between congressional demands that the Postal Service behave like a business and the statute's insurmountable barriers to businesslike behavior. No "business" ever functioned with arbitrators setting wages, without the ability to adjust its prices, without the right to change its services, and without the ability to shut down money-losing operations.

Until recently, postmasters general and postal governors have been reluctant to go public, they said, because such initiatives would be "dead on arrival" on the Hill. Deborah K. Willhite, then USPS senior vice president for government relations and public policy, said: "There is no sense in us getting out there with a vision if we are going to get slammed. . . . Political dynamics necessitate that the agency come forward with a more pragmatic report, detailing how it will manage itself back to health and what legislative tweaks it needs to get there."[11] This mind-set continues to represent Postal Service thinking.

Of course, the USPS will "get slammed" if it proposes substantive changes, whether on labor, pricing flexibility, universal service, monopoly, or whatever. If the operating principle is not to get slammed, by all means hunker down and propose "legislative tweaks."

I believe that political dynamics work in a very different way. Leaders who have the vision and courage to propose clear and bold changes, even if short-term prospects are bleak, begin the debate. That will attract both supporters and critics and, with a sound public information effort, the attention of the citizenry as well. Most postal executives also have come to disagree with the USPS' minimalist approach. In a survey of senior postal executives, of 272 respondents, 7 out of 10 said that the Postal Service should become "an efficient deregulated, quasi-governmental organization focused on supporting universal service through innovative, flexible and market responsive services."[12]

The GAO Report on the "Deteriorating" Outlook

In April 2001 the General Accounting Office urged the Postal Service to act when it placed the USPS's transformation efforts and long-term outlook on its high-risk list, the GAO equivalent of the animal kingdom's "endangered species" list. In a February 28, 2002, report to the chairman and ranking minority members of the Senate Committee on Governmental Affairs (and its relevant subcommittee), the GAO described the Postal Service's financial outlook as "increasingly dire" and its basic business model as "increasingly problematic." The GAO not only called for "prompt, aggressive action" but repeated its earlier advice "that Congress must revisit the statutory framework under which USPS operates and take actions to deal with the systemic problems facing USPS that call for a transformation if USPS is to remain viable in the 21st Century."

Specifically, the GAO's fifty-nine-page report recommended that:

- USPS's Board of Governors and postmaster general provide proactive leadership for transformation by informing its employees, Congress, stakeholders, and the public about the need for change and by identifying in its forthcoming transformation plan (1) actions that USPS can take within its current authority, (2) specific congressional actions that would enable USPS to take a number of incremental steps to address its growing financial and operational challenges, and (3) a process to

address a range of comprehensive legislative reforms that will be
needed to address key unresolved transformation issues;

- USPS improve the transparency of its financial data by posting
monthly and quarterly financial reports on its Web site in a more
timely manner;

- Congress consider and promptly act on incremental legislative changes
that would provide USPS with some additional flexibilities while incorporating appropriate safeguards to prevent abuse. In addition,
comprehensive legislative changes will be needed to address key unresolved transformation issues. Congress could also consider how best to
address issues, such as infrastructure and workforce, which may require input from a variety of stakeholders and will involve some shared
sacrifice. One option could be to create a commission to address unresolved transformation issues and develop a comprehensive proposal
for consideration by Congress.

The Senate Governmental Affairs Committee's four top members, Senators
Joseph Lieberman (D-CT), Fred Thompson (R-TN), Daniel Akaka (D-HI),
and Thad Cochran (R-MS), quickly responded to the GAO report, urging the
USPS to present to the committee a sweeping but workable transformation
plan. They also made plain their support of statutory changes to give the
Postal Service greater flexibility. On April 4, 2002, the 450-page Transformation Plan, signed by board chairman Robert F. Rider and Postmaster General
John E. Potter, was presented to the committee and to its House counterpart.
The following day Potter, a career postal employee and the son of a career
postal employee, described the plan in a speech at the National Press Club and
made copies available to the press and the public.

The USPS Transformation Plan

The Plan set forth steps that the USPS will take which do not require new
legislation and other steps that would require changes in the Postal Organization Act of 1970. In the first category Potter announced that:

We are lifting the moratorium that management put in place four years ago on
closing small post offices;

We no longer need some of the 400 processing centers we have nationwide;

We are going to get even more aggressive in purchasing;

We will improve our dispute resolution processes . . . to reduce the $300 million
a year we spend on labor-management disagreements;
We will move to modernize the rate process under the existing regulatory
framework.

In addition, the plan suggests many operational and marketing changes,
such as a campaign to sell more stamps from vending machines or contract
postal units than in post offices, where the cost for each transaction is much
higher. Many of these initiatives seem sensible and promising, and the USPS
deserves credit for the plan's professionalism and detailed analysis.

Of the steps contemplated by the plan which would require legislative action, the most important is the proposed reorganization of the USPS into a
federally owned "Commercial Government Enterprise" (CGE). Rejecting return of the USPS to its pre-1971 status as a cabinet department and rejecting
privatization, the CGE model would eliminate the break-even mandate of the
1970 statute and permit the Postal Service to retain its "earnings" (i.e., profits),
which would finance capital projects, provide a cushion in hard times, and develop new sources of revenue through the broader use of thirty-eight thousand post offices and the delivery network. Those retail facilities and the delivery network, Potter said, "could be made available to private enterprise as a
joint-profit-making venture."

The Transformation Plan proposes that legislation be enacted to:

- eliminate binding arbitration and substitute mediation and the right to
  strike under the Railway Labor Act;
- permit the USPS to set prices on monopoly mail within broad PRC and
  Board of Governors parameters;
- permit the USPS to set prices on non-monopoly mail at its discretion,
  subject to antitrust and fair competition laws.

Earlier in this chapter I described the consequences of the 1970 strike.
Nothing in the Transformation Plan deals with the possible effects of a nationwide strike, or even local strikes, on our citizens and our economy. Nor does
the plan deal with the precedent such legislation may set for other federal employee unions. Federal employees have never had such a "right." They give it
up, presumably, because of the advantages and benefits of federal employment. In the private sector a strike is a test of economic strength between labor

and management. Labor can withhold its work; management can close its plants or hire replacements. It is hard to imagine the Postal Service closing post offices to combat a strike. If there is a sound public policy argument for such a sea change, it is missing from the plan. Similarly missing is a projection of the probable effects of strikes, in economic and human terms. Labor reform seems to be framed as an "either-or" issue: binding arbitration or right to strike. But postal workers are federal employees, and the model not mentioned is the one that exists for all other federal employees—that is, wages are set under congressional guidelines by government officials authorized by law to do just that. No wage arbitration, no right to strike.

The pricing flexibility proposals raise difficult questions. Monopoly mail would be priced more or less as at present, unless the PRC agreed to change its procedures. Non-monopoly products would be priced by the USPS to meet market conditions subject only to antitrust and fair trade laws. But prices are based upon costs as well as market factors. This would seem to require two cost tracking systems, one for monopoly mail, the other for non-monopoly mail. Would employees who sort or handle both types be clocked to insure that each type bears the appropriate cost burden? Would separate postal vehicles be assigned to each type? Answers to such questions do not appear in the plan.

The Plan Neglects Several Key Issues

The GAO's February 28, 2002, report posed a critical question: "What type of governing board is appropriate for USPS, given the complex mission and role of this $70 billion entity with its nearly 900,000 employees?" The plan is silent on this core issue, without explanation. There are several alternatives, with permutations. For example, the board could consist of three or five full-time appointees who would hire the postmaster general and perhaps other top executives. The PRC would be abolished. The Tennessee Valley Authority, a wholly owned government corporation, has functioned under this structure since 1933, with a three-member board of directors appointed by the president with Senate approval. Under this model the governors (or directors) would establish rates, after due process hearings, subject to appeal to the U.S. Court of Appeals for the Federal Circuit.

Another model, recommended by the Kappel Commission, would also eliminate the PRC and, as in the previous example, would vest rate-making authority in a board of directors, of which the top three full-time postal executives would be members, presumably the postmaster general, the deputy PMG, and the chief financial officer. The PMG would chair the board, thus eliminating—or at least minimizing—the tensions between the board and postal management.

I would add a footnote on foreign postal services, in view of a general impression that they have been privatized. The plan summarizes the changes in seven nations: Canada, United Kingdom, Germany, New Zealand, Sweden, Japan, and the Netherlands. These postal services have been granted more flexibility, in some cases a great deal more. As the plan states, however, each continues to be regulated by its government, "usually through an independent regulator."

In a revealing sentence the plan states that successful transformation depends in part "on adoption of moderate regulatory and legislative reforms." Its right-to-strike proposal is surely not "moderate." It may radically alter the relationship between the federal government and its employees, with unforeseen and possibly grave results.

The other legislative proposals, however, are indeed moderate, in keeping with the long-established reluctance of postal leaders to make the case for management flexibility. The Kappel Commission model that PMG "Red" Blount proposed to the Congress emphasized that the "essential element for the success of the Postal Corporation is a Board of Directors with full authority for postal management." That principle was undercut in the Postal Organization Act of 1970. It should be revived.

The Critical Issues

This is the overarching issue: What kind of Postal Service, if any, would best serve the American people? That is not the same as asking, "What is best for the Postal Service?" The critical subsidiary issues follow.

1. What should be the Postal Service's mission? (Should it be free to engage in any postal-related activity, and who defines *postal-related?*)
2. Should the Postal Service be privatized or "commercialized" with a degree of public control, as in some countries?
3. In view of its present universal service mission, should the Postal Service, now supported by customer revenues, be partly supported by taxes? Or should it return to tax-supported cabinet status?

4. Should universal service be redefined, abolished, or modified?
5. Should the monopoly on letter mail be abolished or modified?
6. How should postal wages be determined? Should collective bargaining exclude binding arbitration? If so, what happens if there is an impasse? Should *comparable pay* be defined by law to refer to similar work in the private sector?
7. Should postal union members have the right to strike?
8. Should the Postal Service be free to close some of the sixteen thousand post offices that lose money? Or are these small post offices justified for noneconomic reasons or to maintain universal service?
9. Should business mailers continue to be required, by law, to subsidize nonprofit mailers? Nonprofits such as Johns Hopkins, Harvard, the AARP, and the Beer Drinkers of America pay only 60 percent of what businesses pay to send advertising mail.
10. Should all or some of the part-time governors be replaced by, say, three full-time governors? Should the statute guide the president's nominations by requiring experience in large corporations or institutions?
11. Should executive salaries in this $70 billion organization continue to be held to levels that are a joke by private sector standards? (The postmaster general's annual pay is $166,700.)

On October 1, 2002, Michael J. Critelli, Pitney Bowes CEO and president of a new group, the Mailing Industry CEO Council, issued a press release stating: "If we are going to have a viable and competitive mailing system in the 21st century, we cannot afford to wait any longer for the serious reforms that will be necessary. It is increasingly clear that we need a Presidential Postal Commission to kick-start the legislative process, and we strongly urge the Administration to consider this idea." The council's board of directors includes the CEOs of companies such as Lands' End, ADVO, Reader's Digest, and Lockheed Martin.

That same month, in an earlier draft, I had written, "There is now some reason to hope." On December 11, 2002, mirabile dictu, President Bush established a commission on the Postal Service by Executive Order (app. 2). Cochaired by James A. Johnson, vice chairman of Perseus, and Harry J. Pearce, chairman of Hughes Electronics, it was hailed by postal officials and most mailers as a responsible step. The largest postal union was highly critical, and others are reserving judgment.

While applauding the appointment of a commission, I was dismayed to note that it was authorized only four staffers and was given a July 31, 2003, deadline. Both are severe handicaps to producing a bold, high-quality report. In fact, its July 31, 2003, report, *Embracing the Future*,[13] failed to grapple fully with the critical issues of binding arbitration and rate setting. A great opportunity to perform a significant service for our society has been lost.

CHAPTER SIX

Professionalism as Third-Party Governance

The Function and Dysfunction of Medicare

Sallyanne Payton

Medicare is the most ambitious and complex social program in the American government: at staggering expense it provides virtually universal coverage to persons over the age of sixty-five for a large fraction of their expenditures on acute medical care.[1] Medicare is also one of the most politically successful programs in the American government, notwithstanding its enormous cost and admitted maladministration,[2] defying the conventional wisdom that the American people will not stand for "big government" and resist assigning functions to government because they perceive it to be incompetent. Medicare is not small, not cheap, and not well run. But it is loved. The affection for it suggests inquiring into why, even though Americans express fear at the prospect of having government take primary responsibility for ensuring the delivery of medical services, as illustrated by public reaction to President Bill Clinton's proposed national health plan, Medicare does not elicit a fearful response. The most urgent current political demand related to Medicare is for an expansion of the benefit package to include prescription drugs and chronic care, and, most startlingly, public opinion pollsters report that a majority of the public have said that they would rather strengthen Medicare and Social Security than have a tax cut.[3]

The Medicare experience consequently cannot be reduced to easy constructs or be judged in accordance with simple ideas. Government programs, like the rest of us, have in addition to their virtues and defects the virtues of their defects and the defects of their virtues. It seems likely that many of Medicare's defects are attributable to its virtues and, conversely, many of its virtues to its defects. Since its great identified defects are (1) its commitment to 1960s-style fee-for-service medicine and (2) the weakness of the federal administrative role, as contrasted with the large powers exercised within the program by nonfederal or nongovernmental entities, these might also be the source of its unique and paradoxical strength. That is the hypothesis that animates this discussion.

A Joint Venture in Governance

Medicare was designed to be a collaboration between two different and equally respected systems of governance: (1) the federal government's constitutional power to tax and spend,[4] used here to purchase medical services for those over the age of sixty-five; and (2) traditional medical professional guild-style collective self-regulation, which is enabled by delegations of power from the states and controlled by institutions in the voluntary sector. Medicare's design is the outcome of the bargain struck in 1965 between the federal government and the self-governing providers of medical services: the federal government would be allowed to become the monopolist and monopsonist in medical services for the elderly only if it constrained its role to that of payer and otherwise allowed the medical services sector to operate in its usual ways through its own usual governance structures, which included state licensing of providers, indemnity fee-for-service payment to providers, any-willing-provider access to the program and its patients, quality assurance through professional self-governance, support of academic overhead and research through patient fees, payment administration through the profession's own fiscal intermediaries, and immunity from payer or state interference with the actual practice of medicine.[5]

Medicare is consequently a florid example of distributed governance and surely the most expensive instance,[6] but its basic form is similar to those of other programs built on extensive partnerships with professionals and their institutions to provide services to a clientele of the government. Apart from its scale and expense Medicare is not greatly different from, for example, scholarship entitlement programs that enable students to attend accredited institutions of higher learning: the government enables its clientele to afford a service rendered by professionals in accordance with professional standards and subject to professional governance.

If designed properly, these partnerships between the state and professionalism, like other partnerships between the state and the instrumentalities of civil society, are not only unproblematic but are extensively beneficial, enabling the competent achievement of public purposes without the creation of large state organizations. In no program are these beneficial effects on display more conspicuously than in Medicare. The less-than-beneficial effects are also extensive and, again, in no program more conspicuously than in Medicare. Medicare furnishes examples of nearly everything that can go right and everything that can go wrong in a partnership between government and a learned profession and is consequently both a beacon and an object lesson.

Problematics of the Partnership

What has gone right in Medicare, given its initial premises, is that Medicare has brought indemnity fee-for-service health coverage to American seniors, as promised. What has gone wrong is that the program costs too much as measured either by the share of the federal budget going into Medicare payment or by the value to seniors and to the public of the moneys spent, that is, by the ratio of medical utility to price. The imminent retirement of the leading edge of the Baby Boom generation makes it imperative to restructure the program to improve its value and capacity to adapt to the new demands about to be placed on it.[7]

The core problem is the fee-for-service provider payment system, which is Medicare's central design element. Contention over the Medicare program consequently tends to focus on, or resolve into, arguments about the payment system. This is about more than money. For most M.D. physicians who came of age professionally before cost containment and managed care, fee-for-service payment is the cornerstone of economic independence and therefore of professional autonomy, the *therefore* being the key element in the connection between the two.

Across the economy fee-for-service payment is the norm for clinical services rendered by professionals to patients or clients where the client is receiving the service and paying the bill. The fee-for-service technique of payment is ubiquitous in the service sector and is compatible with vigorous competition on price and quality if markets are competitive. Fee-for-service payment is used most commonly for transactions in which customized service is necessary and neither provider nor client is prepared to commit in advance to a fixed price and therefore to assume the full business risk associated with uncertainty about the nature of the client's problem and the cost of possible solutions. Where the client holds the checkbook, and the information imbalance is not extreme, client and provider may decide jointly on what actions to take, at what cost, as the project proceeds. Fee-for-service payment is therefore compatible with extreme attention to client requirements and preferences.

Relatively few potential customers for medical services can afford adequate medical care if they must pay for it themselves. Third-party payment is therefore the economic foundation on which widespread access to medical service is built. At the same time that third-party payment expands the market for medical services, then, it creates a tension between the provider's desire to serve the patient and the provider's urgent need to be on good terms with the payer, whose interests may not be aligned with those of the patient. The central issues of health financing policy consequently tend to focus on the terms on which third-party payers will be required or permitted to furnish payment.

The conflict over how physicians will be paid by third-party payers frames the controversies over health policy in the United States. Physicians strongly favor techniques that support rather than displace the direct relationship between physician and patient.[8] They therefore prefer that third-party payment be structured as indemnity insurance when the insurer furnishes to or on behalf of the patient the funds to pay the physician's bills, which are constructed on the lines of ordinary fee-for-service arrangements between individual customers and individual suppliers.

This preference of the physicians is in tension with the rational preferences of the third-party payers. All payers have an interest in using their market position to make better bargains on price than individual patients can obtain, and some payers prefer to employ physicians directly on salary or contract or to pay a capitated rate for bulk purchases of medical services, rather than to pay separate bills for individual services. All of these payment techniques have the effect of making the physician alert to the payer's interests and preferences as well as those of the patient. Unfortunately, the interests and preferences of the payer may be different from those of the patient. For example, the motive of some corporate payers in arranging for the provision of medical services to the pop-

ulations they serve is that the individuals are factors in the corporations' production. Military units, sports teams, and some employers keep physicians and
other health professionals on staff. The patients served by such physicians may
have objectives for their own care that differ from the objectives of the payer,
which creates a conflict for the physician. It also happens that corporations (including governments) need to furnish medical services the purpose of which is
to establish authoritative predicates for taking certain types of action, as when
the certification of a medical condition is necessary to qualify an individual for
a benefit. Such services lend themselves to bulk procurement; as, for instance,
when a payer contracts with particular physicians for all of its workers' compensation examinations. This also is a situation full of potential for conflict:
The payer may prefer to contract with physicians who will keep firmly in mind
the payer's interest in the outcome of the examination. Finally, corporate payers will rationally tend to gravitate toward managing their medical costs the
same way they manage other aspects of their operations: They may seek to
achieve administrative control and promote administrative efficiency, may try
to rationalize the medical work and workforce, and may try to aim for a value
point that they regard as representing an acceptable relationship between price
and quality. Rationalization of medical work and workforce threatens the autonomy of the individual physician, and the payer's idea of value in medical
service may not match the patient's or allow the physician to do what he or she
considers best for the patient.

The clinical professional frequently finds him- or herself under the effective
control of payers who are not alarmed at potential deterioration in the quality
of care or the state of the medical art. Both providers and patients are
commodified when distinctions among them are collapsed into a single summary price for clinical services, which may, in addition, be made the subject of
negotiation or competition. Rationalization and commodification are inconsistent with the idea of a personal relationship between provider and patient
and inconsistent with the idea of the patient as a unique human being and the
image of the professional as a dignified person who is somewhat apart from
the ordinary world of commerce.

Finally, there is the threat of direct administrative control of clinical professionals by organizations engaged in the business of arranging and delivering
medical services. These organizations range from small nonprofit clinics to
very large managed care organizations. What they have in common is that
they employ medical professionals on salary or contract to deliver the medical

services that the organization is responsible for furnishing under its agreement with a patient or payer. These corporations challenge the medical profession itself for control of the practice of medicine, because their dominance in the medical marketplace tends to make employment or contract labor preferable to independent practice and, therefore, to diminish the degree to which medical standards are developed autonomously by medical professionals without regard to the interests of organizations that do not have direct responsibility for patient care or legal liability to patients for injuries caused by failure to abide by professional standards of care.

The stakes in the payment system are consequently high. Fee-for-service payment by payers, for physicians, is not just about money; physicians have historically argued that the basic principles of fee-for-service medicine instantiate a piece of the social compact itself, because fee-for-service payment supports the integrity of the physician's focus on the individual patient.[9] In the 1930s the American Medical Association and its affiliates adopted professional codes of ethics forbidding practitioners to allow themselves to be employed on salary or to contract on any but a fee-for-service basis,[10] and they obtained state legislation specifically forbidding the corporate practice of medicine. By 1965 the normative correctness of fee-for-service payment by payers to providers had been established after hard and continuing battles between organized medicine and the corporations, including the government and the hospitals, which had attempted to absorb physicians into their own operations as paid labor, employed by salary or contract.

The bitterness of this conflict cannot be overstated. In the early decades of the twentieth century organized medicine resisted vigorously the employment of physicians by corporations of any type. Its particular contempt was reserved for the early group health associations, which were integrated medical services firms that hired doctors on salary in order to save money. These were mainly workers' and consumers' cooperatives, staffed by idealistic physicians, and were clearly aligned with patient interests, which were actually represented in their governance structures. Mainstream practitioners denounced these organizations as communist, and their physicians were ostracized on the grounds of their being incompetent and unethical.[11] Government control of medicine was out of the question: The Roosevelt administration dared not even bring up the question of national health insurance at the time when it argued for personal income support through Social Security.

This standoff was resolved by the invention in the 1930s of hospital-

sponsored private health insurance developed in response to the political im-
possibility of creating government-sponsored national health insurance. The
rise of private nonprofit health insurance through the Blue Cross plans,
owned by regional associations of nonprofit hospitals, defused political
conflict by obviating it. By the 1940s employers could buy health insurance
for their workers, guaranteeing them access to mainstream medical care. The
Blue Cross allowed all hospitals and all physicians to participate in the insurance-funded marketplace that it created, thus protecting the structure of universal access of all doctors to all patients, and vice versa. Blue Cross plans paid
ordinary and customary fees to physicians and "reimbursed" hospitals for
their costs, all on a fee-for-service basis, and deliberately eliminated the possibility of price competition and business risk for the providers.[12] Seeing the
success of the Blue Cross, commercial insurers, never having developed the
health insurance market on their own, followed the coverage model established by the Blue Cross and used health insurance as a loss leader for their
more lucrative lines of life and disability insurance, all three sold together as a
package. Once private health insurance became a standard fringe benefit of
employment after World War II, the group health associations became marginal except in their core service areas, and organized medicine continued to
argue with conviction that care given by physicians who were on contract to
corporations was inferior to the care given by physicians in private practice,
who were paid fee-for-service by their patients or, increasingly, by their patients' health insurance plans.

There matters rested during the war years of the 1940s through the economic boom of the mid-1950s. Employer-paid group insurance, tax-favored
by the Internal Revenue Code of 1954, diffused quickly into the employee
compensation packages of mainstream employers. By the late 1950s, however,
the inflationary tendencies of indemnity fee-for-service payment became apparent as workers who had retired found that they could afford neither the
cost of hospitalization nor the cost of health insurance. They turned to their
state legislatures, some of which began seriously to consider price controls on
hospitals, and they importuned the Congress to provide federal funding for
health coverage. This was the political movement that eventually brought
about enactment of Medicare after the Johnson landslide of 1964. Medicare's
primary purpose was to bring retirees' medical purchasing power into parity
with that of workers covered through their employers.

The Medicare program was designed to replicate the standard Blue Cross benefit package and the Blue Cross pattern of administration, the cornerstone of which was fee-for-service provider payment. Institutionalizing fee-for-service payment in Medicare made the program enactable because it allowed government funding of medical services while eliminating the possibility of government control of the practice of medicine. As in the employer-based private insurance programs, fee-for-service indemnification was essential to the establishment of what the medical professionals viewed as a right relationship between and among the government, the providers, and the beneficiaries.

Medicare is therefore structured as a voucher program,[13] one of the oldest and certainly the largest in government. The advantage of organizing a government program as a voucher is that the government purchases the service rather than producing it, ideal where there is a demand for government services but no constituency for growth in the apparent size of government and no desire for government control of production and distribution. In a voucher program the service is produced in the ordinary way, and the matching of beneficiaries and providers is taken care of by the market, as are the management and administration involved in production of the service. The government agency in charge of such a program becomes some combination of payer, regulator, and auditor. The agency also makes policy and handles the program's relationships.

Programs that are designed to stimulate consumption of a professional service through a voucher given to program beneficiaries create a governance partnership between the state and the profession. These partnerships require relatively modest regulatory effort specific to the program because the profession, under the general laws that give it powers of self-regulation, maintains its own licensing or credentialing apparatus and has its own professional standards and techniques of enforcing them. Unless government wishes to add particular types of regulation relevant to the program's particular mission, it can simply accept the actions of the existing professional regulatory and credentialing systems in satisfaction of its own standards. For example, the administrators of the Pell Grant program that funds student tuition can rely on educational institutions' own accreditation systems to identify trustworthy schools and can rely on the accredited schools themselves to control the quality of the curriculum. The Medicare program has a similar structure: One can think of Medicare as the equivalent of scholarship fund for patients, an extreme example of a voucher. A pure voucher program was not what advocates of national health insurance had originally had in mind, so it might be useful to pause to place the specific design and relationship issues in their larger political context.

The Politics and Metapolitics of Federal Health Insurance

The legislative compromise that produced Medicare was achieved after a pitched battle between the competing ideologies that generally shape American politics. In 1964–65 Lyndon Johnson was determined to complete the New Deal by creating a health insurance program to complement Social Security, and, predictably, organized medicine and political conservatives opposed his effort, as they had opposed every previous attempt to create a national health insurance system. The physicians, as noted earlier, thought that Medicare would amount to socialized medicine, which they opposed passionately. The political conservatives, who objected on general principle to expanding the reach of the state and creating a direct patronage relationship between ordinary citizens and the federal government, objected in particular to Medicare's proposed features of direct federal administration and universality. Medicare was not to be means tested, which meant that ordinary Americans would become accustomed to receiving a tax-financed benefit of great importance directly and visibly from federal officials.

Liberals, by contrast, were committed to universality and to a social insurance rather than welfare principle precisely *because* that approach would create a middle-class constituency for the program as it had already done for the income support portion of Social Security. In this they prevailed. They compromised, however, their preference for a strong federal administrative role and for federal control of the shape of the medical industry, even though to do so cut against what were then regarded as fundamental principles of national health insurance as expressed in the health care systems of other industrialized countries. At the time when the Medicare legislation was being considered, Britain's National Health Service (NHS) was a widely admired model of a government-run national health care system. The NHS rationalized medical service delivery by using nurses in place of physicians for primary care, controlled the building of health care facilities, and rationed the specialty care provided in the hospitals. Private health coverage in the United States, by contrast, pioneered by the hospitals to encourage utilization of their services, allowed unlimited access to physicians and specialty care, thus concentrating resources on acute care at the expense of preventive and primary care and public health services and encouraging medically inefficient spending on expensive services aimed at correcting conditions that might more cheaply be prevented or managed. These features of private coverage were deliberate design principles intended to promote the advance of medical science, focusing on acute care to restore function to workers and their families who had employment-based coverage. To create a government system for the nonworking elderly on the model of workers' private coverage was, therefore, to adopt flawed economic and medical principles from the beginning. Any doubts about the prudence of pursuing this course were outweighed, however, by the fact that the political moment for federalizing health coverage had arrived.

The interest group that mediated crucially between the political liberals and conservatives consisted of the private voluntary hospitals, which badly needed a source of funding to augment the charitable resources they were devoting to care of the uninsured, now including retirees. Apart from being former rather than current workers, the retirees matched the demographic profile of the mainstream workforce and electorate. They were thus squarely within the constituency that the nonprofit voluntary hospitals were created to serve. The cost of their care thus became an issue for the leadership of their communities.

The leadership of the voluntary sector generally supported federal assistance to health care but was wary of national health insurance. The governing bodies of private voluntary hospitals tended to be composed of persons who were in the political center-right, committed to serving the public interest and favoring decentralization in government operations and a strong influence of local or mediating institutions on policy. In the mid-1960s these institutions were doing the essential work of medical professional service delivery and governance and were anxious to obtain the resources necessary to continue to carry out their mission as the cost of care and public demand for care both increased. They supported government action to augment private voluntary action, not to supplant it. They therefore advocated federal support for patients who were not covered by insurance and who otherwise lacked the means to pay their bills—those who could be regarded as "medically indigent"—and their interest extended to the under-sixty-five group. They advocated a non-age-delimited, means-tested federal grant-in-aid program to assist the states, in preference to an age-delimited, non-means-tested centralized national program with direct federal administration. In the 1965 political cycle the voluntary hospitals' approach became Medicaid.

For the voluntary hospitals the most problematic aspect of Medicare as proposed by the Johnson administration was that it would be administered directly by the federal government. The liberals' willingness to compromise on direct federal administration made Medicare politically viable, because it enabled the voluntary hospital industry to abandon its historic opposition to federalizing health insurance. Twenty years previously the hospitals had joined the physicians in opposing President Harry Truman's proposal for national health insurance, but by the 1960s much had changed. The voluntary hospital industry, commanding a substantial cash flow from employee benefit plans in the postwar boom, had developed, in collaboration with other voluntary institutions such as universities and foundations, an institutional capacity for governing the health services sector of the economy and administering a private fee-for-service medical coverage system of continental scope. With the Johnson landslide making further resistance in principle to federal funding seem futile, the question was how to tailor an accommodation between the public demand for funding and the health care sector's demand for professional self-governance. The design ultimately settled upon was that the federal government's role would be made to emulate as closely as possible that of a private employer that had purchased coverage for its employees from Blue Cross.[14]

In 1965 employers simply paid capitated fees or premiums for their employees. They did not administer the insurance plans themselves nor set health policy for their employees nor have any direct role in the governance of the health care sector. Governance was done by the states and the voluntary sector. Claims administration was done by the insurers, the main organizations of this type being the hospitals' captive "service benefit" Blue Cross plans. Health policy consisted of guaranteeing that the patients might consult the physician of their choosing and receive whatever services their physicians decided were medically necessary. Health coverage was intended to facilitate essentially private patient-provider relationships governed by private law.

The hospitals therefore bargained for a similar arrangement for the government's clientele, which meant writing these roles into the Medicare statute. The basic structure of the Medicare fee-for-service program has been stable since its enactment. The locus of administration has changed since 1965, some updating of the program structure has occurred with adoption of prospective payment systems, and program integrity operations have been augmented, but the essential tasks of the Medicare fee-for-service medical system and the assignment of powers in the Medicare statute are familiar from the 1965 political bargain. The current functions are set forth in table 6.1.

Table 6.1. Current Administrative Functions in Medicare Fee-for-Service

Function	Done by	Control
Issue regulations and policy guidance	Centers for Medicare and Medicaid Services	Political accountability through Executive Branch and Congress
Qualify and enroll beneficiaries	Social Security Administration	Legal right of beneficiaries (entitlement program), political accountability
Furnish information to beneficiaries	CMS	Political accountability
License and credential providers	States, voluntary sector institutions, e.g., specialty societies, Joint Committee on Accreditation of Healthcare Organizations (JCAHO)	State political and legal processes, governance structures of voluntary sector organizations
Enter providers into Medicare	CMS	Automatic for licensed providers on signing participating provider agreement
Determine payment policies and rates	Congress, CMS	Political accountability
Deliver services	Providers	Professional controls, legal liability to patients
Qualify services for payment	Physicians certify eligibility by determining medical necessity of services	Program integrity enforcement
Administer claims	Nongovernment intermediaries (for Part A) and carriers (for Part B) are designated by provider organizations and become contracted agents for government.	Contract enforcement
Conduct quality control activities	Professional self-discipline, Peer Review Organizations, courts through enforcement of rights	Accountability for professional self-discipline is with profession; PROs are accountable through contract with CMS, courts are a separate branch
Conduct program integrity operations (i.e., fraud and abuse enforcement)	CMS, HHS Inspector General and U.S. attorneys	Political accountability
Manage dispute resolution	First line is carriers and intermediaries, thereafter agency administrative proceedings	Litigation

The enormous virtue of this distribution is that it allows the federal government to borrow the existing governance and administrative capacities of its nongovernmental and nonfederal partners to create a vast and, at least initially from the point of view of beneficiaries and providers, competently administered federal program: Medicare actually began operations at scale within a few months of enactment of the legislation. The defect of the distribution of power is that the Centers for Medicare and Medicaid Services (CMS) do not carry out most of the functions required for the governance and administration of Medicare, which means that the program's performance depends on the thinly supervised performance of the federal government's partners. The situation has been aggravated by congressional underfunding of even the small portion of Medicare administration which is actually the responsibility of government: CMS has fewer than five thousand full-time equivalent employees, many fewer than required to perform competently the core functions assigned directly to it, which include, in addition to managing most of Medicare, responsibility for Medicaid, the regulation of private plans under (HIPAA), privacy protection, and much else. More dangerously, persistent underfunding of the core means that CMS lacks capacity to manage its relationships with its various institutional partners and to make certain that the interests of the government are adequately addressed in their operations.

This is of greatest concern in the case of the Medicare intermediaries and carriers, collectively called the "contractors." The contracting-out of the most important operational responsibility of the program, which is to pay claims, makes Medicare an early example of a business practice now much recommended, which is shrinking an entity to its core competence and contracting out functions in which there is a developed capacity in outside contractors.[15] For Medicare, which could easily have choked on the task of administering a nationwide universal entitlement to clinical medical services, extensive contracting out solved not only administrative challenges but political and conceptual problems as well.

Contracting Out for Fit and Flexibility

The Congress built the contracting out of claims administration deliberately into the governance design as part of the original compromise of 1965. This move solved three problems simultaneously: (1) Medicare quickly acquired a large-scale administrative capacity without building a large government organization; (2) the regionalized payment machinery of the Blue Cross complemented the structure and conformed to the payment preferences of the medical industry, thus avoiding a clash of cultures between payer and the community of payees; and (3) delegating to the Blue Cross authority to pay fee-for-service institutionalized a politically legitimate, culturally appropriate concept and practice of equality in access to clinical services.

Notwithstanding the basic flaws in the Medicare design, these were enormous achievements that should not be underappreciated. Medicare's instant success as a piece of administrative machinery was due to the unique nature of the Blue Cross as an insurance organization. First of all, and most important, the Blue Cross had unsurpassed credibility because it was the nonprofit financing arm of the voluntary hospital industry and so was no ordinary commercial insurer but, rather, was a kind of public service organization that had created the functional equivalent of a national health insurance plan (though not a universal one) which compensated for the failure of government itself. Second, the Blue Cross had a state and regional structure, which meant that every Blue Cross plan was accustomed to dealing with local practice patterns. Third, delegation to the Blue Cross made it possible for the Congress to achieve what Medicare promised, which was parity between Medicare patients and privately insured ones, since by coordinating its coverage and payment practices the Blue Cross could make Medicare policy-in-action match the policy-in-action of the Blue Cross private plans.

The availability of the Blue Cross to run Medicare claims administration helped to solve the problem of relationships with providers. A national voucher-type entitlement program presents the challenge of how to make it possible for a large, centralized, rule-governed, complex hierarchical payer organization such as, for example, the Social Security Administration, to have a comfortable relationship with a payee industry that is a network composed of individuals and relatively small entities that tend to work in specialized or localized communities of practice with very little administrative capacity and extreme antagonism to corporate authority. The medical industry is fundamentally a community of professionals which depends on individual initiative to create new knowledge and technique. Information is disseminated through academic channels or practice groups such as hospital medical staffs and specialty societies, and knowledge diffuses through being adopted into practice by clinical professionals who become persuaded that a particular item or technique works for their patients. The practitioners and organizations that provide patient care have direct liability to patients for injuries and damage caused by clinical failure traceable to malpractice and are therefore the driving force in determining actual practice standards. High levels of individual professional responsibility produce high resistance to being told what to do by persons who are not familiar with the individual patient being served.

The consequence of this extreme lack of hierarchy is that there are in the medical industry hundreds of thousands of small units with nonstandardized practices and procedures of all types. In 1965 the medical industry's organizing principles were still personal professional responsibility, individual and small group practice, collective professional self-discipline, collegial exchange through hospital medical staff organization, and collective commitment to the development and sharing of professional knowledge. The danger for the medical industry was that a monopsonistic payer of the centralized, hierarchical type would develop payment rules and models that would force medical practice, and therefore the medical profession, into its own image. The payment system had to be made in the image of the medical industry, or the industry would take on a shape complementary to the administrative preferences of the payer.[16]

The Blue Cross was an appropriate payer because it had been made in the image of the medical industry. It was a federation of state and substate regional plans, each of which was owned by the local nonprofit hospitals. The Blue Cross plans were deeply familiar with and committed to their local communities of practice and were accustomed to handling fee-for-service claims arising out of them. Enlisting the Blue Cross as the claims administrator for Medicare gave the Social Security Administration, which was a classically hierarchical, rule-bound payer, a capacity that was the functional equivalent of a decentralized, specialized field operation with discretion to tailor general policies to local conditions.

Finally, turning over claims administration responsibility to the Blue Cross eliminated controversy over equality principles. As a universal entitlement program grounded in an equality ethic, Medicare must reconcile the concept of equality with the fact of variations in practice style among health care providers and resource consumption among program beneficiaries. The challenge is to identify the correct index of equality when the service is individually tailored clinical medical care that is normatively correct on it own terms when it treats different persons differently for reasons that cannot be stated as rules of general applicability. The answer for Medicare was to defer to professional standards, which affirm the appropriateness of variance and individuation of both patients and providers within an ethic of treating everyone as being of equal value, equally entitled to have their medical needs met. That equal caring should result in different styles of care and different levels of resource consumption is not then problematic, being grounded in respect for the individual. This fundamentally Kantian (and familial) medical ethic was politically attractive and had the additional merit of being easy to administer. No collective process was required and no rules. The ethic of giving every patient the care appropriate to his or her condition according to medical standards was built into the medical economy itself, requiring only that patient and provider be enabled to find each other in a marketplace in which no third party had power to decide who should consult whom or what the treatment should be.

Fee-for-service payment was a support for the concept of equality as equal caring, and turning over claims administration to the Blue Cross affirmed the Congress's adherence to the values of the medical profession and its adoption of the medical model for equality and entitlement. It also reassured the medical community that its professional model would not be challenged by a centralized administration intent on making national rules, required by the imperatives of rationality to stamp out every variation not illustrative of a principle behind a rule. The genius of this solution was that the institutionalization in federal policy of variation of medical practice was silent and largely invisible. The actual coverage policies that are tailored to local practice patterns are buried in the mountains of claims payments that pass through the Blue Cross organizations.[17]

Automatic Process, Hollow Organization, Permeable Boundary

From the point of view of both providers and patients, the flow of Medicare benefits and payments comes untouched by federal hands. Conversely, Medicare's operations are, from the point of view of the government, automatic, indeed an extreme case of the kind of "automaticity" which Lester Salamon discusses in *Tools of Government*. Salamon notes that analysts generally esteem tools such as vouchers, of which Medicare is an example, because a program that exhibits this characteristic "utilizes an existing administrative apparatus for its operations rather than creating its own special administrative apparatus."[18] The design of Medicare is an extreme case of automaticity in this sense. With respect to the beneficiaries, the program is entirely automatic: They choose their own providers and have their claims paid by the contractors. Many beneficiaries have no need to come into contact with a federal official. For providers the automaticity consists of their automatic entitlement to Medicare participation if they have been licensed by state governments or, in the case of institutions, accredited by the Joint Commission on Accreditation of Healthcare Organizations (JCAHO), which is their own private organization. Payment, under the compromise of 1965, came to them through their own financing arm, the Blue Cross, and followed their preferred practices of provider payment.

Under the compromise of 1965 no federal administrative agency was given a substantial practical role in the operation of the program. Medicare administration is usefully regarded as an early example of a "virtual" organization, held together by contract and coordination rather than by ownership or administrative hierarchy. The virtues of the automaticity and the limitations on the federal administrative role have already been discussed. The corresponding defects are the reverse side of the virtues: The weak federal administrative role has led to the development of a relatively weak federal administrative agency.

"Hollowness" is the affliction of organizations that contract out functions and do not retain or develop within themselves the capacity to perform these functions, with the consequence that knowledge about how to do essential tasks is held by outside entities. The organization's function becomes one of managing relationships with its partners, who are actually doing the work. Inevitably, eventually, the organization's own lack of knowledge and skill translate into an imbalance in bargaining power and in general stature within the domain that mirrors the actual imbalance in intellectual and managerial capacities. This can happen to any organization, from automobile manufacturers to government agencies. It can be a virtue when the organization intends to be a broker or purchaser rather than a producer but is problematic when the organization is actually responsible to third parties for performance of the functions contracted out. CMS is a classically hollow organization, routinely overmatched by "stakeholder" interests.

The hollowness of the CMS, in combination with the automaticity feature of the Medicare program, has the consequence that the relationship between CMS and the stakeholders in the Medicare program is the antithesis of the classic "iron triangle" of industry, agency, and congressional committee depicted in the political science literature. CMS acts only rarely to affect program operations, and when it does so its actions tend to constrict and encumber the flow of benefits and funds, placing CMS in the role of regulator rather than benefactor vis-à-vis the providers. The agency thus tends to find itself in a confrontational posture in regard to powerful elements among stakeholders. For example, recent administrative actions implementing legislation that imposes greater financial accountability on the providers and which intensifies program integrity operations have resulted in provider backlash against the agency, manifesting itself in expressions of extreme lack of confidence. At the present time the relationship between the CMS and the provider communities has something of the flavor of the relationship between the Internal Revenue Service and taxpayers in jeopardy of audit. Congressional support of the stakeholders against the agency progressively erodes the capacity of the only entity in the Medicare system which is committed to the interests of the government.[19]

The Medicare experience suggests that designers of government programs should exercise caution in creating government programs with the characteristic of automaticity and government agencies with the characteristic of hollowness. Designers should be alert to the fact that whatever structure of interests is created by a government program will become part of the political environment, so there is positive feedback to whatever the government does. The governance process is dynamic, not static. Forces set in motion at Time 1 must be contended with at Time 2, and the results of the transactions at Time 2 are the essential context of what happens at Time 3, and so forth. People who are given a cherished bounty will devote some portion of the bounty to activity designed to influence the source of the bounty to continue to act favorably toward them. If part of their bounty consists of a steady flow of funds watched over by weak administration, they have an interest in promoting the flow and enforcing the weakness, except where greater strength is to their advantage. Government creates the powers that then confront it.

Medicare illustrates another peculiarity of government which designers of governmental institutions should keep in mind, which is that the government does not have the kind of boundaries which might allow it to distinguish between its interest as customer and the interest of suppliers as suppliers, and to act in its interest alone. Every supplier to government is a constituent of government and is therefore entitled to participate in the process of attempting to influence legislative and executive action. This means that the government's suppliers are represented in the government's own governance mechanism. By contrast, the officers and directors of private corporations have an enforceable fiduciary duty to the shareholders alone, and suppliers are not represented as a matter of right on the corporation's board of directors.

Private businesses thus have a flexibility to take up and discard various management practices involving outside parties which government as a practical matter does not have. An administrative or payment system once set into statute tends to stay there regardless of its suitability to changing conditions, because it structures flows of government-created powers, privileges, and opportunities to persons who have an interest in retaining them and will use political power to that end. Given the inertia intrinsic to government, it has always been regarded as prudent for designers of federal government programs to allow new ways of doing business to be the subject of experimentation in the states and the private sector, and to evaluate the experience, before committing major federal programs to them by statute.

This brings us to the subject of managed care, enthusiasm for which violates the principle just stated. There are reasons for the federal government to look to capitated HMOs to solve the problems of Medicare, but they are easier to describe in terms of the government's inability to loosen the grip of the present Medicare stakeholders on federal policy than in terms of the intrinsic merits of the kind of commercial managed care which has become popular with health policy experts. Experience has not, apparently, triumphed over hope to dislodge the managed care strategy from the repertoire of respectable policy initiatives despite the unhappy experiences of the Medicare+Choice program and the pandemic failure of the managed care industry as a whole.

The reason for this is obvious enough: The selective contracting strategies developed by large private health plans to manage the procurement of medical services for fee-for-service coverage, which form the most obvious model for the evolution of Medicare, are unavailable as models for Medicare restructuring because of opposition by stakeholders who fear losing Medicare business if they are subjected to an evaluation for quality, price, and value. A competitive market with aggressive purchasers has losers, which Medicare has thus far avoided creating. Re-creating Medicare as a program that offers beneficiaries a choice of plans and a defined contribution, by contrast, promises to create losers by operation of the market rather than by the decision of federal officials and, therefore, offers a way out of the present difficulties created by the federal government's hollow administration and excessive entanglement with suppliers. Indeed, in principle a managed care strategy would move the hollowness of Medicare administration back toward being a virtue, since it would make appropriate the existence of an agency that mainly manages relationships with contracting managed care firms and eschews the close administration inherent in direct contracting. The question, therefore, is how to think about the potential consequences of such a strategy, assuming that it can be made to succeed for the Medicare program.

Managed Care as a Challenge to the Intellectual Authority of the Medical Profession

Before we turn to the specific design issues with respect to managed care, we should pause to note that enthusiasm among policy experts for integrated medical service organizations paid on a capitated basis is the current manifestation of the challenge to medical authority which has been growing since the 1970s. Foremost among these challenges have been those arising from the economics profession and from the legal profession through antitrust enforcement. Economists have noted that fee-for-service medicine paid for by third parties on a cost-reimbursement basis creates an economic machine without a damper and makes it difficult to correlate expenditure with medical value. In the 1970s the legal profession launched an assault on the monopolies and cartels through which professions organized and protected their markets,[20] including most particularly the anticompetitive "ethics" of the medical profession which had been used to prevent physicians from being absorbed by corporations.[21] These two initiatives succeeded in establishing that insurance-funded fee-for-service medicine is economically wasteful and that it is illegal for medical professionals and institutions to act collectively to prevent economic integration and price competition. The turn toward managed care would have been impossible without these two developments.

The other two very important developments have been more subtle. Allopathic medicine has laid its claim to authority on the ground of its being "scientific medicine." In fact, however, very little of what constitutes actual medical practice has been subjected to the rigorous testing that goes into the making of knowledge that has the authority of science.[22] Most clinical practice styles are developed in communities of practice, and, as the Wennberg studies have shown,[23] practices may vary widely in their resource consumption without a corresponding variation in quality. More and more expensive care is not necessarily better care. It also turns out that apart from the rigorous testing of pharmaceuticals and the controlled clinical trials conducted in research centers, there is rather little formal science supporting medical practice. This is surely not objectionable in principle, but it undermines the physicians' claim to scientific authority and allows the entry of nonphysician researchers using rigorous methodologies into the business of evaluating the quality and value of medical practice styles. The ambivalent light shed by these inquiries on the actual science of allopathic practice has diminished the authority of the medical profession in its insistence that it autonomously achieves quality in practice. It also makes it more difficult for the allopaths to distinguish themselves from nonallopaths on the ground alone of the latter's being "unscientific" or to distinguish themselves categorically from nonphysician providers such as nurses on the ground of the superior scientific training of physicians.

In the absence of convincing categorical distinctions in principle, the question of relative merit comes down to one of performance, which is to say medical efficacy and satisfaction for the patients. The decline in the categorical authority of allopathic physicians opens the possibility of rationalizing the delivery of medical services by using nurses, chiropractors, acupuncturists, midwives, and other limited-license but independent caregivers in managed care settings. If quality control can be accomplished by direct measurement of results, then it is possible to rationalize the medical labor force, setting the various practitioners to work in areas of practice in which they have comparative advantage. Managed care is therefore a potential antidote to the inefficiencies created by the rigid occupational boundaries and jurisdictions that characterize professional markets. These efforts at rationalization are in their infancy, but the rise of the medical services corporation that has an urgent need to compete on price and quality and sufficient administrative capacity to achieve quality control creates the possibility of improving medical efficiency and quality simultaneously. Or so it is hoped. On the other hand, the strategy of enlisting the commercial corporation invites enormous difficulties.

Managed Care: Antidote to Professionalism

The managed care strategy, sometimes intensified by forcing health plans to compete on price in a managed competition, throws commercialism, disciplined by a regulated market, into the struggle against the shortcomings of professionalism, in the hope and expectation that the antagonistic forces will check one another and produce as a net result efficiently delivered and afford-able high-quality care achieved without contention over regulatory detail. The success of the strategy depends on the accuracy of the assumption that medical markets can be made sufficiently competitive to achieve dramatic reductions in price coupled with quality-enhancing innovations that will compensate the public for its loss of the quality assurance furnished by professionalism. This assumption is heroic as a matter of theory and has not been confirmed by ex-perience, which leads one to ask why health policy experts favor managed care/managed competition for Medicare when the large private employers, to whose programs the public programs are most closely analogous, have stayed away from it.

The managed care/managed competition model for reform is attractive mainly because, politically speaking, Medicare is trapped in its own success. The governance structure that makes possible its patient benefits and provider revenues was created and has been maintained for these nearly forty years be-cause the American public as a whole has been convinced of the desirability of a certain model of relationship between and among payers, providers, and beneficiaries which is encapsulated in the idea of professionalism and which delivers high-quality care.

Managed care can succeed against this model only if it also delivers good performance at good value in the context of a governance model that assures patients of the trustworthiness and competence of the people in charge. Tradi-tional idea-driven managed care, in the old group health associations, suc-ceeded on both dimensions, as do, apparently, the provider-owned managed care organizations. Commercial managed care, however, which became prominent in the health plan marketplace in the 1990s, has not competed suc-cessfully with professionalism on the question of trustworthiness, which has made the public skeptical and unforgiving with respect to other aspects of its performance, about which the actual evidence is ambiguous.[24]

The success of managed care in the market, as well as in the market of pub-lic opinion, depended on its being an improvement over the fee-for-service system in the view of the employees and voters. To these publics the promise was of service and product innovation that would allow managed care organi-zations to reduce costs and prices while maintaining or improving quality, al-lowing consumers to make the kinds of price/quality tradeoffs they are accus-tomed to making in the rest of their economic lives, with all choices being among medical products of more than acceptable overall quality. The medical services sector seemed especially amenable to this approach, since primary and preventive care can obviate the need for relatively expensive acute care. Costs and prices ought to fall as a natural consequence of helping people to stay healthy rather than concentrating on serving them after they become ill. Medically useful but extremely expensive acute care procedures would not have to be discouraged through rationing if they simply became medically unnecessary because of improvements in the efficiency of providing primary and preventive care. Consumers would reject medical procedures of uncertain utility in the presence of accurate price signals. This was more than a dream; it was an expectation based on microeconomic theory and, just as important, based on actual experience of quality improvement in manufacturing and other types of service.

It was also elegant: If providers would integrate economically and medical markets be made competitive, the accuracy of the price signal would do the rest of the work. The spur of price competition would result in reengineering and innovation, as business methods that had produced immense gains in global competitiveness for American industry would be turned to the improvement of medical care delivery. There would be a Jack Welch of the health maintenance organization (HMO) industry, a Marriott of hospital management, a Toyota of health plans.[25] It did not at the time seem unrealistic: Medical services were so badly managed that even corporate performances that would be mediocre by the standards of mainstream industry would be quantum leaps forward for health care.

Hundreds of billions of dollars have been lost in the attempt to make this projection come true. On the terrain of public opinion, however, commercialism is simply overmatched by professionalism and always will be, for good reason. One of the reasons why commercial managed care has not met expectations is that advocates of capitation who claim that commercial managed care is superior to professionalism as a set of principles for organizing medical care delivery have simply misdescribed the market for medical professional services. Standard microeconomic theory posits the consumer as a person who is buying items for his or her own consumption, making comparisons based on his or her own values, however constructed. The consumer is assumed to be an individualistic *Homo economicus* whose most primitive self-interested market behavior results in constant collective advance toward Pareto optimality if markets can be perfected. Markets for medical services are understood to deviate greatly in practice from optimality, but that has been thought, following Kenneth Arrow's seminal work,[26] to be mainly a function of uncertainty about the efficacy and therefore the value of medical services. Arrow identifies professional trustworthiness as a strategy for moderating uncertainty and overcoming information asymmetry, but his construct is consistent with the assumption that, if the consumer has perfect information, he or she might decide to take greater risks in choosing health care options in exchange for lower prices. Managed care is intended to bring to the consumer an opportunity to make better choices on better information, in order to express personal preferences in cost and styles of care.

In the real world of health care markets, however, purchasers are frequently buying or managing care on behalf of a third party to whom they have fiduciary duty, sometimes legally enforceable. This is the situation of parents with respect to their children and frequently of adult children who are taking care of their elderly parents. Some portion of the end-of-life care analyzed by John Wennberg occurs after the patient has lost cognitive capacity and the physician and surrogates are managing the care. In these situations the question for the purchaser/surrogate is not "What are my preferences?" but, rather, "What are my duties?" The answer is that the duty is to do what is in the patient's best interest. The surrogate's own best interest in such a situation consists of doing the right thing and being seen to have done it. Some tradeoffs that might be made in more individualistic situations are utterly inappropriate here. It should come as no surprise that people whose functions are shaped by their duties will prefer to have health care providers who share a sense of commitment and obligation. The reassurance provided by professionalism is frequently the guarantee that moral obligations are being satisfied. Viewed in this light, the public's suspicion of managed care and preference for professionalism are rational, particularly so when it comes to Medicare, which helps many family members discharge their duties toward their senior relatives.

Because of the pandemic business failure of commercial managed care, it now seems unlikely that Medicare will be restructured to make managed care the dominant form of service delivery or to intensify the managed care model into managed competition. Practicality does not, however, lay to rest the theoretical question: If managed competition were achievable, would it be desirable? The nub of the issue is whether it is a good idea to import into Medicare two elements that do not presently exist in the program: (1) an insurance principle to structure the relationship between patients and organizations that arrange their care; and (2) a principle of economic competition among integrated medical service organizations to determine what services will be offered at what prices.

The answer with respect to the insurance principle is surely negative. The insurance principle creates a vicious relationship between insurer and insured which leads the insurer to wish to terminate the relationship at precisely the moment when the insured most needs the service. There is a good reason why the insurance industry is pervasively regulated: The information asymmetries and the temptations for opportunistic behavior on the part of insurers are such that an individual needs the help of the state at virtually all points in the relationship. The health coverage context is the most daunting because protecting the consumer entails constant surveillance of insurers to ensure that they do not behave rationally in engaging in risk selection, rate manipulation, and unwarranted denials of care.

The insurance principle also creates conflict between the insurer and the professional who is giving the care. When the professional provider's life work is identified as a cost, as part of the "medical loss ratio," to use the insurance terminology, rather than an occasion for taking pride in caring for the sick, the provider is placed in a position of conflict with the organization's values, most intensely when the provider is committed to the care of the sickest patients. The theory of managed care is that this tension will be creative and beneficial rather than destructive and bitter, that it will produce good-quality care at the lowest achievable cost, since the insurer will discourage the providers from providing too much and the providers will prevent the insurer from providing too little. The theory of managed competition is that price competition will stimulate these managed care organizations to develop innovative, distinctive styles of practice, the assumption being that the managers and professionals in a managed care organization will collaborate because of their shared stake in the organization's success. Cooperation and goodwill are difficult to achieve, however, when the organization threatens the professionals' livelihoods. The theory of managed care, ironically, in placing conflict at the heart of the relationship between the organization and its professionals, encourages the creation of organizations with built-in tendencies to fail to inspire their professionals to create beneficial innovations. This theoretical insight is consistent with the observation that the predicted avalanche of innovation in service design and technique which was to have begun with the turn to managed care failed to materialize. The failure is probably overdetermined, but it cannot be good for an organization to be in structural conflict with the professionals on whom it depends for a large part of its capacity to think.

Because innovation is the key to progress, however, incorporating spurs to innovation in the design of any restructured Medicare program should be at the heart of public policy. The medical profession's success in advancing the medical art has resulted from the creation of communities of practice and from institutionalized research, all of which develops knowledge that is diffused into practice. The diffusion mechanism has a self-organizing quality: Those practitioners who keep up with developing practice find that their professional opportunities grow, and those who fall behind find that theirs contract. This mechanism can, in principle, be deployed to investigate and disseminate ways of creating greater efficiency and value. The question is whether managed competition is likely to do better.

There is good reason to think otherwise. The theory of managed competition is that the firms will develop their own practice styles and compete on the basis of strongly differentiated "brand names." This implies that the advances in practice styles will be proprietary information owned by the firms. One can imagine business method patents on medical practice methods. This vision of the integrated medical services firm as the owner of essential medical information is inconsistent with the idea of medicine as part of the scientific community, with its traditions of openness and sharing, and also with the idea of the medical professional as a knowledgeable, mobile person not bound to a single firm nor shackled by covenants not to disclose.

The other problem is to reconcile the goal of optimal patient care with our knowledge of how competition works as a dynamic process. In business a thousand flowers may bloom, but only three survive, and whatever information and benefit was associated with the others is lost. It will therefore happen that features of a product or service which were regarded favorably by the customers will be eliminated if the products have attributes that cause them to fail, even if the desirable features did not contribute to the failure. Conversely, not-particularly-desirable attributes that happen to be in units that succeed will be perpetuated, in preference to more desirable attributes that happen to be in units that fail, even if the not-particularly-desirable attributes did not contribute to the success of their units. The consequence is that the ultimate configuration of the successful units might be random relative to evolutionary desirability except for those particular attributes that actually account for the favorable selection. The survival of traits by association rather than genuine selection is called "hitchhiking" by those who study genetic algorithms; researchers try to eliminate hitchhiking in their models and experiments by making certain that the traits that determine survival are not weighted so heavily that they acquire numerous noncontributing hitchhikers.[27]

This hitchhiking dynamic is as true of organizations as of organisms, and there is no particular reason to believe that the managed care organizations that would survive a vigorous competition on price would be more desirable as purveyors of patient care, price aside, than those that fail. The elimination of competitive units because of small price differentials thus can be expected to have the effect of eliminating from the market useful features. In addition, the consolidation that results from vigorous price competition may well result in the formation of oligopolies or monopolies and therefore potentially put an effective end to the price competition itself,[28] thereby reducing consumer welfare.

These considerations suggest that, if there is a way to stimulate and diffuse medical innovation without using competition as the salient factor in a Darwinian selection process, the results might be better for patients. Consideration of the innovation problem points up the wisdom of the large employers who have tended to avoid adopting either insurance principles or managed competition as structures for their internal health plan markets. Federal health policy experts are convinced, however, that a federal agency would never be allowed discretionary command over the business opportunities afforded by Medicare which would equal the power of the managers of large employers' health benefit programs. Selective contracting is, from the point of view of the providers, a dangerous tool that Congress would probably permit to be wielded only with due process of law.[29]

Still, if the large employers are on the right track in deciding to structure their programs as exercises in prudent purchasing with modified fee-for-service payment, that seems to be the general direction in which to send Medicare. But wait—exactly what makes the large employers attractive as models for Medicare is exactly what Medicare cannot emulate, which is the absence of provider influence in their governance structures. Emulation seems to be out of the question. Partnership, however, might be worth investigating. Perhaps, hoping that the economists might be right in their optimism about the salutary effects of vigorous price competition among commercial entities, the health policy community has leaped too quickly to the idea of having Medicare partner with commercial organizations and has skipped over the question of whether there might not be some benefit in forging closer relationship between Medicare and the types of organizations which have employee or consumer interests represented in their governance structures or have a reason to be more responsive to those interests than to supplier interests.

The old group health associations, the cooperatives, and the union Taft-Hartley plans, all of which have subscriber/patient interests represented in their governance structures, are available as models for such organizations. Partnership between government and these kinds of instruments of civil society is far less jarring to the idea of a social insurance system than is partnership between government and commercial insurers. We should keep in mind that health coverage was developed not by commercial insurers whose relationship to the patients was limited to the insurance nexus but by the cooperative efforts of the voluntary sector and the large employers, which had a far more complicated relationship with their workforces than insurers have with the individuals in their books of business. Both experience and theory teach that in the context of health care coverage the insurance relationship is problematic and should be mitigated rather than intensified. This would be particularly the case with the Medicare beneficiary population, which has never been well-served by the commercial insurance market.

Robustness and Rigidity in Medicare

At the end of this discussion we come to the question of what accounts for the strength of Medicare and what we can learn from this exploration. The strength appears to come from the fact that the partnership between the government and medical professionalism tends to mobilize the strengths and compensate for the defects of each. On the whole, and notwithstanding the conspicuous problems, the great achievement of the Medicare program remains its governance system. Medicare is a gigantic federal program that has the look and feel of a private insurance claims process. The cultures of federal rule enforcement and of medical autonomy have been put together seamlessly, almost without anyone's paying attention to how it is done. Whereas federal entitlement programs tend to be rule bound, alert to deviation and committed to bureaucratic rationality, the medical professional governance system is concerned with individuals, concentrates on tailoring services appropriately to individuals rather than distributing resources equally or fairly, whatever that might mean in the context of clinical services, and tends to operate on a bottom-up, case-based, inductive reasoning strategy rather than a top-down, lawgiving one.

The partnership between these two systems of governance has made the federal government do what it does best, which is to make general policy and provide equal treatment for individuals according to general rules, and to allow the medical community to do what it does best, which is provide clinical services to individuals. The combination has made for powerful satisfaction for the public, which has repaid it with gratitude and consistent political support. The two governance systems have created a durable marriage, which like all alliances can be made to work better together if the parties can be made to understand better the roles and strengths of each, their virtues and defects, the defects of their virtues and the virtues of their defects, and the need to stay connected even as the relationship is being renegotiated.

Part III / Improving Executive Organization and Management

Organization and Management of Federal Departments

Alan L. Dean

From the adoption of the Constitution in 1787 executive departments have been the primary vehicle through which the government of the United States has administered its programs. Over the years their number has increased from three to fifteen, and they have come to vary widely in structure, size, scope, culture, and quality of internal management. Normally, departmental status and membership in the president's cabinet are called for when the size and number of related programs directed to a major government purpose require a secretary to bring about needed coordination. Relevant studies and practical experience support the use of major program purpose as the best way to assemble components of a department which relate to a common mission. Agencies not now included in executive departments—such as the Consumer Product Safety Commission and the Small Business Administration—produce an undesirable increase in the president's span of control. A number of these entities could and should be placed within the appropriate departments.

Laws creating executive departments should authorize the secretary to change the assignments of assistant secretaries and to determine how component bureaus or administrations function. Legislation dealing with agency management, such as the statutes providing for inspectors general, chief financial officers, and chief information officers, should avoid excessive detail in assigning functions and prescribing internal departmental structure.

Experience suggests that a department with a small number of operating administrations reporting directly to the secretary, rather than numerous bureaus supervised by assistant secretaries, is a preferred basic structure. The use of administrations permits a secretary to build better ties with program officials and tends to generate clearer accountability and greater responsiveness by line managers.

Managing Executive Departments

To improve accountability and program oversight, secretaries must be the real—not nominal—managers of their departments. At the same time, a secretary's office always has more to do coping with matters requiring central performance than it can easily handle. Thus, under most circumstances secretaries will facilitate the execution of departmental programs by delegating as much authority as feasible to program administrators, which can improve the secretary's effectiveness and enhance the administrators' role. Such delegations cannot extend to powers assigned by law to the secretary or which need to be handled centrally due to agency-wide impact.

All departmental statutes provide for a deputy to assist the secretary in running the department. This official may become the major force within the department in carrying out the secretary's decisions and helping ensure that the agency runs smoothly.

Quite often, however, things do not work out as expected. This is because the deputy secretary may not be a competent manager or has other interests, such as serving as a policy advocate. The Hoover Commission attempted to strengthen departmental administrative management leadership by proposing the creation of an assistant secretary for administration (ASA) in each department. This official was to be selected from the career civil service and was expected to direct crosscutting administrative activities related to budget, finance, human resources, procurement, management analysis, and support services. From 1950 to 1969 ASAs were important contributors to the professional performance of the responsibilities entrusted to them. Afterward, however, the Nixon administration undertook a successful effort to replace these career officials with similarly titled political appointees. Several panels of the

National Academy of Public Administration (NAPA) have subsequently recommended the creation of an undersecretary for internal management who could oversee all the now scattered aspects of internal management.

Since most public services are provided by field staff, how they are organized and overseen is a major factor in the operation of a department. The demands of programs and the needs of the public being served rule out the use of any single template applicable to all departments. Yet an important factor in determining a specific field structure is the number and complexity of program interfaces in the field. Departments such as Treasury and Commerce administer important services that have little or no need for coordination with other field activities and, therefore, have no need for agency-wide regional directors. Others, such as Housing and Urban Development (HUD), require extensive field coordination and have at times relied on strong regional directors. Historically, many agencies used departmental regional directors with strong authority to coordinate field activities. Some have tried using secretary's representatives who had little or no authority over other field officials. Their influence came chiefly from their personal skills and direct reporting relationship to their secretaries. Both regional directors and secretary's representatives have disappeared from most departments, which now rely on the regional directors of their administrations or bureaus to oversee their respective field operations.

Regardless of structural features, most evidence supports a high degree of departmental decentralization. This can be done through the program administrators, who in turn delegate much of their authority to their field officials. Decentralization can only be effective when field staffs are well informed and the department has reporting, evaluation, and audit capacities to ensure that the delegated powers are appropriately exercised.

One of the most important and complex aspects of departmental management is the design, installation, and refining of the systems needed to perform agency-wide operations on which a secretary must depend. Systems design and implementation usually require the sustained effort of knowledgeable people who receive strong and consistent support from the departmental leadership. Attempts to bring about complex systems reforms may require years to complete, during which time changes in departmental leadership and priorities may occur. These obstacles can best be surmounted by the creation of a permanent management analysis staff whose role has been institutionalized. External consultants can often be called on, but they are most useful when they can work with a stable group of departmental experts.

Overall, no department can function well unless it relies heavily on an experienced cadre of career civil servants. Retaining and getting the most out of career officials depend, however, on a high degree of trust between frequently changing political appointees and the career staff. The tendency over the past thirty years has been to increase the number of noncareer staff. This trend has had adverse impacts on agency stability and even relationships with some congressional committees.

Looking to the Future

It is unlikely that many aspects of departmental organization and management which now need attention can be addressed on a piecemeal basis. It is likely that such reorganization can only be achieved through the enactment of legislation creating a new, independent, and bipartisan commission along the lines of the highly successful first Hoover Commission.[1] Such a group, when supported by both the president and Congress, could propose current approaches to resolving such questions as how many departments are needed, on what basis should programs be assigned departments, what structural features should be preferred, and how the improvement of management systems should be approached.

The Constitution and Executive Departments

Article I of the Constitution contemplated that executive departments would be created to carry out the new government's functions, but it wisely left to Congress and the president the tasks of determining what departments would be created, what their responsibilities would be, and how they would be organized and managed. The First Congress promptly established departments needed to discharge the new government's central functions, and, by the end of 1789, the Departments of State, Treasury, and War were in operation. Since then, Congress and presidents have relied on the executive departments as the primary mechanism to administer federal programs. By 2003 the original three had expanded to fifteen, reflecting increases in the magnitude and diversity of the activities of the federal government.[2]

Evolution of the Executive Departments

About 88 percent of all federal civilian employees[3] and virtually all military personnel are on the rolls of the executive departments. They spent more than 90 percent of federal funds in Fiscal Year 2000.

In citing the dominant place of the executive departments in federal program administration, one should note the existence of major independent agencies.[4] A few of these entities, such as the U.S. Postal Service, the Tennessee Valley Authority, the National Aeronautics and Space Administration (NASA), the Environmental Protection Agency, and the Social Security Administration, have come to play important roles within the executive branch, although they have relatively narrow missions.

From President George Washington to this day, department heads have been included in the president's cabinet by virtue of their positions. Although the cabinet has not evolved into the powerful instrument that similar councils have become in some parliamentary systems, membership carries prestige and reasonable assurance of access to the president and his principal advisors. Presidents have sometimes conferred cabinet status upon specific agencies that are not executive departments for political, programmatic, or prestige purposes, and these delegations are seldom withdrawn.[5]

As they now exist, the departments vary widely in size, importance, and traditions of management. Having been created at different times and having developed different administrative cultures, numerous issues exist with respect to their roles, relationships, and effectiveness. Improving departmental management should rank as one of the most important challenges facing the president and Congress. If it is neglected or given a low priority because it lacks political appeal, program effectiveness will suffer, and the nation will be the loser.

The roles, organization, and management of executive departments have received only cursory attention in public administration literature. There has been little recent authoritative or generic treatment of departmental management, and those who would seek guidance in administering these entities must draw upon past studies that may be somewhat out of date or treat only portions of the subject matter.

In 1948 the first Hoover Commission identified a number of serious deficiencies in the way that departments were organized and functioned and made important recommendations to correct them. Many of these were directed toward vesting authority directly in the secretaries for the departments' programs in order to convert them into real, rather than nominal, managers of their departments. The commission also recommended a Department of Welfare to run Social Security, welfare, and Indian affairs; an Office of General Services for procurement, supplies, and public building functions; and consolidating housing activities into one agency. There were 273 recommendations in all, of which 196 were fully or partially adopted.

The establishment of the Department of Housing and Urban Development in 1965 introduced several important management concepts, some of which were particularly applicable to smaller departments with relatively unified missions. Special efforts were made to balance the parochial tendencies of headquarters bureaus with extensive delegation of program operational authority to regional offices headed by experienced career staff. Although assistant secretaries were empowered to issue directives on behalf of the secretary to the regional administrators, field officials were empowered to respond to community needs within the policies established by the department. This arrangement enabled HUD to administer related programs in an integrated manner, an approach that pleased community leaders. The early positive reputation HUD generated by its initial field structure was later reflected in the Department of Community Development proposed by President Richard M. Nixon, a concept that developed support in Congress. With the passage of time, however, changes in HUD's early management concept contributed to scandals and loss of confidence in the department. After the first four years the career regional directors were replaced by political appointees, and lines of authority became so blurred that regional offices eventually became another time-consuming bureaucratic layer, rather than a mechanism for saving time and expense for state and local clients.

In 1966 a Bureau of the Budget–led task force drafted legislation to create a Department of Transportation (DOT).[6] Because there was no nucleus agency on which to base the department, as had been the case when HUD and the Department of Health, Education, and Welfare (HEW) were established, there was an opportunity to propose the best possible ways of consolidating the transportation functions that were located in various government units.[7] The draft DOT legislation thus reflected the best available thinking on how a department should be organized and managed. The legislation proved relatively noncontroversial, and Congress incorporated the task force's main recommendations in the Department of Transportation Act of 1966. The DOT concepts, which are treated later in this chapter, influenced the content of later proposals related to the reform of executive departments and their internal management concepts.

A more comprehensive effort to improve departmental organization and management grew out of President Nixon's proposal in 1971 to replace seven of the existing executive departments with four larger and more functionally designed entities, each based on a major governmental purpose. Largely reflecting the 1970 recommendations of the Ash Council,[8] the President's Departmental Reorganization Program became a major Nixon initiative. An Office of Management and Budget (OMB) team and several task forces were established to draft legislation to create the Departments of Community Development, Natural Resources, Human Resources, and Economic Affairs. Special attention was given to incorporating and articulating sophisticated concepts of structure and management in the four bills.[9] These concepts and the documents associated with this effort should be of interest to anyone concerned with departmental management.[10]

As the 1972 election approached, the White House abandoned its close cooperation with Congress on organization proposals, a development that brought the departmental reform effort to a halt. After the election President Nixon and White House staff, contrary to the recommendations of both the Ash Council and OMB management staff, tried to avoid legislation by issuing an executive order that centralized control in the White House. This change involved designating certain cabinet secretaries to act as counselors and assistants to the president to coordinate the departments without legislation. This approach lasted for only a few months.

Little of significance affecting departmental management occurred from 1972 to 1988. The messages and hearings on establishment of the Department of Energy in 1977 and the Department of Education in 1979 reveal little evidence of research into the experiences of the existing departments or accepted approaches to sound departmental structure.[11] The Reagan administration's proposals aimed at abolishing these departments also seem to have been developed without a full understanding of the role of an executive department specifically or of executive branch organization generally.

President Ronald Reagan's 1988 decision to convert the Veterans Administration into a Department of Veterans Affairs renewed interest in the criteria for the creation of federal executive departments and their structural design.

Prior studies and presidents had opposed—or declined to endorse—departmental status for the Veterans Administration. Thus, President Reagan's unexpected stand produced much discussion.

The Senate Committee on Governmental Affairs asked the National Academy of Public Administration (NAPA) for its views and to suggest ways that departmental status could best be achieved, if a decision were made to proceed with such status. The resulting panel report listed fourteen criteria on which departmental status could be evaluated (see app.). Applying these standards, the panel found "little evidence" that providing for veterans' needs would be "materially improved" by converting the Veterans Administration into a cabinet department. Congress proceeded to create the department, but the academy's report led to a number of improvements in the statute's structural and management provisions.

This episode essentially replicated the creation of the Department of Labor in 1913 and the Department of Education in 1979, when the demands of organized groups outweighed considerations of executive branch organization. A result has been to fragment executive branch machinery, weaken the "major purpose" approach to government organization, create departments with narrow missions, such as the Department of Veterans Affairs, give excessive influence to some clientele groups, and diminish the importance of cabinet status.

The recent creation of the Department of Homeland Security (DHS) involved factors and considerations that are unique, or have been rare, in the history of our executive departments. Because the department has just become a legal entity at the time of this writing and its secretary has had little time to convert an unprecedented congeries of agencies into a functioning organization, the wisdom or consequences of the restructuring cannot yet be predicted with assurance.

In public administration it is well known that poorly conceived or implemented reorganizations can make even unsatisfactory structural situations worse than before. It will require several years of operating experience before the need for or the effectiveness of the Department of Homeland Security, as it has been established, can be fairly evaluated. Factors that must be addressed in any assessment include:

1. Can any department with so many programs and organizational entities be managed so as to make a positive contribution to the operations of the federal government?

2. Are there programs or entities that should not have been included in the new department (e.g., the transportation security responsibilities of the Department of Transportation)?
3. Is there a need for a permanent executive department concerned with homeland security?
4. Are there more workable ways to improve the coordination and effectiveness of homeland security matters than the DHS as established?

Major Aspects of Departmental Organization and Management

For a department to have effective management and successfully pursue its goals and purposes, a number of prerequisites must be satisfied. A department must bring together important programs with the same major broad purpose and have the authority to advance its mission. The applicable statutes should avoid excessive prescription of structural and procedural detail.

Criteria for Establishing Executive Departments

An executive department is usually called for when programs related to some definable government purpose become so numerous, so large, and so complex that an official of secretarial rank with enhanced access to the president is needed to provide effective oversight and coordination of program management. At the outset of our government the Congress established departments to deal with the central functions prescribed by the Constitution, namely foreign affairs (State), revenue collection and financial management (Treasury), and defense (War). Aside from the splitting off of the Navy Department in 1798, no new executive department was established until 1849, when the Department of the Interior was set up to reduce the clutter in the Treasury Department and to assume the responsibility for emerging programs involving public domain, Indians, and minerals. For much of our history Congress has been cautious in creating new departments. Most have been fully justified, or even overdue, at the time of their establishment.

When political forces lead to the creation of departments that otherwise lack persuasive justification, they may complicate, rather than facilitate, the administration of federal programs. A notable example was the Department of Labor in 1913, which split the then ten-year-old Department of Commerce and Labor. Undertaken in response to organized labor's insistence on having a "voice in the cabinet," the result was a small "clientele" department that raised troublesome questions about whether the secretary of labor's role was to administer the department in the public interest or serve as the advocate for an organized segment of American society. Over the years the Labor Department's mission has entailed ongoing relationship problems with other departments, especially Commerce, Education, and the former HEW, now Health and Human Services.

Similarly, the benefits of separating the Department of Education from HEW were not initially discernible. President Jimmy Carter kept his campaign promises to the teachers' unions, but this action entailed the added costs of establishing another secretarial office and its panoply of associated officials.[12] It also constituted a further retreat from the "major purpose" goal of organizing a department for human resources programs around HEW.[13] Since both the George W. Bush administration and most congressional Democrats now emphasize improving elementary and secondary education, the case for cabinet representation for Education has become stronger. Even with expanded programs, however, it would still remain to some degree a narrowly based, client-oriented department.

Changing conditions may suggest the need to abolish or redesign an existing executive department. Replacement of the War Department with the Department of Defense, for example, was a restructuring that eliminated the Navy Department as a separate cabinet agency.[14] The wartime evidence supporting unification of the defense-oriented agencies and the rise of the air force as a major service made a strong case for these changes, despite the opposition of the army and navy. In 1971 the Post Office Department was replaced by today's U.S. Postal Service to provide better for its business-type functions and to reduce congressional micromanagement.

Many students of government organization believe that most of what President Nixon tried to do in 1971–72 made organizational sense. The proposed structural reforms should be studied by anyone who is considering how to improve government management and effectiveness. Nixon made a strong case for curtailing the number of departments, reducing the president's span of control, and concentrating related programs under a single secretary. "Major purpose" was to be the principal criterion for grouping governmental functions. Each secretary was to have responsibilities broad enough to enable him or her to bring about meaningful direction and coordination of related programs.

The case for combining the programs that relate to a single major purpose within one department is well illustrated by the Department of the Interior. For many years after its creation, the department was noted chiefly for its scandals, its eagerness to give away public lands, and its neglect and abuse of Native Americans.[15] The accession of Harold Ickes as secretary in 1933, coupled with a rising interest in natural resources conservation, improved the department's management integrity and spurred an effort to redesign it into a true Department of Natural Resources. Virtually every president from Franklin D. Roosevelt to Carter endorsed this objective. Unfortunately, the Army Corps of Engineers administers the largest programs involving national water resources, and major flood prevention and forest management programs are lodged in the Department of Agriculture.[16] The National Oceanic and Atmospheric Administration remains a unit of the Department of Commerce, although it was originally intended to be a component of the Department of Natural Resources. Opposition from the directly affected congressional committees and from groups fearing the loss of valued relationships impeded the creation of the proposed department. Consequently, the secretary of interior has been handicapped in providing leadership in many water resource matters, and interdepartmental problems often go to the president which should be handled at the departmental level. The same situation exists with respect to land management; Interior has the Bureau of Land Management and the National Park Service, while the Department of Agriculture has the Forest Service.

DOT, on the other hand, demonstrates the benefits of grouping virtually all transportation programs in a single major purpose department. Since the department's activation in April 1967, important progress has been made in bringing more balance in federal assistance to the various transportation modes, enhancing safety as a crosscutting responsibility in the department, and encouraging each element of the department to take a broader view of the public interest.

The benefits are especially evident in surface transportation matters, where great strides have been made in fostering highway and mass transit cooperation and funding. It also made possible the implementation of congressional initiatives such as the Intermodal Surface Transportation Efficiency Act of 1991. Most recently, the existence of a DOT provided a logical organizational location for most of the functions set forth in the Transportation and Airport Security Act.

The positive developments that contributed to DOT's evolution into a model example of a major purpose department were the acquisition of major transportation responsibilities relating to urban mass transportation, the promotion of the maritime industry, and the residual functions of the Civil Aeronautics Board and the Interstate Commerce Commission. Internal changes were also made to sharpen the focus on programs relating to highway and motor carrier safety.

The comprehensive role achieved by DOT in the administration of federal transportation programs was undermined in 2003 by the provisions of the law establishing the Department of Homeland Security which transferred the Transportation Security Administration and the U.S. Coast Guard to the new DHS. Since both of the transferred agencies carry out responsibilities chiefly relating to transportation safety, this part of the DHS legislation may prove to cause many unintended problems of interdepartmental cooperation.

The Major Purpose Concept

The case for major purpose serving as the preferred basis for establishing an executive department and determining the scope of its mission is far broader than the examples already cited in this chapter. The alternative approaches, when tried, have not succeeded at either the departmental or major agency level. The Federal Loan Agency (FLA) and the Federal Works Agency (FWA), both created by reorganization plans in 1939, provide examples. These were abortive efforts to organize by process or skills. FWA, for example, included the federal government's highway functions and responsibility for public buildings. This experiment was judged to be a failure shortly after its inception, and FWA was abolished in 1949. Today these programs are placed where they clearly should be: in DOT and the General Services Administration. FLA did not endure as long; in 1942 its lending functions were moved to more suitable settings, and the agency was disbanded.

The major purpose concept has been advanced in the proposals of virtually every major group that has broadly studied executive branch organization. These include the first Hoover Commission, the Ash Council, and Nixon's Departmental Reorganization Program. The concept also guided the DOT task force in 1966. Departmental organization based on major purpose has been, and still is, a concept endorsed by legislation. The Reorganization Act of

1949 made this objective a principal intent when it stated that presidents should "determine what changes in such organization are necessary" to carry out such purposes as to "group, coordinate, and consolidate agencies and functions, as nearly as they may be, according to major purposes."[17] When practical experience, major study commissions, presidents, and Congress all agree on a single organizational concept, prudence would suggest that it be given great weight in future departmental reform initiatives.

Efforts to realign the departments are occasionally denigrated as "box shuffling" or seen as too costly. It is sometimes argued that the appointment of able officials and the fostering of interdepartmental coordination can render unnecessary more fundamental reforms. This argument has merit in that talented and committed executives can sometimes make a poor organization work better than it would under less able leadership. An example is the progress made at the Federal Emergency Management Agency under the leadership of James Lee Witt. Deficient scope of authority or defective structure, however, makes it harder for even the most capable agency heads to do their jobs and reach their goals. There is no adequate substitute for clear assignments of responsibility within sound structural arrangements. It is doubtful that we can ever attain the quality of program execution which our citizens have a right to expect until the executive branch departments are converted into more viable entities capable of coping with the complex problems of government. Lesser measures tend to be mere palliatives that seldom produce much in the way of lasting or beneficial results.[18]

Consolidating federal programs into a smaller number of major purpose executive departments could also improve coordination and oversight of many of the so-called independent agencies of the executive branch.[19] Agencies such as the National Archives and Records Administration, the Railroad Retirement Board, and the Small Business Administration could readily be placed in or under existing or restructured executive departments. In many cases the pleas of interest groups or other nonmanagerial factors explain the origin and continuation of independent agencies.

The trend in recent years has been to weaken, rather than broaden, the missions of some executive departments. An example is the removal of education and social security programs from the former HEW, actions that reversed years of effort to build a more comprehensive Department of Human Resources.

Structuring Major Purpose Departments

Ensuring that a department contains programs that form a sound basis for its existence is only the first step in facilitating good management. The department must also be organized internally so that it can best achieve its statutory mission. Both headquarters and field structures must be designed to advance the department's effectiveness.

Legislation establishing a department should avoid excessive detail in prescribing internal structure and the placement of authority. The Department of Transportation Act of 1966 balanced Congress's desire to determine the department's major features with the secretary's need for authority to manage. Only a small number of DOT operating (modal) administrations were set up by law. These statutory constituents initially included the Federal Aviation Administration (FAA), the Coast Guard, the Federal Highway Administration, the Federal Railroad Administration, and the St. Lawrence Seaway Development Corporation. The act generally avoided prescribing the subordinate structures of these first-tier program entities. Moreover, most program authority was placed in the secretary with the power to delegate. The 1967 organization has held up well in practice. The subsequent principal changes have involved absorbing additional functions such as urban mass transportation, vestigial functions of the Civil Aeronautics Board and Interstate Commerce Commission, and maritime programs.[20] There has also been a splitting of the original Federal Highway Administration into construction and safety oriented administrations, but this is the only major change to a program entity included in the original departmental plan.[21]

DOT assistant secretaries function in staff capacities with no direct authority over the heads of operating administrations. Nor are functions assigned to them by law. The secretary alone decides what the assistant secretaries shall do and adjusts their role accordingly. This approach encourages the use of these officials in crosscutting roles such as policy, public relations, congressional liaison, and administrative management. Thus, one assistant secretary may be assigned a general policy role, another public affairs functions, and another budget and program review responsibilities. The secretary can usually make changes administratively without seeking legislation. Many adjustments have been made in the roles and titles of DOT assistant secretaries since 1967.[22]

The DOT approach to internal organization closely resembles the one long used by the Department of Defense. In Defense the principal operations are conducted by the three services, while undersecretaries and assistant secretaries are charged with such matters as logistics, personnel, budgets, and research and technology.

The Defense-DOT management concept contrasts sharply with the organization of departments such as Interior, Agriculture, and HHS. These traditionally contain statutory bureaus or "administrations," which are managerially self-sufficient and concerned with a slice of the department's statutory mission. Program-oriented line assistant secretaries bridge the wide span of control over these entities. Interior Department assistant secretaries have been used to oversee and, in theory, coordinate bureaus concerned with water resources, land management, mineral resources, wildlife and recreation, and Native Americans, with mixed results.

Line officials in departments such as Interior are often unable to manage effectively because bureaus are insulated from the secretary by the intervening assistant secretaries, yet the program-oriented assistant secretaries rarely have the experience, continuity of service, or resources needed to exercise meaningful supervision. In addition, the crosscutting functions that should be handled out of the secretary's office may be neglected or poorly led because most of the assistant secretaries are being used as line officials supervising programs.[23] The Department of Energy was established in a centralized mode with the assistant secretaries directly in charge of operating programs. This was done to avoid the creation of "fiefdoms," as were alleged to exist in DOT. The result, however, has been a weak management structure.[24] More recently, Congress showed its displeasure with the Energy Department's structure by passing legislation that effectively created a department-within-a-department for the nuclear weapons mission.

Another action that the author believes weakened the ability of cabinet secretaries to use their top officials in ways that would be most helpful in managing their departments was the creation of statutory inspectors general during the Carter administration. Public administration scholars and departmental executives have differed on the need for and role of inspectors general, whose actions have at times produced both strong criticism and applause. They are of assistant secretary rank (Executive Level IV) and are appointed by the president and confirmed by the Senate.

The Inspector General Act of 1978 vested federal audit responsibilities and the conduct of investigations involving fraud, waste, or abuse in these unique officials. Congress prescribed the qualifications and functions of inspectors general in detail and specifically required that they be appointed "without regard to political affiliation and solely on the basis of integrity and demonstrated ability in accounting, auditing, financial analysis, law, management analysis, public administration, or investigations." It has become established practice that they are not automatically terminated upon the inauguration of a new president, a development that can add stability to the position. Each inspector general nominally reports to the secretary or the agency's number two officer but may not be supervised by anyone else. Neither the establishment head nor the next in rank may prevent the inspector general from launching or completing any audit or investigation or from issuing subpoenas. Furthermore, the position must be filled, even if a secretary prefers other ways to conduct audits and investigations.

There are now fifty-seven statutory inspectors general. This has partly resulted from a mostly unwarranted congressional distrust of federal managers and partly from concern about waste and failures of integrity in certain programs and agencies. Under the current statutes the dual reporting requirements and the prescription of their functions ensure that inspectors general have a large measure of independence.

Supporters of the inspector general concept contend that the position has improved the operation of departments and agencies by reducing waste and ferreting out abuse that otherwise would not have been discovered until much later, when the consequences would have been more serious. They believe that the position, when utilized as part of the top management team during the formulation of new policies, can help minimize agency vulnerability to waste and abuse.

By flagging problems at an early stage, supporters believe that inspectors general can place agency leadership in a position to claim credit for taking strong remedial action, thereby enhancing the agency's stature and leadership. They also point to the substantial savings that are included in the inspector general reports. Finally, Congress believes that cover-ups of agency failures are more difficult with the presence of the inspectors general. Congress is less likely to question agency statements or actions when the inspectors general have already addressed them as part of their work.

There are some, including the author, who view the inspector general concept differently. This view holds that the inspector general statutes are basically flawed because of their dual reporting to Congress and the agency head, a violation of a basic principle of good management.[25] Those with this view believe the placement of the audit function under an independent official at times delays—rather than expedites—the discovery of problems and can delay an agency head's urgent need for taking corrective action. Such delays can result in the agency head being criticized by Congress or the press for inaction. Because of the broad statutory language describing the inspector general's functions, critics charge that the office contributes to the fragmentation of agency leadership's accountability.

There is some concern that the statutory inspectors general tend to fragment the distribution of staff management functions among the secretarial officers of the departments. This is particularly true of the audit function. In major corporations, state governments, and other national governments, there is provision for internal and external audits. In the U.S. government Congress has assigned the external audit responsibility to the General Accounting Office. The author is not aware of any other situation in which an organization head is subject to external audit and does not have full authority over internal audits. Vesting authority over internal audits in an independent inspector general weakens the agency head's control over resources devoted to the prevention of abuse and inefficiency, which were once directly available to that official. It is clearly anomalous that the chief financial officers established by Congress do not have authority over internal audits.

Given the strong support in Congress for inspectors general and the fact that their number has greatly expanded since the first fourteen were established, there seems little prospect for revisiting the concept except as part of a thorough reexamination of how best to organize executive departments. If this were done, the author would suggest that an alternative approach used by President Eisenhower be considered. The president and Congress could require each secretary or agency head to organize his or her office so that the functions now lodged in inspectors general would be performed by one or more officers designated by the agency head. The adequacy of such arrangements could be reviewed by the General Accounting Office through its audit program and by Congress through its oversight activities.

At the present time the challenge facing departmental secretaries and other agency heads is in trying to make the concept work better. Care in the selection of inspectors general and the training of their staffs should, for example, be given high priority.[26]

The Role of the Office of the Secretary

Notwithstanding some setbacks, the Hoover Commission's goal of concentrating program and managerial authority in the cabinet secretaries has been substantially realized. Many authorizing statutes now vest functions in the secretaries with the power to delegate, rather than lodge authority directly in subordinate officials. This gives secretaries needed flexibility in implementing statutory functions and adapting to changing circumstances.

Departmental secretaries are likely to achieve less momentum and success with their programs if they fail to utilize the talents of their top program officials. A secretary's substantive and administrative powers should be delegated to the agency's administrators or bureau directors, excepting, of course, those that by law or other compelling reasons must be retained. The secretary's office has enough to do without retaining functions that can be performed at lower levels. DOT's initial approach was to decentralize program authority to the modal administrations whenever feasible and to make individual administrations self-sufficient in day-to-day administration. Implementing these concepts was not easy, but it was energetically pursued during the department's first six years and, in the view of Secretaries Alan Boyd and John Volpe (1967–73) and the author, with good results.

Secretarial offices have been charged with micromanaging even such well-staffed subagencies as the Social Security Administration and the Federal Aviation Administration.[27] When this occurs, these offices may become a drag on efficient administration. In both cases perceptions of micromanagement bolstered efforts to give them independent agency status. To survive as the principal mechanisms for executing the nation's laws, executive departments must prove their worth by advancing the quality of administration in ways that produce beneficial results.

Responsibility for Internal Administration

All departmental statutes provide for a deputy secretary to assist the secretary in running the department. The presence of a number two officer should be helpful, but it may prove insufficient unless other institutionalized sources of management advice and assistance are available. This is because few secretaries or deputies are chosen for their experience in managing public agencies.

Moreover, the pressures of policy matters, legislation, interagency conflicts, interest group demands, and public relations often severely limit the time available to run the agency. Some deputy secretaries are able to serve as effective chief operating officers, but others may lack the required backgrounds or interests to fill a management leadership role effectively.

During the first five decades of the twentieth century the official who ran a department's internal administration was the "chief clerk." This official was always a career civil servant whose formidable institutional memory and skill in getting things done were vital in the rigid and overcentralized departments of this period.[28]

The first Hoover Commission concluded that there was the need for a stronger center for administrative services and management advice to the secretary. It recommended the establishment in each department of the post of assistant secretary for administration, whose occupants would be from and in the career civil service, to help cope with this need. With indefinite tenure, the ASAs were expected to oversee internal functions such as human resources, budget, financial management, management analysis, audit, and support services.

The response to this proposal was universally favorable, and it was approved by President Harry Truman. Within months most executive departments were equipped with statutory ASAs. When HUD and DOT were established in 1965 and 1966, respectively, these positions were included without controversy in the authorizing acts.[29] From 1949 to 1969 career ASAs provided each secretary with a single official responsible for virtually every aspect of internal organization or management.[30] In the Nixon administration, however, White House officials distrusted the civil service and especially the career assistant secretaries. The administration acted to remove many ASA positions from career status and substituted political appointments to similarly titled offices. An inevitable loss of institutional memory and objectivity followed.

Congress has also contributed to the disappearance of a single experienced center of internal management. Several laws prescribing how these functions must be organized, and the creation of statutory inspectors general, now make it next to impossible to restore the ASA post as the focal point of internal departmental management. An important obstacle is the 1990 statute establishing the post of chief financial officer (CFO) in each department. This law contributes to the dispersion of internal management responsibilities by mandating a presidentially appointed CFO in each department who must report directly to the secretary. The CFOs were made responsible for "directing, managing, and providing policy guidance and oversight of agency financial management personnel, activities and operations."[31] CFOs were also required for several non-cabinet agencies, including the General Services Administration and the Office of Personnel Management. These, however, are to be career officials and are appointed by the agency heads. More recently, the Information Technology Management Reform Act of 1996—better known as the Clinger-Cohen Act—established chief information officers in the executive departments. This statutory provision has continued the undesirable tendency to prescribe detailed arrangements for internal management through legislation. Similar status has been suggested for human resources and procurement leadership in the departments.

Since the position of career assistant secretary cannot be realistically restored in the present political climate, National Academy of Public Administration panels have proposed new and more effective centers of internal management.[32] The solution preferred by academy panels has been the establishment of the post of undersecretary for management at Level III in the executive schedule. The four executive departments proposed by President Nixon in 1971 all provided for such a position. As the third-ranking officials of their departments, their focus on management issues would free the deputy secretaries to concentrate on substantive program matters. The authorizing statutes for the new undersecretaries should require a background in public management or related experience. The need is now greater than it was in 1971, when an academy panel first recommended the establishment of the position of undersecretary for management.

Recognition that secretaries often need help in overseeing their departments' internal operations has led, in some cases, to establishing a chief of staff or designating an official as chief operating officer (COO). The chiefs of staff are usually special assistants to the secretaries with defined roles that give them special and influential status. The need for and role of a chief of staff are influenced by the way the secretary and deputy secretary function, departmental traditions, the role of a headquarters secretariat, and the skill and personality of the incumbent. This post should not be required by law in civil departments because it would intrude on the freedom of secretaries to arrange their offices to meet their style and requirements. A deputy secretary who is an effective manager and a well-organized secretariat will often reduce or eliminate the need for a chief of staff as an important figure in management matters. This has been demonstrated in several departments, including DOT and HEW. The post may, however, become one concerned chiefly with political matters.

The COO concept usually entails so designating an existing high official. The COO position is common in private sector corporations, and its adoption by public agencies is seen as helping them improve their internal management. Ideally, the deputy secretary should be the COO but, as noted earlier, many of these officials are neither well qualified for nor interested in this role. Thus, it may be desirable to authorize but not require secretaries to appoint COOs but with the option of leaving the position vacant if it is not needed.[33] President Bill Clinton established by executive order a President's Management Council that served as a mechanism for COOs to meet regularly and consider issues of government-wide concern.

Field Organization and Management

The quality of departmental administration depends heavily on the design of the field organization and the degree to which authority is decentralized to field officials closer to the public served. Existing departmental approaches to field management reveal much diversity, and generally applicable models are not to be found.

In contrast to the organization of the secretary's office and the structure of headquarters program elements, in which specific approaches have been suggested, there is no such thing as a one-size-fits-all field organization. Since the field deals chiefly with services to the public, it must be tailored so as to ensure that those services are competently delivered. The nature of the department's mission and the complexity of the interfaces among its programs and various constituencies should be major factors in the design of a field organization.

The departments differ markedly in the way they use regional directors. In HUD the regional administrators were initially career officials. They supervised almost all program responsibilities within their regions. The secretary could empower headquarters officials to issue directives to the regions, but, since only the secretary could hire or fire the regional administrators, the headquarters officials were dependent on the secretary's support. In some agencies regional directors have complete authority across all program areas, yet they are often criticized because their decisions and actions can vary significantly from region to region. At the other end of the spectrum are departments with no crosscutting departmental regional officials, including Justice, Commerce, Treasury, and Transportation.

Some departments have no regional directors with comprehensive authority for a good reason—namely, that their programs require little or no field coordination. In the Treasury Department there are few relationships between the U.S. Mint and the Internal Revenue Service or between the Financial Management Service and the Secret Service. In the Department of Commerce, the Patent Office, the Census Bureau, and the National Oceanic and Atmospheric Administration deal with few matters of common concern in the field. Their field organizations may or may not need strengthening, but there is no persuasive case for inserting regional directors who represent the entire department.

Between the extremes of HUD's original departmental regional administrators and the Commerce-Justice-Transportation-Treasury reliance on bureau field structures are a number of intermediate arrangements. In the 1970s HEW's regional directors lacked comprehensive program oversight authority but played important roles in the field. Especially during the secretaryships of Elliot Richardson (1970–73) and Caspar Weinberger (1973–75), the regional directors acted as general managers, program coordinators, services providers, and evaluators. HEW secretaries decided, however, against making regional directors responsible for technical and nondiscretionary programs whose field operations were supervised by Washington. Examples included food and drug enforcement and Social Security payments.

On the other hand, the interrelationships between the various human resources programs were so complex that regional directors were able to play a strong role in dealing with other government units within the regions. Thus, HEW regional directors were given line authority over programs that did not lend themselves to direct administration through the separate field organizations of the program agencies. This was especially true of activities involving the needs and problems of such special groups in our society as children, youth, Native Americans, the aging, the mentally retarded, and the users of skilled nursing facilities.

In the Carter administration Secretary Joseph Califano abolished the HEW regional directors and replaced them with much weaker "principal regional officials." This reversed the evolutionary process that was producing a field management structure well suited to HEW's needs. Although the principal regional officials were again designated as regional directors early in the Reagan administration, they never regained their former status.

Other departments, such as Interior, Agriculture, and Transportation,[34] do not have regional directors but have from time to time created a field presence through "secretary's representatives." These individuals usually report, actually or nominally, to the secretary but are given little or no program authority. They often handle interagency and intergovernmental relations, and they can also act as conveners of the field directors of the program elements. These representatives may act as the eyes and ears of the secretary and may serve as members of interagency bodies.

The value of regional or secretary's representatives is in dispute, and the supporting evidence to date is inconclusive. DOT's experience suggests that the concept's efficacy depends on the performance of the individual representatives, the degree to which they have real access to the secretary and other senior headquarters officials, and the extent to which they can work constructively with agency field leadership.

As the secretary's representatives disappeared from DOT and other departments, HUD introduced this arrangement in 1994 in an attempt to reduce the stovepiping produced when Secretary Henry Cisneros abolished the regional administrators.[35] When National Academy of Public Administration fellows cautioned HUD officials that reliance on secretary's representatives had failed in most other agencies, they were assured that the secretary planned to treat them as the field equivalents of assistant secretaries. HUD has retained the use of secretary's representatives.

Regional directors are not a prerequisite to decentralized management. Decentralization entails giving field officials the authority to act definitively on matters within their geographic areas, and it is possible to operate a decentralized system through the bureaus or program administrations of departments such as DOT or Treasury. Within DOT the Federal Aviation Administration and the Federal Highway Administration are among the executive branch's most decentralized organizations. The same has been true of Treasury's Internal Revenue Service. These entities create their own regional systems and delegate legal authority, or redelegate secretary-derived authority, to their own field officials. Most such units have regional directors or similarly designated officials, but they report to the head of the program entity, not to the office of the secretary.

The weight of experience appears to favor decentralized departmental management. When field officials can take final action, services can usually be provided more quickly and with a better understanding of local conditions.

Yet a truly decentralized system is not easy to install or maintain. Many headquarters officials are reluctant to rely on field staffs to act on nonroutine matters and may consistently push for recentralization. Successful decentralization also depends upon clear policies and standards to guide field officials and, upon reporting, audit and evaluation systems to ensure that delegated authority has been properly used. If at all possible, principal field officials should be from, and remain in, the career civil service. In numerous departments, such as DOT, HUD, and HEW, field officials with career status have usually imparted experience, expertise, and continuity to the administration of their programs. They may also be capable of enhancing interagency coordination. These are important factors that are frequently absent from short-term, politically sponsored appointees.

The FAA shows the benefits of a carefully planned and implemented decentralization of a major agency. Between 1961 and 1965 decentralization facilitated a reduction in total agency staffing by 10 percent in a period of increasing workload. In some cases delegations to the regions reduced processing time by as much as 90 percent.

Congress has been ambivalent about decentralization, initially supporting it in HUD and for the most part in DOT but resisting it in HEW. From 1969 to 1972 Secretary of Transportation Volpe had little trouble advancing a philosophy of decentralized management, despite the fact that he had to rely on his modal administrators for implementation. In contrast, Secretary Weinberger and Undersecretary Carlucci encountered strong resistance, including legislative interventions, when they sought to advance decentralization in HEW. A department seeking to foster decentralization as a better way of doing business will need a good case and must deal with the concerns of the involved congressional committees.

Management Systems

A department may have a coherent major purpose and sound internal organization yet still have poor management. A well-functioning department also needs systems to enhance its capacity to make sound decisions, to use resources skillfully, to provide a competent and motivated staff, and to generate responsiveness to public needs.

Such a department must invest much effort in designing, implementing, and fine-tuning systems for policy development; preparing regulations; determining budget priorities; keeping track of costs and outlays; recruiting and developing competent people; evaluating existing programs and identifying opportunities for improvement; assembling program information needed by agency management and the public; exploiting new technologies; and procuring and utilizing facilities, equipment, and supplies.

Some departments and independent agencies have excellent programs for developing their employees and managers, while others do little in this area. Some develop first-rate financial information, including usable data on program costs; others have accounting systems that do little more than help avoid violations of the Anti-Deficiency Act. Some have advanced systems to facilitate the monitoring of program accomplishments; others approach target setting and accountability for results in haphazard ways.

Keeping up with and effectively using technological developments have severely challenged agency managers. Coping with new technology requires strong leadership, a competent staff, reliable funding, and the commitment of the workforce. As the Federal Aviation Administration and the Internal Revenue Service have found, the long lead times for acquiring new systems, as well as high costs and the rapidity of change, can frustrate even well-managed agencies. If the obstacles to utilizing new technologies are not energetically addressed, agency managers can pay a heavy price in the form of poor service delivery and a tarnished reputation.

Most departments have a long way to go toward designing and operating the management systems they need to serve the public. Lack of progress in these areas may be traced to top officials' lack of understanding, inadequate or poorly led staff, insufficient funding, and resistance among affected program elements. Except for financial management and selected projects, OMB leadership has also been limited.

Another obstacle to implementing sound management systems is the lengthy period associated with their design and installation, sometimes due to the organization's complexity and the difficulty getting concepts understood and accepted.[36] In other instances the designers themselves may undertake global assaults that falter under their own weight and wear out the patience of even the most supportive management. Systems reforms often should be done on a modular basis and through pilot demonstrations, so that management can evaluate each piece as it becomes operational. This approach is particularly desirable in areas such as management information, productivity improvement and measurement, and cost accounting.

To get results, a department needs to build the in-house capability to design, implement, and operate management systems. External contractors can help, especially in highly technical areas, but systems improvement is a long-haul undertaking, requiring qualified internal staff who can stick with the reforms from beginning to end.

Recent pressures on agencies to downsize have resulted in the weakening, or virtual elimination, of the management analysis staffs who once gave several agencies sustained and sophisticated assistance in meeting organizational and administrative needs. Department heads would be well advised to rebuild the in-house capacity needed to help design and evaluate reforms of their internal systems.

The Government Performance and Results Act of 1993 (GPRA) is the most recent major effort to improve goal definition, priority setting, and results measurement. Since its enactment, agencies have directed substantial resources to carrying out its provisions. There have been wide differences among agencies, however, in achieving adherence to GPRA and integrating its features into their overall management.

It is too soon to predict how much GPRA will in the long run contribute to the quality of agency management. General Accounting Office studies have been helpful but inconclusive, and the process of evaluation is continuing. It also remains to be seen how vigorously this effort will be supported by the new administration and whether the reconstituted authorizing and appropriations committees will begin to make decisions that are significantly influenced by the GPRA process.

The Role of Career Staff

The quality and continuity of departmental management have been jeopardized by assaults on the career civil servants upon whom the political leadership of any agency must heavily depend for the skilled execution of programs. From the beginning of President Franklin Roosevelt's second term through President Lyndon Johnson's presidency, major progress was made in developing institutions needed to foster improved executive branch management. Career staff made major contributions to decisions bearing on the quality of administration. The emergence in 1939 of a highly respected Bureau of the Budget in the Executive Office of the President was a particularly significant event. Staffed almost entirely by career civil servants, it provided presidents with objective advice on government funding and management. The Division of Administrative Management and its successor organizations were headed and staffed by career experts who had developed sound doctrines to guide organization and management decisions.

The Hoover Commission–generated ASAs stayed in touch with one another informally. Their Executive Officers Group met regularly to exchange ideas and to foster cooperation with the Bureau of the Budget. They also undertook or helped coordinate interagency management projects. As neutral professionals, ASAs bridged changes in secretaries and presidents, including those involving shifts in party control. Also during this period, many bureau directors were drawn from the career service. Virtually all regional officials had competitive status, and the entire staff of the U.S. Civil Service Commission, including the executive director, had career tenure.

The Nixon administration feared that career staff could not be counted on to carry out loyally and efficiently the policies of political appointees. The Nixon White House believed that department heads needed their own people if they were to control their agencies effectively. A result was the politicization of many senior positions in Washington and in the departmental field services, especially departmental regional directors and secretary's representatives. As previously noted, the career ASAs were largely replaced by political appointees with similar titles. Many political appointees began surrounding themselves with noncareer special assistants and chiefs of staff who often brought mistrust and inexperience to the management of their agencies. Layers of political appointees were established in OMB and in the Office of Personnel Management.[37]

Placing political appointees in traditional career posts, coupled with the denigration of public servants, has not been limited to a given political party or president. In 1978 President Carter said that his most frustrating problem was the "horrible federal bureaucracy." President Reagan proclaimed: "Government is not the solution to our problem. Government is our problem." The situation has become progressively more serious since President Nixon's aides launched a concerted effort to place political appointees in as many senior positions as possible.

It is worth emphasizing that, whatever the quality of political leadership, a high level of management effectiveness cannot be maintained without a cadre of trusted civil servants. Secretary of War Henry Lewis Stimson once remarked, "The only way to make a man trustworthy is to trust him; and the surest way to make him untrustworthy is to distrust him and show your distrust."

The Departments and the White House

Since President Franklin Roosevelt was authorized to appoint six "anonymous assistants," the White House, and the Executive Office of the President generally, have grown enormously in size and complexity of functions. This evolution has presented many secretaries with serious territorial and relationship problems. These difficulties can arise from how a president and his principal aides view the role of department heads.[38] If given discretion in managing their departments, both the secretaries and the president will usually benefit. If, however, the White House seeks to micromanage the agencies, it may dilute its ability to handle matters that really require presidential attention. At the same time, an interventionist approach can undermine secretarial accountability for departmental program outcomes.

This chapter has argued that a department usually functions best when decentralized. This applies a fortiori to the much larger executive branch. It is often difficult, considering political and personal factors, to remove loyal political allies who cannot run their agencies, but it is even more difficult to bypass them. Fortunately, most departments can continue to function at a reasonable level if they are being held together by competent career managers.

It also helps immensely for a secretary to have a trusting relationship with the president. It then becomes much easier for the department to rebuff intrusive White House staff and to defend departmental turf. A forceful personality and a willingness to resign, if necessary, also ordinarily strengthen the secretary's position.

Looking to the Future

From time to time issues of government management become so serious as to require addressing by external commissions that can focus public, congressional, and executive branch attention on both the nature of the problems and the potential solutions. Examples include the Brownlow Committee of the

1930s, the first Hoover Commission, the President's Commission on Postal Organization, and the Ash Council, all of which played key roles in creating climates favorable to important reforms and developing specific courses of constructive action.

It is unlikely that serious attention will again be devoted to improving departmental organization and management on a government-wide basis without the stimulus of some new entity along the lines of an independent and impartial commission. One effort to utilize the commission device to advance improved government organization and management was the Government for the 21st Century Act, cosponsored by Senators Fred Thompson, Joseph Lieberman, and others in the 106th Congress. This bill, had it passed, would have provided for an independent Commission on Government and Restructuring to examine and make recommendations on reforming and restructuring the organization and operations of the entire executive branch. The commission would have examined such issues as how to restructure agencies and programs to better achieve their statutory missions and how to maximize productivity, effectiveness, and accountability for performance results. The focus would have been broader than that of the commission proposed by Murray Comarow in chapter 5 for the United States Postal Service, but here, too, a commission would be appropriate to help mobilize a constituency behind a well-conceived set of policies.

At Senator Thompson's request, a NAPA ad hoc task force provided comments on the legislation to the Senate Committee on Governmental Affairs. As was stated in chapter 5, the task force noted that successful commissions have possessed five fundamental characteristics:

1. Their mandate involves a fairly specific social, economic, or political problem that the legislative process apparently cannot handle. A charge too sweeping in nature generally results in failure.
2. They have real support from the president and key members of Congress and from a fair number of affected interest groups and the media.
3. They are composed of objective, highly respected people, with no close ties to directly affected groups.
4. Members are personally prepared to follow up on their recommendations and help convince decision makers to act.
5. A high-quality professional staff supports them; the notion of several wise individuals brainstorming their way to a solution is illusory.[39]

The new administration and a closely divided Congress present a new opportunity to launch a commission on executive branch organization on a bipartisan basis. NAPA fellows would be glad to lend their support to such an effort.

APPENDIX TO CHAPTER 7

At the request of the Senate Committee on Governmental Affairs, a NAPA panel in 1988 developed criteria to be used in committee deliberations about whether or not the Veterans Administration should be elevated to cabinet department status. The panel identified fourteen criteria and found that they provided the most appropriate bases for determining whether any set of government programs are best conducted by a cabinet department. Posed in the form of questions under five broad categories, these criteria are listed here.

Establishing a National Priority for the Agency's Programs

1. Does the agency or set of programs serve a broad national goal or purpose not exclusively identified with a single class, occupation, discipline, region, or sector of society?
2. Is there evidence that there is a significant need of the veterans' population which is not now adequately recognized or addressed by the Veterans Administration, the president, or Congress which would be better assessed or met by elevating the agency to a cabinet department?
3. Is there evidence of impending changes in the needs of, or the circumstances surrounding, the veteran population which would be better addressed if the Veterans Administration were made a cabinet department? Are such changes expected to continue into the future?
4. Would a cabinet department increase the "visibility" and thereby substantially strengthen the active political and public support for programs assisting veterans, including the volunteer service and donated cash assistance currently being provided through veteran service organizations and the nonorganized citizenry?
5. Is there evidence that becoming a cabinet department would provide

better analysis, expression, and advocacy of the needs and programs that constitute the agency's responsibilities?

Improving Program Effectiveness

6. Is there evidence that elevation to a cabinet department would improve the effectiveness of service delivery to veterans and their beneficiaries?
7. Is a cabinet department required to better coordinate or consolidate programs and functions that are now scattered throughout other agencies in the executive branch of government?

Improving Veterans Program Efficiency

8. Is there evidence that a cabinet department with its increase in the centralized political authority of the secretary's office would result in a more effective balance, within the agency, between integrated central strategic planning and resource allocation and the direct participation in management decisions by the line officers who are responsible for directing and managing service delivery? Would the staff officer–line officer interaction be improved?
9. Is there evidence that there are significant structural, management, or operational weaknesses within the Veterans Administration which could be more easily corrected by elevation to a cabinet department?
10. Is there evidence that there are external barriers and impediments to timely decision making and executive action which could be detrimental to improving the efficiency of Veterans Administration programs? And would these impediments be removed or mitigated by elevation to a cabinet department?
11. Would elevation to a cabinet department help recruit and retain better-qualified leadership within an agency?

Improving Federal Policy Integration

12. Is there evidence that a cabinet department would facilitate more uniform achievement of broad, crosscutting national policy goals such as

better integration of biomedical research; a national AIDS program; drug prevention and treatment programs; health care cost containment; equitable needs tests in areas beyond disability compensation benefits; government-wide personnel and budgetary controls; more efficient management and disposition of federal real property assets; and the comprehensive coordination of health care, income maintenance, education and training, and other service delivery strategies?

13. Would elevation to a cabinet department for the Veterans Administration weaken or strengthen the cabinet and the Executive Office of the President as policy and management aids to the president?

Improving Accountability to Elected Public Officials

14. Would the elevation to a cabinet department have a beneficial or detrimental effect upon the oversight and accountability of the agency to the president and Congress?

CHAPTER EIGHT

Modernizing Federal Field Operations

Dwight Ink and Alan L. Dean

The majority of federal employees are located outside the Washington, D.C., area in thousands of field offices scattered throughout the nation. These field employees are the source of most of the personal contacts between the federal government and citizens, businesses, and state and local governments. How these offices are organized and staffed, how they relate to their headquarters and one another, and the degree to which their program and administrative management systems facilitate effective program delivery all have an enormous impact on the extent to which our government works well. Yet field operations seldom register in the minds of management reform leaders. Moreover, for years there has been little effort to coordinate field operations among agencies in ways that make them most effective in serving the public. Such coordination will be of critical importance in homeland security, which has become a critical concern in the United States following the attacks on the World Trade Center and the Pentagon.

Despite the importance of federal field offices, one looks in vain for the attention from either the Office of Management and Budget (OMB) or federal agency leadership that was seen in earlier years. Congressional interest is nearly nonexistent except when a department attempts to eliminate an office that is no longer needed.[1] At one time OMB had six to eight management personnel working full-time on field office issues and several more part-time; now it has none. When departments undertake internal reform efforts, they involve the field only after the changes have been designed by headquarters. Field staff is then informed, without having had a role in planning the changes. This deprives the reform of the benefits of field knowledge and experience and also fails to provide the field offices with any incentive for successful reform that would result from a sense of ownership gained through participation.

Some say this reduced emphasis on field operations is a natural change in response to the growth of the electronic information age, which is making obsolete a significant portion of what field offices used to provide. According to this view, with the help of new data systems and far better communications, headquarters simply does not need as much help from the field. Further, the design of many domestic programs, and consequently also the role of field offices, has changed, especially with the growth of block grants. Although it is true that changing circumstances have had, and will continue to have, a significant impact on the role and the characteristics of field offices, even before the terrorist threat recently gave greater recognition to field operations, they have remained a vital part of our governmental system over a span of many years.

If ignoring field operations was unwise in the past, such neglect is especially dangerous today, with so many American communities now potentially vulnerable to terrorist attacks. Early proposals for organizing the government to address the threat of terrorism gave only limited attention to field operations, despite the critical role of the field in working with state and local officials to prevent and respond to attacks. Inexplicably, the White House failed even to mention field organization in its legislative proposal that led to creation of the Department of Homeland Security.

It is time to rediscover the field. The new homeland security challenges demand it. Major changes in our federal field arrangements must be made rapidly. This chapter provides a number of observations about field operations, particularly in the difficult area of coordination, which may be helpful in bringing about the necessary improvements.

Sorting Out the Role of Field Offices

Even when OMB and agencies do get around to addressing field matters, they give little thought to the basic role of field offices. Yet an awareness of their role should serve as the backdrop for the manner in which a field office is structured and the way in which it functions. There is much diversity among departmental approaches to the details of field management, as there should be, but several general observations regarding roles have rather broad application.

Some people regard field offices as simply an extension of headquarters, performing routine tasks while deferring important actions to Washington. This view fails to take full advantage of the vital resource that field operations offer and thus contributes to ineffective departmental performance. It undervalues the importance of effective program and policy implementation. Downgrading the role of field operations shortchanges those whom the department is designed to serve.

The principle can be easily stated: *The basic role of field offices is to administer the programs and policies enunciated by headquarters,* including both policies that originate with presidential and congressional actions and also lower-level policies enunciated by the departmental secretary. This operational role usually involves extensive interaction with different elements of the public, often including middle- and lower-income people who are rarely seen by Washington. Field personnel are in a better position than headquarters to monitor the effects, good and bad, of most programs on the citizens, families, and communities who are the intended beneficiaries of departmental programs, and the field has a responsibility to keep Washington informed on such matters. The field is also the part of a department or agency which can best ascertain the extent to which the planning and delivery of agency programs need to be coordinated with related programs of other agencies, thereby avoiding conflict and overlap as well as providing opportunities for mutual reinforcement.

Headquarters offices have the well-known role of formulating and evaluating policy. They also have the role of continuing oversight of field operations, a role that is often performed poorly. The headquarters policy role is demanding and involves close interaction with the White House and the Congress, relationships requiring skills that are also frequently in short supply. Much effort has to be devoted to the media and to dealing with the many interest groups that descend on every agency. At the same time, headquarters also needs to take care to provide clear guidance to the field which is necessary for policy implementation and translation of legislation into program actions. Monitoring field operations requires considerable skill in knowing how closely to follow field activities without meddling in their work and stifling innovation.

These headquarters roles are vital and time-consuming. To the extent headquarters also actively involves itself in field operations, particularly those requiring discretionary decision making regarding individual grants and contracts, less resources will be available to pay attention to the basic headquarters roles of policy development and oversight. As a result, both headquarters and field are weakened.

There is seldom a sharp dividing line, however, between policy and implementation. It is both inevitable and appropriate that headquarters will have some involvement in operations and that field offices often will advise on policy. Policy and implementation are interdependent components of government which cannot stand alone. Further, as will be discussed later, not all programs are administered in the field. Whatever vision a department has for its field offices, *the key to organizational success is to make sure that the structure, operational systems, and staff composition foster the assignment of clear accountability to individuals and organizations in both headquarters and field offices.*

Homeland security will increase the importance of the operational role of field operations, and its exacting demands on operational success will likely expose future accountability failures in a highly visible way. The damage from such lapses could be severe.

Designing the Field Structure

There is no one-size-fits-all field organization. The mission and size of departments and agencies vary greatly, as do their constituencies. Therefore, it is not surprising that the structure of field offices also varies greatly. Certainly, no one would argue that the highly technical field operations of the National Aeronautics and Space Administration (NASA) should be structured like those of people-oriented departments administering social programs. Each should be designed de novo, but with a few basic concepts in mind.

Perhaps the most important factor in designing the structure of field organizations for domestic programs is an understanding of how program delivery arrangements can best serve that segment of society for which the programs are designed. The resulting ideal structure will likely be much different than the more traditional design based on the perspective of high-level Washington officials located far from the program recipients. This is particularly true of departments, such as Health and Human Services (HHS) and Housing and Urban Development (HUD), which administer social programs with numerous small grants to common recipients, particularly families or neighborhoods. In these cases it is especially important that the field structure be designed with close attention to how the total department-wide field system affects the recipient.

The current stove-piped organization of most agencies, and the fragmentation of federal agencies, suggests that the structure of the federal government often fails to pay adequate attention to the needs of those whom it serves. Officials in Washington too easily forget how government looks to those outside the beltway who are struggling with a conglomerate of related programs, each of which has its own bureaucratic regulations, requirements, and red tape, often involving several federal offices separated by hundreds of miles.

The fragmentation of government agencies and programs has been a boon to the leaders of special interest groups residing in Washington but contrary to the needs of people and communities. Neither individual people nor their neighborhoods can be carved up and divided along the jurisdictional lines of the hundreds of federal assistance programs or the numerous separate field systems that administer them. Unfortunately, our federal delivery system has evolved more from the perspective of Washington than from that of the public.

One of the most controversial structural issues is that of regional offices. Small departments and agencies have the option of choosing regional offices that are "line" organizations with direct operational authority over all field operations and programs in the region. Policy determination, of course, remains in Washington. Larger departments, however, generally view such regional arrangements as impractical. In departments such as the Department of Transportation (DOT), in which the different modal administrations have much less need for day-to-day interaction, department-wide regional offices with line authority are neither necessary nor desirable, though regional offices for the individual components are often needed.

Large departments sometimes utilize secretarial representatives, without line authority, in the field. Although they can be useful as eyes and ears of the secretary, they have very limited utility in terms of departmental operations. Frequently, they simply get in the way and muddle lines of accountability. They have been so ineffective in some departments that Congress has terminated their funding.

To be effective operationally, a Homeland Security Department will need to have a far more closely integrated field structure than most departments.[2] The field will also need to interact rapidly at times with other federal agencies and with state and local governments and nonprofit and profit organizations. Many of the best examples of effective design and implementation come from several decades ago, when field operations were a major focus of management reforms.

The HUD Field Structure

Housing and Urban Development was a department originally established to provide internal field integration and close interaction with state and local government and nongovernmental entities though to a lesser degree than homeland security will require, but its history has relevance to the future need for greater field linkages.[3]

Conceived during the Kennedy administration, HUD was born in 1965 as an important part of President Lyndon B. Johnson's Great Society response to the unrest and violence of the inner cities. It had become increasingly clear that urban problems were so interrelated that individual efforts to improve only one dimension of community life—whether housing, schools, jobs, health care, or transportation—were not addressing the root problems, which were multifaceted. Increasingly, several federally assisted programs had to be packaged as a single project, and some type of inter-program and interagency glue was needed for these broader attacks on decaying neighborhoods. HUD was to help provide this glue.

In addition to the functions picked up by the new department from the Housing and Home Finance Agency (HHFA), HUD received a range of new responsibilities designed to meet the complex needs of urban communities, especially the inner cities. The novel Model Cities program was led by HUD, for example, and involved all the domestic federal departments. HUD also administered programs to help local governments improve their capacity to manage local affairs, requiring broad knowledge of both federal and local programs. HUD also received a convening role in an effort to coordinate the array of federal programs affecting individual communities.

The original HUD field organization reflected both this sweeping role originally intended for the department as well as early recognition by the Bureau of the Budget (BoB) management staff that the Great Society programs were overcentralized, with no capacity for field coordination.

It would have been impossible to equip the seventy-five Federal Housing Administration (FHA) field offices with the resources and technical staff needed to administer this new, complex HUD role that was to involve nearly every aspect of the government's domestic programs directly or indirectly. Further, it was believed that these field offices scattered throughout the country were too vulnerable to the local political pressures when it came to approving grants. Therefore, with BoB support, the department was designed with strong regional offices that would have not only the capacity to administer the broad scope of HUD programs but also the stature to coordinate effectively with other federal agencies and with state and local governments.

This meant equipping the regional offices with the technical expertise to handle operational problems across the spectrum of HUD activities, with a few exceptions concerning the FHA. Except for the very largest projects, career regional administrators received decision-making authority regarding grants and contracts, although they were to give headquarters an advance alert for those decisions that were controversial or politically sensitive. These regional administrators reported directly to the secretary, rather than to an assistant secretary or other intermediary. Assistant secretaries could issue directions on behalf of the secretary but not on their own. This greatly reduced the stove-piping effect that could have led individual parts of HUD to deal with their clientele through separate fiefdoms rather than on an integrated basis. And it helped to focus assistant secretaries on their policy and program oversight roles, rather than devoting so much time to operational issues for which most were not as well equipped as were the regional directors.

The assistant secretary for administration provided the institutional support needed by the regional offices to help the secretary ensure effective operation of the new system. That office also provided constant monitoring of field operations, plus a yearly in-depth review. Appointed by the secretary, the career regional administrators were at the GS-17 and 18 levels, at the top of the career service. Secretary Weaver was severely criticized by leaders of the Democratic National Committee, especially Richard J. Daley, the prominent mayor of Chicago, for departing from the traditional use of political appointees to head major field offices. Weaver said he would not repeat his HHFA experience of having a number of incompetent political appointees forced on him to head field offices, many of whose loyalty was to their personal political sponsor such as a mayor or special interest group rather than to him or the president. In fact, Weaver told the White House he would resign if not permitted to have experienced career men and women lead these important positions. This unusual stand on principle did not endear him to President Johnson, but the White House recognized there was some merit in his argument; moreover, the thought of the first black member of a presidential cabinet resigning in protest was not a welcome one. In the end Weaver was permitted not only to appoint career persons as regional administrators, but he also proceeded to appoint FHA office heads on the basis of merit as vacancies occurred.

As part of the HUD effort to respond to community problems on a holistic basis, several regional administrators were equipped with "metropolitan expediters," who traveled from city to city, as well as visiting state offices, to ferret out problems state and local officials were encountering with federal grants and contracts. Expediters could spot a problem at an early stage and quickly arrange for the appropriate expertise from the HUD regional office to solve it. Problems involving other federal agencies were simply referred to the appropriate agency for their handling. The expediters had no line authority to correct problems, yet they were very successful in triggering prompt corrective action from the regional and field offices. These expediters quickly became very popular with local officials, but several members of the House Appropriations Committee, without warning, deleted their funds because they were solving problems that had hitherto been addressed by members of Congress, who thereby earned political points with their constituents.

HUD never fully succeeded in its broad mission, but the department was successful enough in broadening its approach to community problems to become the core of President Richard M. Nixon's more ambitious proposal five years later for a Department of Community Development, which had the congressional votes for passage until the abuses of the Watergate period derailed it.

All of this sounds at odds with later HUD experience. The department's reputation plummeted in the 1970s and 1980s as the field offices came to be headed by political appointees, the assistant secretary for administration position was politicized and reduced to a shell, and the departmental philosophy of preventing scandal and abuse was watered down and often replaced with the inauguration of investigations that usually closed the barn door after the horse was gone. In addition, as early as 1969, the delegations to the field began to be blurred and weakened, and headquarters institutional support and oversight of the field declined. As a result, the field system became ineffective, illustrating the necessity for sustained management attention to complex field operations.

DOT Field Structure

The Department of Transportation, established in 1967, faced a very different situation than that which confronted HUD at its inception and thus required a different field structure. DOT was much larger than HUD so that the department-wide regional structure employed by HUD would have been impractical and unwieldy for DOT. Equally important, some of the modal components of DOT did not require the day-to-day interaction among the modes of transportation which characterized the more interdependent programs brought together in HUD.

The new department inherited several field organizations, including those of the Federal Aviation Administration (FAA), the Coast Guard, the Bureau of Public Roads, and Railroad Safety. It was evident that most of the department's programs would be carried out through the field offices and installations of the modal administrations.

The first DOT task force developed a management concept paper that necessarily contemplated that the administrations would continue to direct their own field operations and that there would be no cross-departmental regional directors. The rationale was the demonstrable fact that, while all components of the department were concerned with transportation, some had little day-to-day field interaction. The Coast Guard, for example, rarely needs to cooperate with the Federal Transit Administration, nor does the St. Lawrence Seaway Development Corporation need to work closely with the Federal Railroad Administration. Under these circumstances department-wide regional directors would create more problems than they could help solve.

From the first, the department was committed to the decentralized management of the organizational units that administered each mode of transportation. This approach was addressed in the Department of Transportation Act, which envisioned extensive delegation of the secretary's authority to the statutory modal administrators. One of the first policy directives of the second DOT secretary, John Volpe, was to affirm his support of a decentralized department.

The desire to have the various administrations achieve an optimal level of cooperation in the field compelled the secretaries to seek organizational devices with less authority than the HUD regional directors or those the FAA or the Federal Highway Administration (FHWA) could exercise. DOT Secretary Boyd opted for a system of field coordinating committees (FCCs) composed of the senior field officials of the modal administrations.

The initial twenty-six field-coordinating committees did not represent regions. They were established in any location where there was a cluster of departmental field activities. The secretary named the chairs from senior field directors of the administrations. Although they had no directive authority, the FCCs came to play a number of roles through cooperation. Regional officials who had never before met came to know and help one another, and committee members learned about the activities of other parts of the department, cooperating with the interagency Federal Executive Boards, sharing information on matters such as combined federal campaigns, and generally advancing the recognition that they were all in the same department. No negatives developed other than that there was no official present who directly represented the secretary.

The FCCs, in spite of their limited powers, have proven durable as a field mechanism. They continue to function today, albeit in reduced number, and in recent years have undertaken significant initiatives for the secretary. An example is the nationwide effort to induce educational institutions to emphasize transportation as an academic field that offers many career opportunities. As might be expected, the most active and effective FCCs are those located in major urban areas with numerous DOT field offices.

The original field arrangements had to be supplemented when President Nixon decided to establish ten standard regions with designated headquarters cities and a system of Federal Regional Councils (FRCs) for each new region. Senior field officials of the member agencies, which included the DOT and other major departments concerned with the administration of grants-in-aid to state and local governments, chaired the councils. FRC members were required to represent entire agencies, and, after an initial period of operation with career leadership, they were increasingly pressed by White House staff in subsequent years to be noncareer (i.e., political) appointees.

DOT had no field officials who could speak for the entire department and had no noncareer people in its regions. For several months, therefore, DOT utilized regional directors of its modal administrations as departmental members of the FRCs. Ironically, these DOT career civil servants won praise for their knowledge and dedication in councils composed chiefly of political designees with limited federal experience.

The Nixon administration soon made it clear that, if DOT wished to retain FRC membership, it would have to provide appointees directly representing the secretary who were not from the career civil service. Secretary Volpe then accepted the approach previously rejected by Secretary Boyd—namely, the appointment of secretarial representatives, chosen by the secretary from outside the career civil service.

The noncareer requirement proved to be a near fatal impediment to the effectiveness of DOT's participation in the FRC. In a department with many Coast Guard, FAA, FHWA, Federal Railway Administration (FRA), and Federal Transit Administration (FTA) career officials with field experience, the secretary now had to bring in a new set of people of varying competence and experience. In some cases the new secretarial representatives were irretrievably unqualified. Some were political favorites who had failed in other assignments. In one instance a career aide was needed to awaken the member when meetings adjourned. Only a few noncareer officials with prior DOT or state or local experience were capable of effectively representing the department's interest in the FRCs.

The secretarial representatives did, to some extent, initially report to the secretary. This relationship was their only real source of power or influence. They also were named chairs of the FCCs in the headquarters cities of the standard regions. After the Volpe administration the position of secretarial representatives declined rapidly in value. Later secretaries paid little attention to these field officials, and the decline and eventual abolition of the FRCs removed the principal reason for their creation. The Congress recognized what was happening and in 1981–82 eliminated funding for the secretarial representatives. They were scarcely missed. Most other experiments with secretarial reps as field officials have been found wanting. This approach to field coordination has been abandoned in most agencies, although HUD Secretary Cisneros initiated an effort to use secretarial representatives in the mid-1990s.

DOT has had to pursue its goals of acting as a single department in the field as well as at headquarters by coping with growing needs and occasional congressional intervention through the appropriations process. The fate of the secretarial reps has been described. Congress later directed the elimination of the FHWA regions and refused to fund the FHWA regional offices. Although the effectiveness of the regional structure was debatable, this congressional in-tervention—in a matter of internal management—required FHWA's fifty state divisional offices to report directly to the headquarters.

The department has taken several steps to compensate for the disappear-ance of the entire FHWA regional structure. These include the establishment of four service centers to provide the field divisions with technical advice and services. The current centers do not approve proposed actions of the divisions. Nor do they exercise directive authority.[4]

Essential FHWA and FTA cooperation on urban projects was set back by the changes in FHWA, because FTA continues to use a field organization with ten regions. DOT has sought to ameliorate the adverse effects of this situation by establishing metropolitan offices in large urban centers which contain both FHWA and FTA staffs. They are expected to coordinate projects with both highway and mass transit components.

The success of these recently activated field offices in pulling together DOT's interrelated field activities remains to be seen. It is still an option to consolidate the FHWA and FTA into a single Federal Surface Transportation Administration as recommended in a report prepared by the National Acad-emy of Public Administration (NAPA) at the request of former DOT Secretary Sam Skinner.

Field Structure of the Department of Health, Education, and Welfare and Health and Human Services

The Department of Health, Education, and Welfare (HEW), now HHS, has had great difficulty in finding an effective structure that facilitated field com-munication and coordination. Until the removal of education and social secu-rity functions, the Department of Health, Education, and Welfare (1953–79) was unquestionably the largest and most complex of the civil executive de-partments. What it and its successor, the Department of Health and Human Services, did in the way of field organization and management is, therefore, of substantial interest to all who are concerned with how large, complex depart-ments can approach this vital aspect of agency administration. The experience of the department since the early 1970s is most relevant to the theme of this chapter.

When Caspar Weinberger and Frank Carlucci, respectively, became secre-tary and undersecretary of HEW in 1973, they found a department that had benefited from the astute management of the preceding secretary, Elliot Richardson. One feature of the inherited organization was an extraordinarily competent group of regional directors. Most of these officials were experienced in public management, some had long HEW experience, and several still enjoyed career status. Moreover, in spite of the broad range of programs administered by the department, these regional directors exercised substantial authority to influence, or even direct, line programs.

Weinberger and Carlucci had established an excellent working relationship during prior service in OMB, and this helped ensure a harmonious and highly effective direction of the department. Central to this success was a division of labor between the two men: Weinberger concentrated on the policy and relationship needs of HEW, while Carlucci focused on policy implementation and internal management matters.

The new leadership quickly recognized that, in spite of Secretary Richardson's past efforts, much still needed to be done to improve the department's functioning in both the headquarters and the field. To aid in designing further reforms, Carlucci created a new position of management advisor and activated a Departmental Management Council, which he personally chaired.

The new leadership launched an immediate examination of the way the field was managed, with the management advisor directing the staff work. This review aimed to strengthen the effectiveness of the regional directors by improving their access to the secretary and undersecretary, by decentralizing authority best expressed in the field, and by broadening the range of programs under the direction of the regional directors (RDs).

A first corrective measure was to remove a layer between the undersecretary and the RDs—in this case, an assistant secretary for regional affairs. Accordingly, the role of the assistant secretary was changed to remove any role in field management. The move was successful, in spite of protests from White House sponsors of the assistant secretary.

The opening of direct channels to the top leadership of the department had the immediate effect of making the RDs more important actors in all aspects of HEW management. The increased involvement of these experienced officials, who had detailed knowledge of what was happening in the field, materially contributed to the quality and feasibility of headquarters decisions. Such an outcome is possible only when the senior field officials are made a vital part of central management and are not in any way deprived of direct access to the heads of an agency.

HEW was different from both HUD and DOT. It lent itself to a regional director system with line authority because many programs involving the aged, the handicapped, children, and societal groups with special needs required coordination of service delivery. Some large departmental components, such as the Social Security Administration and the Food and Drug Administration, were less subject to control by RDs and managed their own field operations.

Decentralization was also emphasized, because the RDs could not coordinate actions performed in or directed by headquarters offices. Implementing decentralization in HEW proved much more difficult than in DOT or HUD, however, because the Washington headquarters of influential interest groups, such as the National Education Association, either failed to support or actively opposed moving more authority to the field. These stances produced congressional questioning and the threat of legislation to prevent or delay major decentralization moves. The motivations behind this resistance to measures designed to simplify and expedite service to citizens and state and local governments were not always evident, but it appeared that some Washington lobbying offices of interest groups preferred to handle issues directly with the departmental headquarters rather than being cut out of the loop by having decisions made at the regional level.

The departures of Weinberger and Carlucci several years later brought regional reform to a quick end. The new secretary understood neither management generally nor field organization. The Departmental Management Council and its staff also disappeared. The regional directors gradually lost their involvement in major department management matters, and their roles and influence steadily declined. Finally, Secretary Joseph Califano in the Carter administration abolished the regional directors and replaced them with weak "principal regional officials." Subsequently, a number of approaches to regional management have been tried by various secretaries of HEW and HHS, but the strong, institutionalized regional director system of the Richardson-Weinberger period has never been restored.

The experience just recounted demonstrates the damage that can result from placing regional officials under the direction of anyone who is not directly running a department. It also suggests that a decentralized field structure needs either a secretary or deputy secretary who is concerned with field operations.

Relationship of Structure to Staff and Systems

Field structure should not be designed in isolation. Management systems are intertwined with structure and should be developed in concert with it, and both structure and systems must consider the number, type, and level of staff required to make the organization work. Structure, systems, and resources are the three legs of an organizational stool which must be fitted into the design of field operations.

What Kind of Field Staff?

No structure or management system will work if it is staffed by unqualified personnel. Few things are more obvious than this, yet the staffing of field offices has dropped to a low position on the totem pole of departmental priorities. Some attribute this decline to a view that, with greater reliance on "e-government," there is less need for field personnel in most social programs. Indeed, there are areas in which the number of field personnel need to be reduced and not only because of the greater application of technology. The Department of Agriculture, for example, has been striving with only limited success to reduce the unnecessarily large number of field offices that were established many years ago in an age of muddy roads and limited rural communications.

On the other hand, the streamlining of administrative processes which reduces some field staffing needs may create new fieldwork that requires a higher proportion of high-skill responsibilities than before. Centrally aggregated statistics can provide invaluable data concerning the state of programs, but most program evaluations require onsite observation by people who live and work in the field. To the extent that presidents succeed in their efforts toward decentralization and citizen-centered approaches to domestic programs, there should be an increased priority for placing experienced people in the field who are equipped to handle more challenging managerial responsibilities.

In these circumstances it is important to increase the proportion of high-level career positions in the field relative to those remaining in headquarters. Several agencies regarded at one time as leaders in effective management, such as the Atomic Energy Commission (AEC), NASA, and DOT, had a high proportion of their top career positions located in the field. In fact, AEC had difficulty attracting good people to Washington, which was regarded by most employees as less important than the field, "where the real work" took place. As noted earlier, when the Federal Aviation Administration was decentralized in the early 1960s, a number of supergrade positions were transferred to the field. The same was true of the founding of HUD.

This emphasis on qualified field personnel points up the need for greater attention to the training and development of field personnel as they face new responsibilities. It is unfortunate that, as changes in the roles of agency personnel have accelerated in recent years and the need for retraining federal employees has increased significantly, the capacity of the Office of Personnel Management (OPM) to provide employee training and development leadership within the executive branch has plummeted. For years it has been clear that domestic agencies attach far less importance than the military to employee development. They fall even farther behind the priority assigned to training by most major corporations. Inexplicably, this deficiency grew worse during the 1990s at the very time that President William J. Clinton was striving to change the culture and role of federal personnel. The need to reverse this negative trend is especially acute as it applies to social services agencies that have the most difficulty securing funds for training but in which work assignments are most fluid. Homeland security adds a new sense of urgency in this regard.

As part of the development of career leadership, the government should find a way to foster mobility of nontechnical personnel among field offices and with headquarters, especially at the Senior Executive Service (SES) levels, as contemplated by the Civil Service Reform Act of 1978. At one time several agencies required field experience before advancing people to top career positions in Washington, a practice that has considerable merit. The practice of using mobility for punitive purposes during the middle 1990s has made career people wary of participating. The Merit Systems Protection Board and Special Counsel have failed to deal with this abuse in the way contemplated by the 1978 Civil Service Reform Act.

One reason for the decline in stature of field operations has been the politicization of field leadership through both Republican and Democratic presidencies. Despite some excellent political appointees, the political process has not produced the general level of qualified field leadership which a well-managed merit system can provide. Grant and contract awards by political appointees are more vulnerable to attack as being politically motivated than those awarded by career managers. Indeed, grants denied to communities or local governments because of political considerations would seem to constitute mass discrimination against those who live there.

Political appointees in the field frequently possess more loyalty to their sponsoring political leader or special interest group than to the department head or the president. They are more susceptible to pressures from their sponsors than are career leaders, who may have questionable ties to interest groups but are rarely as dependent upon such groups for their appointment or advancement. Further, political appointees may be well versed on policy issues, but, because of their much shorter tenure, they are seldom as well informed on program operations as the senior careerists and generally do not develop a good grasp of their job until they are about to begin looking ahead to their next job outside government. Most do not provide continuity, and their vision for the agency and its programs tends to be coterminous with their expected tenure. Finally, the number of low-level political appointees is much higher than one finds in other advanced countries, to the extent that White House personnel offices lack the capacity to screen them adequately to ensure high quality.

It should be noted that the report on which the 1978 Civil Service Reform Act was based recommended that field offices be headed by career men and women.[5] The prestigious Volcker Commission wisely urged that the number of political employees in government be reduced by one-third. Political appointees play a vital role in policy making, but policy is not the role of field offices.

Modernizing Management Systems

One of the problems produced by the typical approach of addressing Washington first when modernizing systems and then turning to the field almost as an afterthought is that this sequence places too much emphasis on Washington convenience and not enough on either the needs of field personnel serving the public or the needs of the public being served.

Modernization of management systems should be based on information gained by reviewing them in their entirety, on a life cycle basis, integrating both headquarters and field activities, rather than in segments, or in sequence, even though implementation may need to be phased. Programs involving discretionary decision making in their operations should be decentralized as much as possible, underscoring the importance of including the field portion of a redesign at the outset. The discussion of decentralization later in this chapter illustrates how President Nixon and the BoB found decentralization critical to reforming domestic program management systems.

Through the use of the life cycle process reviews and strong decentralization, the New Federalism program of President Nixon reformed hundreds of grant systems, often saving 75 to 90 percent of the time and effort devoted by both federal and local officials to grant preparation and approval activities. This reform reduced positions, cut processing time to a fraction, and provided accountability that had been missing. Finally, this streamlining permitted more flexibility to respond to the unique conditions of widely varying conditions. As one would expect, the results garnered considerable bipartisan support in Congress and among state and local government leaders.

No comparable range of in-depth analyses have occurred since that time, yet homeland security operations will require a renewed streamlining effort in order to develop greater compatibility among agency field operating systems and to increase their capacity for operating quickly. Undertaking this effort necessarily requires looking at both administrative and program systems in their entirety.

Field Coordination

In view of the formidable coordination task presented by the war on terrorism, it is helpful to reexamine past experience in striving to make interagency and intergovernmental coordination more effective. Despite considerable rhetoric about the need to consolidate related programs and eliminate those that perform marginally, government continues to fund hundreds of domestic programs administered by dozens of agencies, each with its own culture and way of doing business. Many of these programs involve all three levels of government—national, state, and local. The array of different delivery systems is often something of a nightmare when viewed from the vantage point of those being served. Unfortunately, OMB no longer analyzes such problems in enough depth to ascertain their prevalence or to take corrective actions comparable to those in earlier years.

This fragmentation of government agencies and programs has been a boon to the leaders of special interest groups. It has offered a tempting vehicle for members of Congress to gain credit for fighting on behalf of appropriations for their special programs, no matter how much their efforts contribute to further splintering of the programmatic landscape or to fattening the budget. But neither individual people nor their communities can be carved up and divided along the structural lines of the hundreds of assistance programs or the variety of agencies that administer them.

For example, it is difficult for local city or county officials to integrate a federally assisted rapid transit system with other federally assisted projects that affect economic development and social services if the federal field offices are located in different cities, require different planning approaches, and do not work closely together. Neighborhoods in Des Moines, Iowa, or Los Angeles, California, cannot be expected to try to coordinate the federal government. Yet, beyond continued efforts toward block grants, the federal government no longer gives much attention to making coordination of federally assisted programs easier.[6]

This has not always been the case. Again, a case study from some decades ago provides the best example of a concerted federal effort to provide field coordination. It began with a unique response to a large-scale tragedy, a response that turned out to be the prototype for a nationwide coordination program some years later for a number of departments. In 1964 the most powerful earthquake in the history of the North American continent struck Alaska, registering about 9.2 on the Richter scale and lasting an incredible four minutes. Over sixty-four thousand square miles of surface rose or sank permanently eight feet or more. Two-thirds of the Alaskan population resided in the affected area, where all public facilities were damaged or destroyed. Water and sewer lines were broken and often had to be redesigned and relocated as a result. Hundreds of homes were destroyed, some disappearing into the ocean, as did the terminus of the Alaskan railroad. Alaska's main economic base, fishing, was put out of business because many boats were destroyed and the small boat fishing harbors were inoperable, needing to be rebuilt. Property lines shifted, creating legal problems for rebuilding which had to be resolved within weeks. Alaska faced the prospect of rampant inflation. In addition, despite the short Alaskan construction season, most reconstruction could not begin until extensive drilling by heavy equipment barged from the lower forty-eight states could first enable engineers to determine where it was safe to rebuild.

No engineer thought the relocation, redesign, and reconstruction of basic facilities such as harbors and water and sewer systems could be accomplished before the frigid fall weather would halt construction, causing much of the population to flee to the lower forty-eight states. As a new state with limited population in days before oil revenues enhanced state coffers, Alaska had little capability to cope with this calamity. The federal role was paramount if there were to be any chance of success.

President Johnson responded quickly by reconstituting most of his cabinet as the Federal Reconstruction and Development Planning Commission, to be chaired by a powerful ally in the Congress, Senator Clinton Anderson, a former secretary of agriculture. A senator could not direct action, so Johnson appointed a senior career person as executive director of the commission who also reported to him to ensure that the rebuilding moved forward with great speed. The task was more complex than any disaster recovery in our history because of the range of damage, the unprecedented urgency, and the fact that the president determined that the whole recovery effort would not merely rebuild, as in prior disasters, but also would incorporate changes to enhance future Alaskan economic development.[7]

Every state and local agency in the area, as well as virtually every federal agency plus three foreign countries—Canada, Norway, and the Soviet Union—became involved in the reconstruction effort. The federal government faced an unprecedented challenge in meshing the work of so many groups, especially because urgency permitted only a few days in which to organize.

Simplicity and innovation were the guiding themes for managing the process. Streamlined management approaches avoided the establishment of special procedures, except for a system of rapid reporting. Nine specialized interagency task forces were established, plus the Alaskan Field Committee, which ushered in a new approach to coordination that became the prototype for the nationwide regional councils that would come later.

The Field Committee was composed of the highest-ranking field person from each federal agency with field offices in Alaska. The executive director appointed the field coordinator of the Interior Department to chair the committee. No special authority was given the committee, and each member relied on the authority he or she had as an agency official. The committee's task was to coordinate, and help expedite, the operations of the various agencies with one another and with their counterparts at the state and local level. Under no circumstances was it to become another decision-making layer in the federal system.

Alaska Governor Eagan established a State of Alaska Reconstruction and Development Planning Commission as well as a state coordinator who accompanied the federal executive director on his frequent visits to Alaska and participated in all the federal meetings. The attorney general of Alaska was given an office in Washington next to that of the executive director and attended the Washington staff meetings as well as those of the federal commission.

Coordination was further enhanced through the "circuit-riding" visits of the federal executive director, who would come to Alaska roughly every ten days for a ten-day visit of all the communities that had been struck by the earthquake. In each community the director would conduct public meetings in a school auditorium or gymnasium. Around a large table sat members of the Field Committee, together with state and local officials. Members of key task forces and community organizations gave brief reports, after which the interagency/intergovernmental group of officials, chaired by the executive director, moved forward to develop community plans and set schedules, assign priorities, and resolve problems. Of particular significance is the fact that there were no separate federal plans, no state plans, and no local government plans. By virtue of this coordinated effort, the group instead produced joint rebuilding and redevelopment plans, such as the "Valdez Plan," the "Seward Plan," and the "Turnagain Plan," which incorporated the thinking of all three levels of government and the citizens. There were no secret meetings or executive sessions.

Back in Washington, department heads worked together in their role as commission members to develop policy, and the deputy department heads were available to help the executive director resolve any problems relating to their department. Several departments quickly delegated more authority to their member of the field committee and were surprised at how well their field representatives performed with so little guidance from departmental headquarters.

This unique interagency, intergovernmental coordination arrangement was given enthusiastic support from the Bureau of the Budget and achieved great success in meeting the president's goals. Peacetime construction records were broken, inflation was prevented, and legislation was passed regarding debt adjustment, disaster loans, and civil works. As a result, people did not have to leave Alaska as the fall arrived with freezing temperatures, and the state survived the earthquake's destruction. Five months after the earthquake, in an editorial entitled, "Government at Its Best," the *Anchorage Daily News* praised the innovative leadership and coordinated action of the Reconstruction Commission staff before concluding, "If more government officials functioned with the same type of attention to needs and details, the word 'bureaucrat' would fast disappear from popular dictionaries."

The Alaskan experience provided a model for regional coordination of federal programs more generally. As management problems of the Great Society programs increasingly plagued the Johnson administration, Phillip "Sam" Hughes, deputy director of BoB, drew upon the Alaskan experience to establish four pilot regional councils patterned after the earlier Alaska Field Committee but with each council covering a group of states. The results were promising, though the councils were handicapped because their members were scattered among cities, often hundreds of miles apart. At the outset of the Nixon administration this regional concept was extended to create ten regions with regional councils and coterminous boundaries that covered the whole country. Further, those agencies having most of the federal assistance programs co-located their regional offices in the ten regional cities designated by BoB.

As in Alaska, each of the ten councils was composed of the ranking field official from each department in the region. The councils had no authority per se but relied on the departmental authority possessed by each member. Similar to the Alaskan prototype, the role of the councils was not decision making but, rather, coordinating and expediting actions and plans. In lieu of the president's executive director, who had overseen the Alaskan operations, the BoB Office of Executive Management now designated several of its staff to be "Council Watchers" and to spend much of their time in the field monitoring the work of the councils. Their role was to assist the councils and to make sure they served as expediters of federal services and did not become another level of bureaucracy. An Undersecretaries Group was established to assist in the Nixon streamlining programs, with special emphasis on decentralization and the operation of the regional councils. The seven major public interest groups of state and local governments (e.g., mayors, governors, and city managers) sent several joint letters to the White House commending the administration on the entire BoB (later OMB) grant reform program, of which the regional concept was an important part.

After a few years of success, however, White House pressure led most departments to replace career field leaders with political appointees, thereby lessening their credibility as impartial administrators of federal grants and contracts. Further, in 1973 the OMB management staff was broken up so that the councils no longer had the Washington support that had been so important. The Undersecretaries Group also deteriorated into relative unimportance. As a result, the whole regional coordination concept faded and died.

No serious effort at operational coordination among the domestic departments and agencies has been made since the early 1970s. No broad survey has been made in years concerning the extent to which the current lack of federal interagency or intergovernmental coordination presents a problem with or without terrorist threats.

Now the performance bar has been raised dramatically. The battle against terrorism presents a far greater coordinating challenge for the United States than we have faced before, requiring the most effective interagency field coordination performance in our history. Yet the federal government no longer has anything in place to build upon since the Advisory Commission on Intergovernmental Relations is gone, and the capacity of OMB to address crosscutting management issues and the integration of related operations is nearly nonexistent. Management leadership in the departments is fragmented.

We must find a way quickly to develop new approaches to coordination. Since we have no idea at what day or hour our field organizations may be tested by an unexpected attack, there is great urgency. The experiences outlined here are not adequate for the needs of today, but they will be useful in designing systems to meet new challenges.

Decentralization

Few federal management concepts have been more widely promoted, but more poorly administered, than that of decentralization. With its populist overtones it is easy to understand why politicians continue to wax eloquently about the need to bring government closer to the people. President Bill Clinton and Vice President Al Gore pressed for government to be more "customer" oriented and called for decentralization as part of the "Reinventing Government" program. One of the five key elements of President George W. Bush's Management Agenda is "Citizen-Centered Government."

Many career leaders also advocate decentralization. Why so much support? First, the flowcharting of program delivery systems shows that, when properly managed, discretionary programs that are operated largely in the field move forward far more rapidly with less cost and fewer staff members than when they are administered largely in Washington. Field personnel are closer to the people served by federal programs than their Washington colleagues and understand their problems more clearly. Washington is not in as good a position to tailor agency actions to the unique circumstances of individuals and their communities.

Washington-run operations tend to generate unnecessary paper flows as headquarters officials substitute detailed reports from the field for firsthand knowledge of the circumstances under which the federal assistance has been requested. Reports that provide quantitative information are essential, but these reports cannot convey the information on the qualitative circumstances of the recipients and their particular needs which is available to field personnel through their personal observations and interactions. Earlier studies have shown the difference in effectiveness to be enormous in many cases.[8]

Second, as mentioned earlier, the more that headquarters immerses itself in conducting operations, the less time and attention it can give to its primary roles of policy development and direction, the monitoring of program performance, and program evaluation. The last two functions are perennially shortchanged because of a combined lack of attention and skill.

Not all domestic programs are candidates for decentralization. Operating payrolls, aggregating data, and processing standard forms that involve large numbers of people and families throughout the country, such as social security, appropriately involve considerable centralized data processing. But even in these areas there still is a need for employees in the field who are accessible to the public. Too often discussions take place in the simplistic terms of programs being either centralized or decentralized, when in fact most have a combination of centralized components, such as policy, as well as decentralized operations.

Despite the pledge of incoming political leadership to bring government closer to the people, relatively few such programs are successful over a period of time. If decentralization has so many advantages when properly managed, why is this so? One major reason is that decentralization is seldom well managed. The Reinventing Government decentralization was ill designed and implemented for the most part, and the Citizen-Centered portion of the Bush Management Agenda has had difficulty getting off the ground. Since President Nixon's New Federalism program, no government-wide effort to decentralize has met with great success.

Decentralization is a surprisingly sophisticated concept that requires skill and experience to design and manage. The well-intentioned Office of Personnel Management decentralization of the 1990s illustrates some of the problems. The agency followed the intent of the earlier Civil Service Reform by delegating authority for certain personnel actions to departments and agencies. But its leadership forgot that the organization doing the delegating retains responsibility and accountability for whatever is delegated. Exercising that responsibility requires: (1) first ascertaining that the delegated organization has the will and the resources to handle the delegation; (2) providing sufficient training to those who receive the delegations; and (c) ensuring that the delegating organization has in place the necessary internal monitoring capacity and is able to respond quickly to emerging problems. OPM carried out none of these critical elements and has had to struggle to regain its leadership role.

Decentralized Structure of the Federal Aviation Agency

The Federal Aviation Agency (FAA) provides an early example of a major independent agency massively (and successfully) reforming its field structure and strengthening the role of its regional officials in the period from 1961 to 1964. At the time of its creation, in 1959, the FAA had inherited the extensive field structure of its predecessor, the Civil Aeronautics Administration (CAA), which had been a part of the Department of Commerce. The CAA was a stovepiped, centralized entity with hundreds of field offices, which took their directions from specialized divisions in Washington. The CAA had six regional managers, but these officials were chiefly concerned with administrative services, rather than the oversight of line programs such as air traffic control systems, maintenance, and the enforcement of air safety standards and regulations.

During its first two years the FAA grew rapidly. Little was done to alter the way that the CAA had carried out field operations. The first FAA Administrator, Elwood "Pete" Quesada, was preoccupied with matters of policy, jurisdiction, headquarters staffing, and the construction of Dulles International Airport and preferred not to make any major changes in how the field functioned. Late in Quesada's two years as administrator, the new FAA Office of Management Analysis performed a major study at the direction of the associate administrator for administration, a career official. This study documented numerous problems in how the agency was functioning in the field and proposed placing more line authority in the hands of a new group of powerful regional directors. Quesada made only minor adjustments to the authority of the existing regional managers, but the report was not forgotten.

Najeeb Halaby, who became the administrator in 1961 under President

John F. Kennedy, had been deeply involved in the studies that led to the passage of the Federal Aviation Act. Among the first questions he put to the associate administrator for administration was "Why is the FAA so centralized?" Halaby quickly adopted most of the recommendations of the earlier report and, after a meeting of senior FAA officials, announced his decision immediately to decentralize the agency. The principal changes implemented by the administrator were:

- placing most of the seven regions under top-level GS-18 regional directors, all of whom were in the career service, and abolishing the position of regional manager;
- delegating all authority of the administrator to the regional directors, except where specifically withheld by an agency order;
- replacing all previous line bureaus with "services," which functioned chiefly as staff offices concerned with improving or advising in the execution of line programs;
- prescribing that regional directors were to report only to the administrator and deputy administrator and that they would receive mandatory directives only from these officials;
- reducing the size of headquarters substantially, to reflect the many authorities and approvals that were shifted from Washington to the field; and
- sending several powerful bureau chiefs to the field to serve as regional directors.

This radical reform required three years for full implementation and was opposed by all the bureau directors. It was based, however, on careful management studies that convinced the administrator and deputy of its necessity. The result was a more efficient and responsive agency, which was able to reduce total staffing by four thousand positions in the face of increasing workloads. The success and increasing acceptance of the field reorganization was in large measure due to a strategy specifically intended to reduce internal resistance whose principal elements were:

- issuance of an agency order prohibiting any reduction in force or reductions in employee compensation, if the action was due to decentralization or other management improvements;

- the delegation of all headquarters' authority to the regional directors, except where specifically withheld by agency order;
- the appointment of several high-level headquarters officials, most of whom had strongly opposed the reorganization, to the post of regional director (these officials quickly became ardent advocates of decentralization); and
- the utilization of a strong staff of management analysts and industrial engineers who designed the reforms and identified needed changes during the implementation phase.

The design and implementation of sweeping changes such as those enacted in FAA field operations can only take place when there is strong persistent leadership. There must also be the capability for management planning independent of the parts of the agency most directly affected by changes. Resistance to reform is often encountered from headquarters officials fearful of losing power or status.

Decentralization to the field can be sustained only under agency managers who understand how it should function and who are prepared to resist frequent headquarters efforts to pull authority back from the field. Unfortunately, there have been a number of recent changes in the FAA's distribution of authority which have tended to undermine some of the Halaby reforms. Contributing to the general weakening of the field directors was the increase in the number of contiguous state regions from five to nine. This change, undertaken in an effort to conform to President Nixon's standard regions, spread out and thinned the staff available to assist the regional directors in carrying out their responsibilities. Nonetheless, the FAA reorganization stands as a case study of the benefits to agency performance of a well-conceived and well-implemented decentralization plan.

Conclusions

American political leaders need to rediscover federal field operations and the important role that the field plays in the capacity of departments to carry out their missions effectively. With the dramatic arrival of the new dimension of homeland security, effective field operations should regain a crucial role, which has faded since the days of Johnson's Great Society and Nixon's New Federalism. In fact, if the United States fails to modernize federal field machinery and dramatically improve its ability to foster close teamwork among federal, state, and local leaders around the country in a way that is essential to meet the new challenge of terrorism, the failure could easily endanger the lives of many thousands of U.S. citizens.

Revitalizing our field operations to meet current challenges suggests two steps for consideration. First, the Department of Homeland Security will require far more early steps to be taken quite rapidly to equip federal field organizations to address terrorism issues.

Second, the longer-term needs not only of the antiterrorism effort itself but of the impact of homeland security on other nonsecurity field operations require a careful, deliberate, and in-depth review of the whole field structure of the domestic agencies. This second step will require a special mechanism that does not currently exist.

At one time a president could look to the management staff of BoB, subsequently OMB, for leadership in making both our federal field machinery and our intergovernmental arrangements more effective. Today OMB no longer has the capacity to play those roles as the management component is largely missing from that institution. Adding to the problem, agency management has become increasingly stovepiped by both Congress and the executive branch, with the result that department heads no longer have a continuing institutional management leadership arm within their department to help them.

Therefore, in order to address the broader long-term issues that affect the whole federal field system, we recommend establishing a presidential task force to examine executive branch domestic field operations thoroughly in light of today's changed conditions. The task force should be given six months to a year to recommend longer-term actions for modernizing homeland security field operations and their impact on other domestic activities. This charter should include how our federal field operations might most effectively partner with state and local public and private institutions where appropriate.

Developing recommendations for reshaping federal field structures and processes will require highly sophisticated management analyses against a complex political background. The task force should include people with substantial federal headquarters and field management experience as well as members with state and local government backgrounds. It should also utilize analyses and advice from nonprofit organizations.

In addition, this task force should also submit recommendations regarding an institutional support unit that could be established in the Executive Office of the President to provide continued oversight of the functioning of inter-agency and intergovernmental arrangements in both headquarters and field. It would also provide oversight and assistance in strengthening the management capacity of individual domestic departments and agencies, including their program and administrative management analytic capabilities. Installation of new structures and systems over the years will require continuing leadership for ensuring the necessary experimentation, pilot operations, and simulations to test new systems, structures, and coordinating mechanisms as they are put in place.

We recommend against locating this institutional support in OMB. Beginning a few years after the Bureau of the Budget's reorganization, in 1970, into the Office of Management and Budget the management capacity of OMB has steadily declined, despite numerous reorganizations and congressional legislation designed specifically to restore the *M* in *OMB*, a management leadership role that thrived only in the first several years of its existence. It is now evident that the budget will always dominate this institution to the detriment of the president's need for broad management leadership in the executive branch.

The challenge of homeland security and its relationship with other domestic activities calls for innovations in field operations and coordination which provide reform, not mere tinkering. New institutional management leadership will be essential to bring about the necessary reforms and to sustain them.

CHAPTER NINE

Technocracies

Can They Bell the Cat?

Barbara S. Wamsley

> A certain cat was so vigilant and active, that the mice, finding their numbers grievously thinned, held an interagency meeting to consider what they should do. Many plans had been started and dismissed, when a young mouse rose and said, "If the Cat wore a bell around her neck, every step she took would make it ring; then we would always be aware of her approach and could run to our hole." The speaker resumed his seat with a complacent air, and applause arose from the audience. An old gray mouse, with a merry twinkle in his eye, said that the plan was an admirable one; but he feared it had one drawback. The young speaker had not told them who should put the bell around the cat's neck.
>
> —AESOP, *THE MICE IN COUNCIL* (CA. 620–560 B.C.)

Today we have many groups seeking and sometimes succeeding to reform various aspects of the federal administrative management process. Yet comprehensive, integrated reform continues to be elusive. No one is "belling the cat." Central leadership is nonexistent or inadequate to direct and lead the reform effort that is needed to make our management systems compatible with twenty-first century needs in a coordinated and coherent way. Instead, reform is riding the back of individual technocracies.

Technocracies—What Are They?

Technocracies are organizations or groups of professionals aligned along a specialized management or administrative function. They function with the sole legitimate purpose of providing support and services to those responsible for setting public policy and delivering public service.

Until the 1950s a department's internal administration was headed by a career "chief clerk." As Alan Dean explains in this book's chapter 7, this official was vital for his or her formidable institutional memory and skill in getting things done in rigid and overcentralized departments. Today it is hard to find such an individual who is part of the career civil service and has broad-reaching authority and oversight over internal administration. There are two major reasons for this. First, the Nixon administration replaced career assistant secretaries with political appointees. Second, Congress continues to prescribe how management functions are organized, for example, having chief financial officers in each agency. Technocracies, to some extent, have evolved to fill this leadership vacuum. Today administrative and management reform or new techniques and practices are often driven, and at the very least heavily influenced, by these technocracies.

Components of Technocracies

Technocracies include members of traditional staff and policy offices within agencies (e.g., human resources, budget, and finance), and organizational operating services units (personnel and procurement offices). Technocracies also include the professional organizations geared to that specific technology (e.g., human resources management), colleague-established user groups (e.g., the Senior Executive Association), and formally established interagency committees (the Chief Information Officers Council).

Technocracies' Influence

The purpose of technocracy groups is to share information, ideas, and practices. In doing this, they can influence outcome of specific laws or regulations affecting their specialty area, through both formal and informal processes, both as career service members of the executive branch and as members of professional organizations. These professionally focused groups "constitute a form of private government." As a "private government," they "can influence the construct of policy through their consultations with congress and interest groups."[1]

Although professional guilds rarely have a formal charter from Congress or the president, they can be called upon to serve in an official capacity in formal processes. The inclusion of the Public Service Consortium in Vice President Al Gore's National (Labor/Management) Partnership Council is an example. Their inclusion was brought about because no other central government entity existed to represent managers at the Executive Office of the President (EOP) level, so that employees' organizations banded together and successfully lobbied to represent management at the table. While professional public service groups have existed for decades, they traditionally have not had the strong influence they exert today not only on substantive government policy but also on the effectiveness of government management.

Technocracy Leadership

Technocracies have evolved, and their leaders have evolved with them. How well leaders of these technocracies perform within the organization determines their merit in helping the organization succeed. At a minimum they are filling a leadership void created by too little attention to overall management at the president's level and, on the other hand, too much incremental management attention by Congress.

Technocracies also are important players in incremental reform in their specific areas. Yet the incremental nature of technocracy reform tends to segment management leadership, which contributes to avoidance of the tougher challenge of integrated reform measures. In 1982 Frederick Mosher recognized this growing trend toward specialization (or incrementalism). As he predicted, it was a trend that did not go away, leaving much of government in the hands of professionals: "The choice of these professionals, the determination of their skills, and the content of their work are now principally determined, not by general government agencies, but by their own professional elites, professional organizations, and the institutions and faculties of higher education."[2]

Technocracies and the Law

The growth in technocracies came about naturally from a growth in the complexity of government and the ever-increasing impact of technology on how business is done. The power of professional groups on government management policy rose with the increased use and importance of technology. In the federal government structure their increased power and influence on policy has been a natural evolution of new leadership structures responding to the absence or deficiency of central leadership on management issues. In considering the evolved roles played by technocracies, it is important to consider the foundation in history and law for the management responsibilities of government.

General Management Laws

General management laws (GMLs), introduced by Ronald Moe in chapter 2,[3] are the principal tool used by Congress and the president to comanage the executive branch. They include crosscutting laws regulating the activities, procedures, and administration of all agencies of the federal government. GML's provide appropriate uniformity and standardization for government organization and governance processes. Finally they may be broad in scope such as the Administrative Procedure Act and Freedom of Information Act or narrower, focusing on a specific technology such as the Chief Financial Officers Act or the Inspectors General Act.

From late in the nineteenth century until the late 1940s GMLs were few in number each decade and limited for the most part to civil service and financial management, budget, and accounting issues. Among these were the Antideficiency Act of 1870, the Budget and Accounting Act of 1921, and the Classification Act of 1923. A report of the Congressional Research Service (CRS), *General Management Laws: A Selective Compendium,* prepared for the 107th Congress on January 8, 2001, provides a comprehensive analysis of GMLs. (The chapter appendix includes a list of all general management laws included in the CRS compendium.) As Moe notes:

> In recent years, two somewhat contradictory trends are evident. First, there have been enacted many new general management laws (e.g., Inspectors General Act, Chief Financial Officers Act) each supported and justified on its supporters' definition of a problem, but often with what some observers believe to be little consideration of its probable impact upon other related general management laws. Second, increasingly agencies and interest groups have been successful in gaining exemption from the coverage of these acts, especially exemptions in the fields of personnel, compensation, and intra-governmental regulations.[4]

Table 9.1 tracks the growth in the number each decade of general management laws, notably in the latter part of the twentieth century. It also shows that until World War II much of general management concentrated on a limited number of functions of government at the federal level. With the buildup of

Table 9.1 General Management Laws Enacted by Functional Areas, by Decade

Functional Area	1870–1900	1901–1910	1911–1920	1921–1930	1931–1940	1941–1950	1951–1960	1961–1970	1971–1980	1981–1990	1991–2001	Total
Institutional and regulatory management and evaluation	0	0	0	0	1	5	0	3	5	1	5	20
Human resources and ethics	2	0	3	1	0	6	2	4	5	4	1	28
Financial management, budget and accounting	1	1	2	1	0	2	2	1	1	1	9	21
Procurement and real property	0	0	0	0	2	1	2	0	0	3	3	11
Intergovernmental affairs	0	0	0	0	0	0	0	1	1	2	2	6
Total	3	1	5	2	3	14	6	9	12	11	20	86

third-party means of governance (grants to states, contracts with the private sector, new organizational forms such as government corporations) there was a growth in laws governing institutional and regulatory management and procurement of goods and services.

Departmental Positions Established by Law

In the last decades of the last century more GMLs were related to specific technologies and included an increase in congressional action to establish administrative positions in statute (e.g., the Inspector General Act of 1978, the Chief Financial Officers Act of 1990, and the Clinger-Cohen Act of 1996—which created the position of chief information officer in each agency). In Clinger-Cohen, Congress also acted to repeal the primary role of the General Services Administration (GSA) in setting policy and regulations for federal information technology acquisition, transferring most of this authority to individual federal agencies. These laws required that the statutory positions report directly to the agency head.

The departments chose different administrative means to implement this requirement, for two pragmatic reasons. First, the people with the technical knowledge in these highly technical fields of finance and information technology were most often career civil servants at the Senior Executive Service (SES), or GS-14/15, level. Second, it was improbable that agency political leaders would add career staff to the political leadership structure. Thus, the dual-hat appointment was born in some agencies; with the political assistant secretary being designated extra hats of "chief" (e.g., chief information officer or chief financial officer) and with their senior career staff assuming a new hat of "deputy chief."

Although this approach meets the letter of the law, it is not clear that it meets congressional intent. Yet it is an approach that is more practical in application. Cabinet members have a limited amount of time to focus on their policy agendas. It was unrealistic of Congress to expect that political leaders would have time to devote to internal management areas of the agency, except for high-priority management areas affecting program priorities. This is why political support structures exist for the secretary—deputy secretary/undersecretary and assistant secretaries.

One reason that these technical positions were legislatively mandated to report to the agency head could be that the individual technocracies, reacting to a vacuum in leadership attention on their management issues, lobbied Congress to have their positions/functions elevated in the agency hierarchy. In the summer and fall of 2002, as Congress worked on legislation establishing the new Department of Homeland Security (DHS), the technocracy for personnel successfully lobbied for a new legislated position of chief human capital officer (CHCO) for departments and agencies. Unlike the other legislated positions, the CHCO may report to the secretary or another official, as the secretary may direct. The good news is that this is a move away from Congress mandating organizational placement of management positions. The bad news is that each department and agency can place the positions at many different levels, as later evidenced in table 9.2. But on the whole it is a move in the right direction. The Department of Homeland Security has chosen to place all legislated management officers under an undersecretary for management.[5]

Notwithstanding the new approach to legislated management positions for the DHS, if the individual statutory positions organizationally established by Congress are in fact carried out by career staff, we might be seeing the emergence of a permanent higher civil service—that is five or six functionally oriented career staff at the secretary's level which would not leave when the secretary left or the president changed. The fragmentation of responsibility in this new structure would be quite different from the previous career "chief clerk" or assistant secretary for administration who previously integrated and coordinated all of these functions.

Besides advancing the interests of technocracies, Congress could have had another purpose. Members of Congress had reason to encourage the Executive Office of the President, through the Office of Management and Budget (OMB), to exercise better management leadership and oversight responsibilities. It was not illogical to think that, if the Congress elevated these positions to report directly to the secretary, OMB would react by building a capability to provide oversight and leadership. Instead, the opposite happened: OMB, and specifically the deputy director for management function, relies on ad hoc groups (i.e., technocracies) composed of representatives of the chiefs to advise and assist on particular initiatives.

As noted in table 9.2, five departments with similar type operations have placed responsibility for different functional areas at different levels in their organization—including those positions statutorily mandated to report to the secretary. In the fall of 2002, by law only the finance and information technol-

Table 9.2 *Level in Organization for Senior Responsibility for Key Technical Functions*

Department	Planning	Human Resources	Procurement	Finance	Budget	Information Technology
Education	3	6	4	4	3	4
Housing and Urban Development	6	6	4	4	6	6
Veterans	7	5	5	5	5	4
Labor	6	6	4	4	6	6
Health and Human Services	6	5	5	5	5	5

Note: Level definitions: (7) branch chief; (6) office director; (5) deputy assistant secretary; (4) assistant secretary; (3) undersecretary; (2) deputy secretary; (1) secretary.

ogy positions were required to report to the secretary. Of the five departments only Veterans Affairs (VA) and Education have designated these two positions specifically to be at the assistant secretary level. Where there was no specific position such as CIO or CFO, at the assistant secretary level, this analysis determined that the agency is applying the "two-hat" model and that the actual official (the person serving on government-wide workgroups and directing day-to-day administration of the function) is the deputy CIO or CFO.

Besides the two statutorily established positions, there is inconsistency among the five departments about where they place responsibility for each of these very basic management functions. For example, Education placed the positions for budget and planning in staff offices reporting to the undersecretary, and they are noted at level 3, while HUD and VA have placed responsibility at level 6, in an office director.

Placement of responsibility at different organizational levels in departments is not necessarily either a good or bad practice. What is important is the consistency with how the leadership structure works within the individual department. When government-wide management reform is in the hands of technocracies and the people at the table representing their departments come from different levels of the organization, however, the disparity causes ineffective meetings and outcomes. In meetings the CIO at the assistant secretary level has much more authority and confidence in committing his or her agency to certain positions or resources than would a branch chief or office director from another agency, who might feel bound to return to his or her organization to obtain approval for further commitments and actions. David Garrison, former deputy assistant secretary of the Department of Health and Human Services, notes that the confusion can be especially pronounced when OMB or the White House attempt to coordinate interagency meetings. Based on his experience, he observes that, "if interagency collaborations are to move beyond process into joint programming and the like, then steps need to be taken to build working linkages to and among White House, OMB and departmental policy and budget staff."[6]

OMB Positions and Offices Established by Law

Congress legislated that there be three specific management policy and oversight offices in the Office of Management and Budget: the Office of Federal Financial Management (OFFM), the Office of Federal Procurement Policy (OFPP), and the Office of Information and Regulatory Affairs (OIRA). In the Chief Financial Officers Act of 1990, as mentioned earlier, Congress created the new position of chief financial officer in each agency. In addition it created two new positions within OMB's Office of Management: a comptroller appointed by the president to direct the new OFFM; and a deputy director for management (DDM), also appointed by the president, to serve among other management duties as the chief financial officer of the government.

The Tension between Technocracies and General Management Reform

The need for reform of management of government has been documented for decades. Yet, without any direction for comprehensive reform from central leadership in the executive branch and Congress, reform continues in piecemeal fashion, technocracy by technocracy. Reformers continue to talk about proposals to revise the human resource management systems, more procurement reform, biannual budgeting, and so forth. But no measures are being proposed to look at how well the overall machine of government is running—not just the tires, or spark plugs, but the whole car. The rise of technocracies, concomitant with a decline in central leadership and the micromanagement actions of Congress, has not created a climate for comprehensive and coordinated management reform.

The Need for Management Reform in Government

Earlier chapters of this book have reported on the need for federal management reform. A short list of the most often cited examples of the need for integrated reform includes the following arguments:

- The Civil Service System is coming apart. Agencies continue to seek and obtain separate personnel authorities.
- The annual budget process is ill equipped to deal with long-term, expensive technology or capital improvement projects.
- Congress continues to define specific positions within the executive branch for specific functional areas such as finance and information management. This has led to the fragmentation of management structures in the Executive Office of the President and agencies.
- Procurement reform did not go far enough; procurement still takes too long and is too burdensome to procure simple items.
- The federal grants administration system was designed for a different model of federal/state relationships and needs revision to reflect the devolution model begun in the 1980s and today's move toward electronic government (e-government).
- The organizational and management analysis capability is limited or nonexistent at the president's level and in some or even most federal agencies.
- When reform happens, it is incremental, without an understanding of the impact of that reform on other functions or the greater need for a look at systemic, comprehensive, and integrated reform.
- The current administration is repeating the approach to management reform followed by its three predecessors: Incremental reform by special initiative and continued downsizing and delayering of staff. The administration assumes that these efforts will bring about efficiencies and effectiveness in government operations. But the analysis and strategy behind the assumptions and the management capacity to provide the Office of the President with such much needed information does not exist.

With a decline in management leadership capacity at all levels and an absence of major reform, management reform moves into a crisis mode. The squeaky wheel gets the limited amount of oil (i.e., resources, leadership time and attention). In this environment management issues get attention when they become impediments to a political agenda. The Year 2000 (Y2K) computer problem is a good example. The problem of Y2K and computer systems' capability to record only the last two numbers for years had the potential to disrupt seriously every government program, not to mention the private sector. Yet few people outside those in the information technology (IT) technocracy were paying attention to this problem in the early part of the 1990s. This is yet another example of how management oversight was lacking at all levels of government. Y2K reached a crisis point and then received leadership attention at all levels, and especially from the president. The president created a new position in OMB to provide the oversight and direction that successfully avoided the crisis.

If this issue had been earlier on the agenda of central leadership, then the crisis management stage of Y2K may have been avoided. Everyone knew the year 2000 was approaching. Certainly, computer technicians and some agencies, such as the Social Security Administration, were trying to get in front of the problem. But most leaders did not know what was coming. And those who did had the usual short tenure of political appointees. When the recognition hit home that a major crisis was looming, money and other resources (including people) were diverted away from other important work to deal with the crisis—there could be no better recent example of crisis management in its worse sense. Lack of continuity in political leadership and fragmented agendas for management improvement can lead, at best, to neglected management and reactive management and to crisis management, at worst.

The National Academy of Public Administration published a study in 1983 which included findings and recommendations for management reform by each major management function. Most of those findings are as relevant today as they were in 1983.[7] Studying and documenting the problems occur frequently. But progress on resolving them is slow.

Lack of Oversight and Evaluation Capacity

The decline in management leadership capacity in the executive branch began in the 1970s. OMB staffing trends suggest that the decline at OMB began even earlier. Yet the greatest change to the quality of overall management oversight began in the 1980s, when the new Senior Executive Service, established in 1978, was not fully implemented, specifically as the SES concept related to creating a corps of generalists through reassignments. Presidential administrations began to place more emphasis on privatizing government functions and less on reforming government management, and the decade saw significant reductions in management, planning, and evaluation offices and staff in OMB and the agencies.

OMB's Current Management Capacity

OMB's management capacity is questionable. First, consider that in the 1970s OMB's management division had 224 employees. Thirty years later "the director for management [could] call on less than a dozen employees."[8] Even though Congress has created three new offices in OMB, staff capacity has declined significantly since the 1970s. The position of deputy director for management remained vacant under President George W. Bush until August 2002, almost two years into his presidency.

Former House Governmental Reform Committee Chair William Clinger wrote to Vice President Dick Cheney on July 24, 2001, expressing his deep concern that "the management interests of the President, the executive branch generally, and even Congress are not being fully served by the current organization of OMB. The management capacity available to the President in OMB has steadily declined and now barely exists." He went on to say that the constitutional responsibility of the president to manage the executive branch has not been a high priority for recent presidents, with the result being a vacuum that is filled by ad hoc executive management organizations, and others.[9]

Aside from concerns about capacity to manage, others question the authority of the new DDM:

> The relationship of the DDM to the three statutory offices (OFFM, OFPP and OIRA) is somewhat unclear. Congress established these offices before the DDM position was created, and PAS appointees head them. It was not specified when the DDM post was established by the CFO Act whether these three officers are subordinate to the DDM. Regardless of the official relationship, it seems clear that these three offices represent an unfortunate establishment of "stovepipe" structures in OMB, whereas their functions are clearly inter-related.[10]

In summary, there are four reasons to be concerned about the capacity of OMB to provide management oversight for the federal government:

1. OMB's staff capability compared to the 1970s is negligible, even though Congress is creating new statutory offices and responsibilities.
2. The position of OMB deputy director of management was vacant for two years, and since has had only short-time occupants who soon move on to other positions in government.
3. When filled, the position of deputy director has uncertain authority over the statutorily created offices.
4. Functional stovepipes now exist in OMB, and OMB increasingly relies on ad hoc executive management organizations and professional interest groups to carry out and provide oversight of the administration's management priorities.

Some may argue that this assessment fails to recognize the involvement in management issues of the four major Resource Management Offices (RMOs) in OMB. In the first years of President Bill Clinton's term, OMB was reorganized to merge what was already a significantly reduced management staff with the budget staffs to create so-called Resource Management Offices. The four RMOs are organized around major government programs—Natural Resources, Human Resources (e.g., health, education, and labor), General Government Programs, and National Security Programs. Without a doubt the RMOs do get involved in major management issues. It is safe to assume that, if there is a management initiative that carries a large price tag, it will have heavy involvement from the RMOs.[11]

Technocracies are prime players in filling the void in OMB management leadership. Their power and influence grows over the setting of management agendas and priorities. The downside to relying solely on technocracies, however, is that agendas and priorities set or heavily influenced by individual technocracies will fail to provide an overall agenda and priorities for reform of how government should best be managed.

The void in management leadership capacity at the president's level is one that cannot be filled by ad hoc committees or technocracies and should not come to the fore only at a time of crisis. For example, the effectiveness of applying government resources to combating terrorism will depend largely on leadership, management, and coordination of different technologies and their related constituencies and interest groups. In the instance of terrorism both the EOP and Congress recognize a need for strong central management leadership. Expectations are that the new Department of Homeland Security will fill this void. But in a way the process of creating the legislative template for that department has provided further evidence of the limited capacity of OMB to provide management leadership for the president.

Presidents' Management Agendas

While it is questionable whether the president has the necessary structure and staff capacity in his Office of Management and Budget, it would be unfair to suggest that presidents and their staff have not concentrated on improving management. Those improvements are usually introduced in a president's budget as management initiatives and form the president's management agenda for that budget year.

President Ronald Reagan in the 1980s used a commission (the Grace Commission) to review government operations and find opportunities for improvement. Significant improvements in federal accounting and debt collection came about as a result. President Clinton appointed Vice President Gore to "reinvent government." Gore directed the National Performance Review (NPR), which in its first two years directed teams of volunteers to look at each of the major functional areas (e.g., budget, finance, and personnel) and recommend improvements. Individual technical improvements came about from this effort—for example, the use of credit cards for small purchases. Yet success eluded the NPR's search for comprehensive reform in human resource management, the budget, and other areas.

In early 2001 President George W. Bush issued his *Management Agenda for Fiscal Year 2002,* which includes five government-wide management initiatives and fourteen program-based initiatives (e.g., privatization of military housing).[12] The five government-wide management initiatives are functionally based (i.e., by technology): (1) Strategic Management of Human Capital, (2) Competitive Sourcing, (3) Improved Financial Performance, (4) Expanded Electronic Government, and (5) Budget and Performance Integration.

In its focus on narrow aspects of particular functional areas, the 2002 agenda follows the traditions of presidents since the early 1970s. What is missing is an emphasis on more comprehensive reform. A more comprehensive management agenda could include important initiatives directed toward major comprehensive management reform, such as a project to assess the adequacy of resources, structures, and legislative bases for OMB and agencies to manage government programs; and a project to assess how well OMB and agencies are integrating the strategic plans of individual technocracies (management support functions) into and with the organizations' strategic plans.

OMB has developed a unique approach for overseeing and monitoring the progress of departments and agencies in implementing the 2002 presidential initiatives. On October 30, 2001, OMB announced a "scorecard" to track agencies' success in accomplishing the management initiatives. Agencies are given green, yellow, or red lights for their performance.

OMB's scorecard does not, however, link budget strategy to the initiatives. This linkage is necessary to help agencies achieve improvements on the president's management initiatives. For example, the first initiative continues the 1990s downsizing (e.g., encouraging delayering and a decrease in number of managers) without first determining what effect such action will have on important program and management initiatives. This "numbers game," if implemented by an agency to achieve a "green light," will probably affect the agency's effectiveness, including its ability to implement the president's initiative to improve technology for e-government. Information technology relies on a pool of professionals which, like others in the public sector, is facing large turnovers and heavy competition from the private sector in the recruitment and retention of employees.

In his letter to Vice President Cheney, William Clinger expressed concern about the inability of OMB to contribute to the resolution of important federal management issues. He went on to say that Congress has seen its oversight capacity diminish, in part because of the weak management capacity in OMB. He gave as an example the abandonment of the general civil service system to individual oversight committees that work directly with agencies to provide special exemptions or exclusions from the general law. Clinger noted that the weakening of OMB has also led to a weakening of the corresponding committees on the Hill, especially including the House Government Reform Committee and the Senate Governmental Affairs Committee.

The Management Capacity of Federal Departments and Agencies

Just as OMB's capacity to provide oversight and leadership on management and organization has dissipated over the last few decades, so has the management capacity of departments. As discussed previously in this chapter (and more thoroughly in chap. 7), from 1949 to 1973 career assistant secretaries for administration provided each departmental secretary with a single official responsible for virtually every aspect of internal organization or management. Today, with the disappearance of these career senior administrative officials, responsibility for internal management has been distributed among various functional positions.

Not coincidentally, with the weakening and even loss of departmental and OMB management capacity, we are also moving away from a general civil service system and back to the pre-1950 environment of several dozen separate systems. The decline in capacity in OMB has led to reactive management and crisis management, and the same can be said for many departments. Departments are faced with inadequate capabilities for management and evaluations, the internal audit capability rests now with independent inspectors general, and Congress continues to take actions that muddy the water on reporting relationships and responsibilities within departments and agencies. The flexibility given by Congress to the secretary of the Department of Homeland Security for determining the reporting structure for legislated management positions is needed by all departments and agencies.

Technocracies Cannot Substitute for a Lack of Capacity or Leadership

As was discussed previously, there is a leadership vacuum that drains any effort to bring about comprehensive integrated reform of how government does business. This vacuum is created by a lack of organization and management capacity at both the president's and agency head levels. It is also a vacuum that extends to Congress, where integrated approaches to reform have been replaced by reform by particular committees—often appropriations committees—for specific technical areas. Congressional oversight of departmental management has diminished. These causes are not new; they have been building for decades.

Over time the individual technocracies have partially filled that vacuum. But this is not enough. By their very nature reforms pursued by a technocracy are specific to that technocracy (e.g., separate personnel authorities for individual agencies) or are reforms in isolation from the changing needs or practices of the broader context of federal departments and agencies. It was no surprise when Congress established the new chief human capital officer position. From the technocracy perspective the logic is compelling. When two administrative positions get statutory backing and are organizationally elevated, then it is only natural that the leaders of other administrative technocracies want equal standing. Few should be surprised if in time there is a new legislated position for chief procurement officer.

Yet reform left to technocracies, without central leadership, provides no means to integrate reform efforts into a cohesive, compatible government-wide strategy. Incremental reform pursued by technocracies will not be seen as disinterested and cannot carry the same weight as a broad-based reform endorsed by the president.

Other Factors Contributing to the Increased Influence of Technocracies

Political Appointees

There are currently about twenty-eight hundred political appointee positions within the federal government.[13] From 1970 to 1992 the average service for political appointees in their current positions varied between 1.7 and 2.6 years. This transience makes teamwork difficult, as political executives are unlikely to know one another or to be bound by other unifying ties.[14] More realistically, with an average of two years to accomplish anything on their agenda, most appointees will be looking upward for direction on management issues, not out and across their organizations. The "President's Management Agenda for 2002" means each department is implementing and being graded on five individual nonintegrated management improvements. Is it likely that these initiatives are the top five management priorities for every department and agency? Where does the automation of the antiquated air traffic controller system fit within this agenda? Do such important issues compete for time and resources with the five presidential initiatives? These are questions not answered by the "President's Management Agenda for 2002."

Senior Career Managers

At the federal level there is no one school or one avenue for becoming part of the SES. Elevation to that rank is largely determined within the various agencies and departments. Initially, it was anticipated that the SES would become a corps of generalist managers with high mobility between the agencies.[15] Most senior SES officials began and continued up the ladder in their careers in a specific technical area. Prior to the implementation of the Senior Executive Service, some departments ran management intern programs to train a cadre of future managers. These programs were designed to give professionals broad experience across many different technical management areas. When the SES came into being, departments also had SES candidate programs, with the same goal of giving individuals striving for entry into the SES a broad background among various technical management areas. Unfortunately, it is not a requirement that a candidate graduate from the SES candidate program in order to be appointed to the SES. Also, it is not a guarantee that, once having graduated from the program, a candidate would be appointed to the SES:

> Focusing . . . on the top career executives, the proportion of those who have served in an agency other than the present one is similar in 1991–92 to what it was in 1970: between 22 and 24 percent. These figures exemplify the general tendency to promote from within those who have worked their way up the ladder within an agency. These individuals are extraordinarily well prepared in educational terms . . . and they have honed their specialized knowledge of the programs and functions of their agencies through years of service. What they may lack is the broader perspective that can come from service in agencies with different constituencies and missions.[16]

Although these statistics relate to cross-agency experience, it is probable that most members of the SES as they move up the ladder also are staying within their technical field, with little or no cross-training or experience in other technical areas. Too often, this lack of understanding of the shared responsibility among functional management areas results in one technocracy making improvements while having a negative impact on another area. An example is the recent reform of procurement rules, which resulted in lowering the threshold for noncompetitive procurements from $10,000 to $2,500. A senior procurement official explained this was done to appease the small business community and gain their support for the legislative package. It would be difficult, however, to convince the laboratory director or a scientist at the National Institutes of Health that this particular "reform" benefited them. The lab director had to write a justification and obtain three price quotes and wait three months before he could get a replacement for his broken computer. A visiting research scientist said he was spending more than 40 percent of his time justifying purchases needed for his research. Before procurement reform the lab director could have purchased a computer at a local retail store the same day his old computer crashed.

Through broader experience and perspectives managers and leaders can learn to operate more collegially and inclusively to build on the positives and offset the negatives of technocracies.

Institutions of Higher Learning

According to Ronald Moe, "There are over 100 major graduate degree programs in public management offered across the country, plus several thousand programs offered at both the undergraduate and graduate levels in areas related to government management."[17] Some of these graduate programs promote technocracies by conferring graduate degrees in specialized areas such as computer science and human resources. Yet more important than specialized degrees within the field of public administration is the need for schools to build into the curricula at both the undergraduate and graduate levels emphasis on working in technocracy environments.

Edgar Schein, in his essay "On Dialogue, Culture, and Organizational Learning," *Organizational Dynamics* (Autumn 1993), contends that it is not surprising to see poor communication and understanding between different groups that are emotionally attached to their "culturally learned categories of thought." These groups, whether Congress, unions, or senior government executives, have specialized languages and sets of assumptions which help define their unique cultures. This leads to misunderstandings among groups and consequent breakdowns in coordination and halfhearted efforts at cooperation as well as manipulations to preserve a particular status quo.[18]

Attitudes of individuals and institutions toward leadership qualities and responsibilities must adapt to reflect the ever-increasing complexity of managing in an environment of technocracies.

What Is to Be Done?

In a 1965 annual report to the Carnegie Corporation of New York, John Gardner addressed "Some Maladies of Leadership: The Failure to Cope with the Big Questions": "Nothing should be allowed to impair the effectiveness and independence of our specialized leadership groups. But such fragmented leadership does create certain problems. One of them is that it isn't anybody's business to think about the big questions . . . where are we headed? Where do we want to head? What are the major trends determining our future? Should we do anything about them? Our fragmented leadership fails to deal effectively with these transcendent questions."

Before government leaders can address the big picture and answer the hard questions, they must have the willingness and capacity to do so.

Increase the President's Capacity to Manage

Earlier in this chapter two steps were outlined which could improve the president's current management agenda to include broader initiatives that would start in the direction extolled by Gardner. The first was an initiative to assess the capacity of government to manage. The second was an initiative to integrate the mission, goals, and objectives of technocracies with those of the president and agencies. But this assumes that presidents and their leadership teams recognize that a void in management leadership and oversight exists. And that void results from the president's abrogation of his responsibility as chief executive officer to oversee and improve the government.

Equally important, policy makers need to recognize that reforms enacted in a piecemeal fashion, or without benefit of a solid foundation for change, do not lead to better government and in fact may hinder the accomplishment of any political agenda. Together with the president's commitment to lead, he needs the capacity to take on broad management initiatives such as those recommended here. That capacity does not exist today. The use of ad hoc groups to support the president's staff is not the answer. Instead, as others have recommended, the president needs to formalize a management office within the Executive Office.

Legislation submitted by Representative Steve Horn (R-CA) on February 14, 2001, would have transferred OMB management responsibilities to a new Office of Federal Management. This is a move in the right direction, but it would only succeed if it were combined with leadership support, adequate resources, and clear lines of authority for management responsibilities at all levels. Unfortunately, this legislation died in committee at the end of the 107th Congress in December 2002.

Restore Departmental Capacity to Manage

With or without increased capacity in the Executive Office of the President, it is imperative that agencies move back to the future and reestablish the assistant secretary for administration positions. The title can be adjusted to whatever fits within today's organizational structures, but the purpose should be the same: a senior career official, nontenured, responsible for providing continuity in leadership and oversight in the integrated planning and execution of an agency's management functions (including technocracies). All statutory positions would report to this individual, who if necessary could wear many dual hats of chief, if the applicable legislation cannot be changed.

Improving the Quality of Executive Leadership

Public managers often narrow their focus to their area of responsibility, rather than paying attention to the larger management context. Management fragmentation will continue to exist and probably grow. Accepting this, it would seem less important to concentrate on stopping fragmentation than to concentrate on giving managers and leaders the tools they need to manage in a fragmented environment. Technocracies have started this in one respect by building the strong communication channels within their groups. Leaders need to adapt this approach to build strong communication channels among many different technocracies. Not only should leaders do this externally with other organizations, but also, more important, they should serve as the internal coordinator for better communication and cooperation among technocracies within their agencies.

Improved leadership must start with political appointees, especially since they have assumed the mantle previously worn by chief career administrators. Appointees need to be introduced to the complexities—and the importance to their own political agendas—of government management. They should be trained to recognize their responsibility for leadership in the environment of multiple technocracies with different networks of influence and control.

If the Senior Executive Service had met the original intent of the 1978 reform law, our cadre of senior executives would have the broad experience among various technocracies. This broader knowledge and experience base would support better communications and connections, as espoused by Gardner. Yet this did not happen to the degree intended.

It is not too late to use experience to improve leadership capacity. In order to move to higher levels in the SES, managers should be required to have short rotational assignments, of at least several months, in other disciplines. Presidents continue to want the government to be more like the private sector. The practice of requiring broad experience and knowledge for progression in the corporate hierarchy should be one that is adopted for senior executives in government.

Leaders who have experienced a "walk in the shoes" of other technical managers will have a broader understanding of where their functional responsibilities fit with the overall operations and success of an organization. Also, collaboration and inclusion are most likely to occur if a leader has a basic understanding of functions and responsibilities of other technical leaders who have a stake in the outcome of particular projects. There are few management objectives that do not have shared accountability distributed among several different management technocracies in a federal organization.

The Contribution of Institutions of Higher Education to Building Leadership Capacity

Today's educational institutions are responsible for the sound knowledge and skill base of the federal executive, a base that is comparable to that in the private sector. Curricula should be expanded to concentrate specifically on the environment of technocracies in organizational theory and practice. Graduates must understand the environment in which they will be working. Whether they work in today's environment or one that has better management oversight and direction, they still will require skills necessary for communicating and integrating their interests and concerns with technocracies. Prospective career agency leaders need to understand the evolution and nature of technocracies, and they need the skills to work with the technocracies to accomplish their goals.

Conclusion

Leadership or reform by committee or interagency groups led by individual technocracies will be piecemeal and will fail to improve the overall system of government. The structure, tools, and leadership capacity to integrate and coordinate management is needed at all levels of the federal government. This is necessary to accomplish reform that works to improve our system of government without causing the kind of unintended harm that has resulted from past reform efforts.

The Boy Bathing

A boy bathing in a river was in danger of being drowned. He called out to a passerby for help. The traveler, instead of holding out a helping hand, stood by unconcernedly, and scolded the boy for his imprudence. "Oh sir!" cried the youth, "pray help me now, and scold me afterwards."

AESOP (CA. 620–560 B.C.)

Counsel without help is useless. Similarly, leadership without capacity is meaningless.

APPENDIX TO CHAPTER 9: **General Management Laws**

Institutional and Regulatory Management and Evaluation

Federal Register Act
Administrative Procedure Act
Federal Tort Claims Act
Federal Records Act and Related Chapters of Title 44
Government Corporation Control Act
Federal Advisory Committee Act
Reorganization Act of 1977, as Amended
Congressional Review of Regulations Act
Freedom of Information Act
Privacy Act
Inspector General Act of 1978
Government in the Sunshine Act
Federal Vacancies Reform Act of 1998
Government Performance and Results Act of 1993
Paperwork Reduction Act of 1995
Regulatory Flexibility Act of 1980
Negotiated Rulemaking Act
National Environmental Policy Act
Clinger-Cohen Act

Financial Management, Budget, and Accounting

Budget and Accounting Act of 1921
Budget and Accounting Procedures Act of 1950
Balanced Budget and Emergency Deficit Control Act

Budget Enforcement Acts of 1990 and 1997
Congressional Budget and Impoundment Control Act
Chief Financial Officers Act of 1990
Government Management and Reform Act of 1994
Federal Managers' Financial Integrity Act of 1982
Federal Financial Management Improvement Act of 1996
Line Item Veto Act of 1996
Antideficiency Act
Federal Credit Reform Act of 1990
Federal Claims Collection Act of 1966
Federal Debt Collection Act of 1982
Federal Debt Collection Procedures Act of 1990
Debt Collection Improvement Act of 1996
Cash Management Improvement Act of 1990
User Fee Act of 1951

Human Resources and Ethics Management

Title V; Human Resources Management
Civil Service Functions and Responsibilities
Office of Personnel Management (Chapter 11)
MSPB; OSC; and Employee Right of Action
Special Authority (Chapter 13)
Political Activity of Certain State and Local Employees
Employees (a) General Provisions—Definitions (Chapter 21)
Merit System Principles (Chapter 23)
Employment and Retention: Authority for Employment
Examination, Selection, and Placement (Chapter 33)
Part-Time Career Employment Opportunities (Chapter 34)
Retention Preference, Restoration, and Reemployment (Chapter 35)
Employee Performance: Training (Chapter 41)
Employee Performance: Performance Appraisal (Chapter 43)
Employee Performance: Incentive Awards (Chapter 45)
Employee Performance: Personnel Research Programs and Demonstration Projects
Pay and Allowances: Classification (Chapter 51)
Pay Rates and Systems (Chapter 53)
Pay Administration (Chapter 55)
Travel, Transportation, and Subsistence (Chapter 57)
Allowances (Chapter 59)
Attendance and Leave (Chapter 61)
Attendance and Leave: Leave (Chapter 63)
Labor-Management Relations (Chapter 71)
Antidiscrimination in Employment and Employees Right to Petition Congress
Suitability, Security, and Conduct (Chapter 73)
Political Activities (Chapter 73, Subchapter 3)
Adverse Actions (Chapter 75)

Appeals (Chapter 77)
Services to Employees (Chapter 79)
Insurance and Annuities: Retirement (Chapter 83)
Federal Employees' Retirement System (Chapter 84)
Federal Employees Health Benefits Program (Chapter 89)
Ethics in Government Act
Ethics Reform Act of 1989
Lobbying with Appropriated Monies Act
Independent Counsel Act

Source: CRS Report for Congress, General Management Laws: A Selective Compendium—107th Congress, Jan. 8, 2001.

CHAPTER TEN

Program Design and the Quest for Smaller and More Efficient Government

Thomas H. Stanton

Together the Clinton administration and the Republican Congress reduced the federal workforce by more than 300,000 positions during the 1990s. By the end of the decade federal employment was at its lowest level since the Kennedy administration. Measured by the size of the federal workforce, government became smaller. But did it become more efficient? If federal agencies simply substituted private contractors for their former employees, then the answer is in doubt.

Moreover, large-scale contractor failures, in the Department of Education's Student Loan Program and in the Air Traffic Control System of the Federal Aviation Administration, for example, show that government agencies need strength, in resources, staffing, and procedures, if they are to benefit from contracting out. Key elements relate to the capacity of federal employees to select high-performance contractors and maintain high-quality relationships with them. Numbers-driven downsizing can simply hollow out the wrong parts of an agency and reduce its ability to provide public services, either directly or through third parties.

This chapter suggests that smaller and more efficient government is attainable, but only for some government programs and agencies and only if the priorities are reversed to emphasize sound program design rather than downsizing. Good program redesign is needed before downsizing can be contemplated, to ensure that a government agency can maintain or increase its service levels while reducing the number of employees needed for certain tasks.

A note of caution: While downsizing is popular politically, depriving government programs of administrative resources has weakened many of them significantly. On the other hand, there are areas in which downsizing can promote more efficient government, especially if some of the profound changes in the U.S. economy and in technologies have made current ways of doing business unsustainable for government programs. Such programs will need to redesign themselves, or be redesigned, merely to survive.

Effective Downsizing Requires Program Redesign

Downsizing Is Not Always the Answer

Policy makers should approach the issue of downsizing with caution. Unwise cuts in resources can destroy an agency's ability to provide important public services. Numbers-driven downsizing can slash an agency's staffing whether it is operating efficiently or not. Thus, with the benefit of hindsight, policy makers recognize that it was foolhardy and costly in the 1980s to slash the federal examiner staff, which was responsible for policing the financial safety and soundness of the savings and loan (S&L) industry. Among other factors, the lack of effective government supervision contributed to the failure of thousands of S&Ls over the decade, at a cost to taxpayers of $150 billion. Numerous other examples exist of federal agencies cutting their oversight staffs, and the related travel and training budgets, and thus permitting avoidable financial losses to occur.

The corporate world has discovered that "chain saw" approaches often don't work. Businesses that deal with government may find that an understaffed agency lacks the kinds of flexible responses that might be possible if adequate staff were available. Years of federal buyouts may have led to the early retirement of the seasoned agency officials who understood why flexible application of rules is necessary; their fresh replacements may insist on going by the book until they eventually gain the experience needed to make more informed decisions.

Over ten years ago Charles Bowsher, then the comptroller general of the

United States, warned about the problem of "disinvestment in government."[1] A 15 percent reduction in the executive branch civilian workforce (not counting the Postal Service), from 2.2 million full-time positions in 1993 to 1.8 million in 2003, has exacerbated the problem.

Frustrated lawmakers have sought to punish poorly functioning agencies with high-pressure oversight hearings and new laws and appropriations restrictions ranging from micromanagement to draconian acts of displeasure. These measures have added yet another layer to the problem of inefficient government, especially because of the way that congressional activities can distract an agency's leadership from attending to important management responsibilities that might help to solve problems of the type that the Congress is unhappy about.

Browbeating is unlikely to increase government performance. As the private sector learned long ago, well-designed positive incentives, which create motivation to improve performance and take reasonable risks, are far superior to command-and-control approaches. A bureaucrat who will be pilloried for even a minor mistake will be motivated to do little but take a defensive posture and dodge decisions.

Indeed, for some agencies the solution to poor performance lies with the provision of more, rather than less, resources. The United States Commission on National Security/21st Century, which made its report before September 11, 2001, found that the Department of State was "starved for resources." Moreover, according to the commission, "the Customs Service, the Border Patrol, and the Coast Guard are all on the verge of being overwhelmed by the mismatch between their growing duties and their mostly static resources."[2]

The problem is not confined to agencies and departments with national security responsibilities. In 1999 a bipartisan group of fourteen health care experts published an open letter calling for increased resources to be devoted to the Health Care Financing Administration (now renamed the Centers for Medicare and Medicaid Services): "No private insurer, after subtracting its marketing costs and profit, would ever attempt to manage such large and complex insurance programs with so small an administrative budget."[3]

The United States Commission on National Security/21st Century stated the general problem in stark terms: "As it enters the 21st century, the United States finds itself on the brink of an unprecedented crisis in competence in government. . . . Both civilian and military institutions face growing challenges . . . in recruiting and retaining America's most promising talent."[4]

Thus, redesign of government programs is not a panacea. Poor leadership, unmotivated staff, insufficient resources, and glacial or irrational procedures will not be overcome merely by redesigning programs.

Conditions for Effective Downsizing through Program Redesign

That said, redesign does have a role in facilitating effective downsizing of some programs. In particular, program redesign permits government downsizing under three conditions:

1. the federal government withdraws completely from a particular activity;
2. a government agency adopts new ways of doing business that requires fewer employees to produce the same or greater levels of program performance; or
3. a government agency uses selective and intelligent outsourcing to reduce demands upon scarce agency resources.

The second and third conditions may combine in some cases. Consider each of the three conditions in turn.

Complete Federal Withdrawal from an Activity

In theory the federal government's withdrawal from a program should be the easiest of the three ways to reduce the size of the federal workforce. In practice it is among the most difficult, especially for large activities that employ many federal workers.

For years members of Congress have sought to "zero out" entire government organizations. These efforts have largely foundered on a lack of political agreement that the government should in fact withdraw from the activity that the agency or department carries out. Thus, an effort to abolish the entire Department of Commerce failed when policy makers realized that they would need to reconstitute the major components of the department, including such agencies as the U.S. Patent and Trademark Office, the Bureau of the Census, and the National Institute of Standards and Technology. The consequence would have been creation of a large number of smaller agencies or their incongruous placement within other agencies.

The result of these efforts in the early 1990s was to close a handful of federal organizations that had been backed by weak constituencies, rather than closing organizations that possessed weak justifications for their existence. The closed agencies—the Office of Technology Assessment, the Advisory Commission on Intergovernmental Relations, and the Administrative Conference of the United States—read like a who's who of small but valuable organizations that were intended to improve the quality of governmental decisions without serving any particular constituency.

The best examples of complete federal withdrawal involve privatization or devolution of an activity rather than outright termination. In 1998 the government sold the Elk Hills Naval Petroleum Reserve, a small but profitable venture that traces its government origins back to the need to provide for conversion of naval vessels from coal to oil in the early part of this century. The government may ultimately privatize the entire office of Naval Petroleum and Oil Shale Reserves.

The sale of the Consolidated Rail Corporation (Conrail) in the 1980s was another privatization success story. The government sold Conrail at a profit and thereby divested itself of a rail freight company that employed over fifty thousand people. The success of the Conrail privatization is traceable to creation of the capacity within government, in an organization known as the U.S. Railway Association, to design and carry out a long-term privatization plan. After selling Conrail and winding up litigation stemming from Conrail's original establishment, the U.S. Railway Association was terminated as a U.S. government agency.

Privatization requires careful planning.[5] Especially important, government must disentangle the financial objectives of privatization from questions of public mission. The government privatized the U.S. Enrichment Corporation in 1998, over the objections of the chairman of the Council of Economic Advisors and members of Congress. As Dan Guttman observes in chapter 3, this particular privatization was unwise: the processing of uranium is an activity that relates closely to U.S. foreign policy objectives, such as ensuring that radioactive materials from the former Soviet Union do not fall into the wrong hands.

Devolution is the process of turning over to states and localities some functions that the federal government currently performs. Because it maintains public activities and brings them closer to the people and communities served by a program, devolution is a potentially promising way to reduce the size of the federal government.

The 1987 Federal Clean Water Act created the state revolving fund program under sponsorship of the U.S. Environmental Protection Agency, as a part of the U.S. government's transformation of the federal clean water grant program into a state program. The federal government also considered whether to devolve federal highway programs by providing seed money for revolving funds to provide financing for highways within the state. John Petersen, financial advisor to state and local governments and a recognized expert in this area, has observed that the revolving loan fund continues the transformation of federal recurring grant programs into self-sustaining state loan programs.

Adopting New Ways of Doing Business

New technologies increasingly provide the basis for federal agencies to carry out their activities more efficiently and with less staff. Federal credit programs provide a prime example. The Internet, toll-free numbers, and information-based response systems allow federal agencies to serve their constituencies, including veterans (the Department of Veterans Affairs [VA] loan program), small businesses (the Small Business Administration), and rural borrowers (the Department of Agriculture). Federal agencies now can offer round-the-clock service in place of earlier requirements that a user of federal services always come to a federal office during regular office hours to conduct business with the government.

The new ways of doing business also can permit some federal agencies to close field offices and centralize their services in large state-of-the-art servicing centers. The political process imposes limits, however, upon the ability of a federal agency to downsize by closing unneeded offices. The U.S. Department of Agriculture and the health care system of the Department of Veterans Affairs provide prime examples. A concerted effort by the secretary of agriculture together with congressional leaders was able to achieve only limited reductions in the department's huge size, amounting in 2003 to about ninety-nine thousand employees. A similarly determined effort by the head of the Veterans Health Administration led to a shift in medical care to outpatient settings and permitted the VA to close twenty thousand hospital beds, amounting to a 40 percent reduction. Yet the political process precluded the VA from closing more than a handful of aging and unneeded hospitals.

The Department of Agriculture also provides a success story of business process improvement, including a reduction in federal staff levels, which could stand as a model. The Rural Housing Service (RHS) of the department engaged in a multiyear program to centralize servicing of rural housing direct loans, to add new technological capability to field offices to help with loan origination and servicing, and to relocate and downsize staff to accommodate the changes. The Rural Housing Service obtained a multiyear commitment from the Office of Management and Budget for the funds needed for the new technology and staff training. All parties lived up to their commitments, and the new office was able to operate on the basis of state-of-the-art servicing technologies.

Selective and Intelligent Outsourcing

The secret of effective outsourcing is the sound design of a working relationship between the government agency and its private partners. A resource-strapped government agency often focuses on price and takes the lowest bid for contract services. Then, too, government often neglects to structure the relationship with its contractors to ensure that they have incentives to perform well.[6]

The Department of Education displays positive and negative examples of outsourcing in its student loan programs. On the positive side the department's Office of Student Financial Assistance has created a roster of approved collection agency contractors that it uses to collect on delinquent or defaulted student loans. The department applies a stated policy of allocating more workload to successful contractors and less to those whose performance is lower. The department also applies a balanced scorecard of performance criteria, including the quality of treatment of student borrowers as well as the amounts collected. This balanced approach has led contractors to invest in customer-friendly approaches that help students to become borrowers in good standing instead of hounding them unfairly.

On the other hand, the department has contracted with a single giant service provider to process payments for the large and growing direct student loan program. By deferring to cost considerations and selecting only a single contractor, the department becomes one among many government agencies that seem to create the monopolist with which they do business. The problem with relying on a single supplier of services is that the government has little leverage in dealing with low or barely adequate performance. Upgrades in technology tend to become potentially costly change orders rather than the product of the contractor's motivation to perform well and thereby earn more business.

To the extent that government can outsource functions but keep control over the delivery of public services, agencies can use the resulting efficiencies either to downsize or to perform other functions better. Perhaps the best current examples of intelligent outsourcing relate to loan asset sales.

Building upon the lessons learned from the Resolution Trust Corporation, both the Department of Housing and Urban Development and the Small Business Administration (SBA) have conducted successful loan sales. In both cases substantial downsizing, and the prospect of future staff reductions, led the federal agencies to review their business processes to determine whether any could be outsourced effectively. HUD discovered that the process of dealing with defaulted single-family and multi-family (e.g., low-income apartment building) mortgages was extremely staff intensive.

Short staffing and other problems meant that HUD offices lacked the capacity to deal with the defaulted mortgages or the problems that concentrated defaults could create for many communities. HUD engaged in more than a dozen sales of billions of dollars of defaulted mortgages. The department took care to ensure that private purchasers of the mortgages would not treat borrowers unfairly and that the low-income nature of some of the housing would be preserved. The results were substantial revenue for the government, compared with the department's own efforts to collect on the mortgages, freeing up workers to carry out short-staffed functions, and preserving the department's ability to carry out its mission despite significant downsizing.

The Small Business Administration also felt the pressure of staff reductions. The SBA, too, found that defaulted loans placed heavy burdens upon staff to perform functions that the private sector might perform as well. Again taking care to ensure that borrowers would be treated fairly, the SBA has engaged in a series of sales that by the end of 2002 amounted to over 140,000 loans with an aggregate unpaid principal balance of over $5 billion. The SBA is now engaged in a process of reengineering to apply its scarce staff resources to the origination of loans and the program's financial management, rather than consuming an inordinate amount of time on the back end, trying to deal with troubled or failed loans.

These three approaches—privatizing or devolving activities, business process reengineering, and effective outsourcing—offer significant promise.

Moreover, for many government activities, program redesign is a necessity rather than an option.

Why the Old Way of Doing Business Is Untenable for Many Programs

In architecture form follows function. Similarly, in organizational design form should follow purpose. Government agencies and programs must be designed around their purposes if they are to be successful.[7] Unfortunately, questions of appropriate purpose are up for grabs. Issues of purpose and function are in flux in three different dimensions: (1) political disagreements about the proper role of government which can call into question the current functions of a program or agency; (2) technological developments that can change the way that functions are carried out; and (3) economic developments that can supersede the need for government to perform certain functions in the old ways.

Each of these effects makes itself felt in different ways. Questions about the proper role of government are reflected in the many pieces of legislation which seek to zero out or privatize or devolve some or all of an agency's existing program activities. Thus far, many more pieces of such legislation have been proposed than enacted. That is not unusual, but the mere fact that an agency's functions are called into question can have significant consequences, especially in the budgeting and appropriations process. When the Office of Management and Budget and congressional appropriators begin to question certain activities, they are likely to begin to reduce their funding, in favor of higher-priority programs.

Technology acts to take apart old activities and ways of doing business and put them back together in new ways. Driving forces of some technology-based systems include new economies of scale and the superiority of information-based technologies over older approaches. Like the improved economy that comes from using the Internet and toll-free numbers and their ability to provide more extensive service compared to face-to-face meetings at a federal office the availability of optical imaging and electronic data interchange similarly can make many paper filing systems—and the tasks of the people who maintain them—obsolete.

Finally, the economic context is changing at a rapid pace. Many federal activities, such as power production and delivery of paper-based mailings, find themselves threatened by new forms of competition. Thus, increased consumer use of electronic transactions is eroding the Postal Service's profitable service of carrying bills and financial payments by mail. In one area of service delivery after another, private companies are able to use new technologies to skim off customers who would have been part of the government's customer base in earlier years.

The private sector also has become adept at screening customers to attract the most profitable segments among consumers of power, housing, communications, or financial services. The screening process leaves government with a smaller customer base composed of people and firms that the private sector considers too costly to serve. For the agencies and programs that bear the brunt of such adverse selection, a downward spiral is possible, with diminished resources available to serve an increasingly needy segment of the population. The Federal Housing Administration (FHA), for example, operates in an environment in which the private sector has developed sophisticated credit scoring systems that allow the private market to serve creditworthy people who previously would have sought an FHA mortgage. The result has been to drain the proportion of creditworthy borrowers from the FHA program, leaving the agency with much higher levels of delinquency and default than ever before. Although present trends for FHA are unsustainable, no strategy has been developed to deal with the threat of the government's technology-based competition.[8] Such agencies and programs may find that smaller and more efficient government has become a necessity rather than merely an option.

Essential Preconditions for Making Government Agencies Smaller but More Efficient

There are several preconditions for designing smaller and more effective government, including: (1) leadership from the top; (2) a capable workforce; and (3) adequate resources. All are needed if redesign is to lead to a win-win outcome rather than a train wreck.

Support from the Top

Support from an agency's leadership is the most important factor. Effective redesign of an existing program or agency requires a redefinition of its purposes to accord with current needs and commitment from stakeholders. Statecraft also is needed, to ensure that organizational changes do not become enmeshed in a politicized process of taking unilateral credit or laying unilateral blame. This is a tall order.

As a General Accounting Office (GAO) forum on organizational transformation concluded, support from top leadership (i.e., the agency secretary, deputy secretary, or other high-level political appointees) is needed. It is also important to have a cadre of champions (such as political and career executives) to work with high-level leaders to ensure that changes are thoroughly implemented and sustained over time.[9] The same type of top-level support is needed for fundamental transformation of agency programs.

Only support from an agency's leaders can provide the basis for bringing stakeholders together and brokering the necessary tradeoffs. A sense of vision is needed, along with credibility, so that stakeholders understand the need to compromise as a way to save what may be an otherwise unsustainable program. Top-level support also is needed to ensure the commitment of resources that will be needed to invest in technology, train the workforce, and meet the legitimate needs of those federal employees who may not have a future with some of the new organizations.

The Federal Housing Administration provides a useful example of some of the complex stakeholder issues that leaders must address in the process of redesign. The 1990s saw the unveiling of two different proposals for FHA, one to change the nature of the financial services offered by the agency and the other to change its organizational form to create a flexible and efficient wholly owned government corporation to be called the Federal Housing Corporation.

The first proposal came from the Office of Management and Budget. Under this idea FHA would stop providing long-term mortgage insurance. It would, instead, piggyback on the private market by providing extra subsidies so that private financing would be available for the underserved population, including first-time homebuyers, minorities, and lower-income people, whom FHA serves and who are not nearly as well served today by the private market. Many mortgage lenders opposed this proposal, and it died.

The second proposal came from the secretary of housing and urban development. He proposed to transform FHA into a government corporation. The wholly owned government corporation operates on a financially self-sustaining basis and uses business-type accounting and budgeting. Many government corporations, including Ginnie Mae in the Department of Housing and Urban Development, have established enviable track records for providing government services efficiently and effectively. A different part of the mortgage industry, private mortgage insurance companies, opposed this proposal and it, too, died.

The secret of success for such proposals may be to combine ideas for changes in the form of FHA financial services with a change in the agency's organizational structure. FHA would provide credit enhancements that complement rather than compete directly with the private sector; in return, private firms might drop their objections to turning FHA into a more effective financial services organization. It is possible that common ground cannot be found. On the other hand, a credible leader may be able ultimately to broker a win-win resolution. Such an outcome may be possible with some stakeholders when a credible leader marshals convincing evidence that FHA is unlikely to be able to sustain its substantial and increasing rates of troubled loans, especially if the economy hits a protracted downturn.

Workforce

Having a capable workforce is the second important ingredient for downsizing government after support from an agency's leaders. Workforce issues include the need (1) to retrain and equip federal employees for their responsibilities in a redesigned organization; and (2) to provide incentives for some employees to work themselves out of a job. Both issues are important. The theory of a smaller but more efficient government is that the remaining employees will be more productive than before. This requires a commitment for training and equipment. The case of the reengineering of the Rural Housing Service is instructive because of the way that the agency's leaders were able to work with the Office of Management and Budget to obtain the necessary commitment to adopt new information-based technologies, train the employees to use it, and equip them with new laptop computers to plug into the new centralized loan servicing system.

Effective redesign also requires attention to the legitimate needs of federal employees who may leave the organization after working themselves out of a job. This is a matter both of fairness to the employees and of the best interests of government itself. U.S. government employees have shown a pattern of loyalty, even when their own jobs may be on the line. Thus, field offices at HUD were remarkably supportive of asset sales, even at a time when it was not certain how they would fare in the subsequent reorganization. Similarly, the civil servants of the Office of Naval Petroleum Reserves complied fully with the legislation that called for sale of the Elk Hills oil field. Indeed, they generated reports and otherwise helped ensure that the government received full value from the sale.

It is time to create a special incentive system to reward federal employees who work themselves out of a job in a professional manner that benefits the government. Fear of employee opposition imposes a serious constraint upon government's ability even to contemplate reorganizations that would involve downsizing. Finding a way to share savings from downsizing with the employees who help to make the savings possible is necessary.

By themselves, today's buyouts are not the answer. The law creating the Department of Homeland Security authorizes buyouts across the federal government. For many agencies buyouts are likely to provide a severance package of up to $25,000 to each federal employee who agrees to leave the organization and not reenter federal service for at least five years. The problem with buyouts is that they are not selective. They tend to be most attractive to older workers who have been at the agency for some time and have valuable experience that is forfeited when they leave. Sometimes this is appropriate, but sometimes it is not. One federal agency after another has lost its institutional memory to buyouts that have swept their upper and middle ranks. Some of these people may be essential to a successful transition and to the performance of the newly redesigned organization.

Also needed is a separate incentive package for transitional organizations which can be used to negotiate transition packages with employees. The agency may want to retain key employees for a fixed period of time, for example to train their replacements, and may want to let others go sooner, for example if field offices are selectively downsized. The package should be available to reward departing employees for a job well done.

Resources

The third element in running a small yet effective government is a multiyear commitment of resources. Absorption of new technology is not a single-year process. As Robert Alloway, of the Massachusetts Institute of Technology, has pointed out, technology absorption can be especially demanding if it cuts across organizational units in the way that it reconfigures an agency's work processes. That means that a multiyear commitment of funds will be needed to procure and install any new technology and to incorporate it into the agency's activities.

In the case of the Rural Housing Service, absorbing the new loan origination and servicing technology required a three-year commitment of $48 million to install the new technology and train RHS officials on how to use it well. The net result of the change, once the new system was up and running, was a net savings for the government, increased capacity to manage an $18 billion loan program and protect against financial losses that had not been well managed under the earlier system, and better service to RHS borrowers.

Because of the significant up-front costs of such process improvements, multiyear commitments of resources are essential. This is true as well for nontechnological changes such as asset sales, which require agencies to hire financial advisors and other contractors before the first sale actually takes place. Again, support from agency leaders, from the Office of Management and Budget, and from the relevant congressional subcommittees is essential to obtain the advance commitment of resources which must be made years before the savings may materialize.

Statecraft and the Need for Judicious Compromise

There is an illusory goal in the search for smaller but more efficient government. This is the goal of trying to confine political disputes to questions of the proper role of government while protecting the general agreement that government must be efficient in carrying out its authorized activities.

This goal is an illusion because neither politics nor congressional processes work that way. Opponents of a government activity often attack the agency that implements a program, even if they do not succeed in eliminating the program itself. Indeed, the Congress is organized so as to permit parties to bypass the authorizing committees and instead persuade the appropriations committees to deny resources to agencies and programs. Regulated companies can use the appropriations process to restrain activities of regulatory agencies such as the Food and Drug Administration, the Federal Trade Commission, and the Securities and Exchange Commission.

The converse is also true: Proponents of a particular activity may protect a functionally inefficient form of service delivery—and numerous Medicare contractors, HUD multifamily projects, and VA hospitals come to mind here—because they fear that more efficient structures would be politically too exposed. In many cases government programs would perform much more efficiently, for example, if the benefits were simply cashed out and turned into

vouchers or direct payments. This type of transformation is infrequent because it is much easier to repeal, shrink, or divert funds from an outright
transfer payment than it would be, for example, to disestablish the programmatic infrastructure of a housing or loan program. Thus, issues of organization and effectiveness of each government agency tend to reflect the political
environment of that agency and its programs. Contending constituencies
make strategic use of the bureaucratic structure.[10]

Inevitably, the search for smaller but more efficient government comes
back to a search for leadership and statecraft. Among the more promising candidates are agencies such as the United States Postal Service (as Murray
Comarow points out in chap. 5), the Federal Housing Administration, and
federal power administrations. They each serve constituencies that insist upon
effective service delivery and which have a stake in ensuring that the government continues to provide the services. These agencies are especially promising candidates because of changes in economics or technology which call into
serious question their old ways of doing business.

Also promising are selected smaller programs such as grant programs that
provide noncontroversial services, and especially programs that support activities such as economic development which might be devolved to state or local
governments and whose transformation thus might be backed by an informed
and significant constituency.

In short, the search for smaller and more efficient government is more than
a search for an illusion. But it is also no easy pursuit. The search for smaller
and more efficient government can be achieved with the right combination of
political leadership, thoughtful design, and persistent effort by those whose
lives are affected by the outcome.

Abbreviations

AARP	formerly known as the American Association of Retired Persons
ACEC	Advisory Commission on Electronic Commerce
AEC	Atomic Energy Commission
APWU	American Postal Workers Union
ASA	assistant secretary for administration
BoB	Bureau of the Budget
CAA	Civil Aeronautics Administration
CCPR	Citizens Committee for Postal Reform
CDC	Centers for Disease Control
CFO	chief financial officer
CGE	Commercial Government Enterprise
CHCO	chief human capital officer
CIA	Central Intelligence Agency
CIPCO	Citizens for a Postal Corporation
CMS	Centers for Medicare and Medicaid Services (formerly the Health Care Financing Administration)
COLA	cost-of-living adjustment
Conrail	Consolidated Rail Corporation
COO	chief operating officer
CRS	Congressional Research Service
CSRS	Civil Service Retirement System
DARPA	Defenses Advanced Research Projects Agency
DDM	deputy director for management
DHS	Department of Homeland Security
DOT	Department of Transportation
EOP	Executive Office of the President
EPA	Environmental Protection Agency
FAA	Federal Aviation Administration
FAIR Act	Federal Activity Inventories Reform Act of 1998
FBI	Federal Bureau of Investigation
FCC	field coordinating committee

FDA	Food and Drug Administration
FHA	Federal Housing Administration
FHWA	Federal Highway Administration
FLA	Federal Loan Agency
FRA	Federal Railway Administration
FRC	Federal Regional Council
Freddie Mac	Federal Home Loan Mortgage Corporation
FTA	Federal Transit Administration
FWA	Federal Works Agency
FY	fiscal year
GAO	General Accounting Office
GML	general management law
GOCO	government-owned contractor-operated
GPRA	Government Performance and Results Act of 1993
GSA	General Services Administration
GSE	government-sponsored enterprise
HEW	Health, Education, and Welfare
HHFA	Housing and Home Finance Agency
HHS	Health and Human Services
HIPAA	Health Insurance Portability and Accountability Act of 1996
HMO	health maintenance organization
HRT	hormone replacement therapy
HUD	Housing and Urban Development
ICBM	intercontinental ballistic missile
IRS	Internal Revenue Service
ISTEA	Inter-Modal Surface Transportation Efficiency Act of 1991
IT	information technology
JCAHO	Joint Commission on Accreditation of Healthcare Organizations
LIHEAP	Low-Income Home Energy Assistance Program
M&O	management and operating
NACA	National Advisory Committee for Aeronautics
NALC	National Association of Letter Carriers
NAPA	National Academy of Public Administration
NASA	National Aeronautics and Space Administration
NASI	National Academy of Social Insurance
NHS	National Health Service (U.K.)
NIH	National Institutes of Health
NPM	New Public Management
NPR	National Performance Review
NRA	National Rifle Association
OECD	Organization for Economic Cooperation and Development
OFFM	Office of Federal Financial Management
OFPP	Office of Federal Procurement Policy
OIRA	Office of Information and Regulatory Affairs
OMB	Office of Management and Budget
OPM	Office of Personnel Management
PAC	political action committee

PMG	postmaster general
PRC	Postal Rate Commission
PSRO	Professional Standards Review Organization
RD	regional director
R&D	research and development
REGO	reinventing government
RHS	Rural Housing Service
RIF	reduction in force
S&L	savings and loan
SBA	Small Business Administration
SES	Senior Executive Service
TANF	Temporary Assistance for Needy Families
UPS	United Parcel Service
USAID	U.S. Agency for International Development
USEC	U.S. Enrichment Corporation
USPS	U.S. Postal Service
VA	Department of Veterans Affairs
VISTA	Volunteers in Service to America
Y2K	Year 2000

Notes

O N E : Citizens into Customers

1. William N. Chambers and Philip C. Davis, "Party Competition and Mass Participation, 1824–1852," in *The History of American Electoral Behavior*, ed. Joel Silbey, Allan Gogue, and William Flanigan (Princeton: Princeton University Press, 1978), 180–85; Paul Kleppner, *Who Voted? The Dynamics of Electoral Turnout, 1870–1980* (New York: Praeger, 1982), 18–19.

2. Michael McGerr, *The Decline of Popular Politics: The American North, 1865–1928* (New York: Oxford University Press, 1986).

3. Sidney Verba, Kay Schlozman, and Henry Brady, *Voice and Equality: Civic Voluntarism in American Politics* (Cambridge: Harvard University Press, 1995), 72–73, 531; Steven Rosenstone and John Mark Hansen, *Mobilization, Participation, and Democracy in America* (New York: Macmillan, 1993), 61.

4. Michael Schudson, *The Good Citizen: A History of American Civic Life* (New York: Free Press, 1998), 299.

5. Norman Nie, Jane Junn, and Kenneth Stehlik-Berry, *Education and Democratic Citizenship in American Politics* (Chicago: University of Chicago Press, 1996), 131: Verba, Schlozman, and Brady, *Voice and Equality*, 530.

6. Jeffrey M. Berry, *The Interest Group Society*, 2d. ed. (Glenview, Ill.: Scott, Foresman, 1989), chap. 4; Frank Baumgartner and Jeffrey Talbert, "Interest Groups and Political Change," in *The New American Politics*, ed. Bryan Jones (Boulder, Colo.: Westview Press, 1995); Verba, Schlozman, and Brady, *Voice and Equality*, 72–73; Steven Rosenstone and Hansen, *Mobilization, Participation, and Democracy in America*, 61.

7. Sidney Milkis has offered one persuasive account of the origins of the public's detachment from conflict. See Sidney Milkis, *The President and the Parties: The Transformation of the American Party System* (New York: Oxford University Press, 1993), 16–17.

8. V. O. Key, *Politics, Parties and Pressure Groups*, 4th ed. (New York: Crowell, 1958), 221–23.

9. Benjamin Ginsberg, Walter Mebane, and Martin Shefter, "The Changing Relationship between Conflict and Mobilization in American Politics" (paper presented to the 1993 annual meeting of the Social Science History Association, Baltimore, MD, November 1993).

10. Max Farrand, ed., *The Records of the Federal Convention of 1787* (New Haven: Yale University Press, 1966), 1:49.

11. See Michale X. Delli Carpini, and Scott Keeter, *What Americans Know about Politics and Why It Matters* (New Haven: Yale University Press, 1996); Michael J. Avey,

The Demobilization of American Voters: A Comprehensive Theory of Voter Turnout (New York: Westport Press, 1989), 27–28.

12. See E. Pendleton Herring, *Group Representation before Congress* (New York: McGraw-Hill, 1936).

13. See Brooks Jackson, *Honest Graft: Big Money and the American Political Process* (New York: Knopf, 1988).

14. Charles Merriam, *The Making of Citizens* (Chicago: University of Chicago Press, 1931).

15. Guidelines provided to New York State teachers by the State Education Department reflect the lessons in electoral politics designed for very young children:

> To illustrate the voting process provide an illustration such as: Chuck and John would both like to be the captain of the kickball team. How will we decide which boy will be the captain? Help the children to understand that the fairest way to choose a captain is by voting.
>
> Write both candidates' names on the chalk board. Pass out slips of paper. Explain to the children that they are to write the name of the boy they would like to have as their captain. Collect and tabulate the results on the chalk board.
>
> Parallel this election to that of the election for the Presidency.

University of the State of New York, State Education Department, Bureau of Elementary Curriculum Development, *Social Studies—Grade 1: A Teaching System* (Albany: University of the State of New York, 1971), 32.

16. Karlene Hanko, "College, University Presidents Pledge to Encourage Participation in Politics," *Daily Pennsylvanian,* July 13, 1999, 1.

17. Dale Blyth, Rebecca Saito, and Tom Berkas, "A Quantitative Study of the Impact of Service Learning Programs," in *Service Learning: Applications from the Research,* ed. Alan Waterman (Mahwah, N.J.: Lawrence Erlbaum, 1997), 42–43. Only 19 percent of service-learning students interviewed indicated that their activities were "political"— efforts to change laws or collecting signatures on petitions. See also Jianjung Wang, Betty Greathouse, and Veronica Falcinella, "An Empirical Assessment of Self-Esteem Enhancement in a High School Challenge Service-Learning Program," *Education* 99 (Fall 1998): 99–105.

18. Elizabeth Crowley, "More Young People Turn Away from Politics and Concentrate Instead on Community Service," *Wall Street Journal,* June 16, 1999, A28.

19. Nina Eliasoph, *Avoiding Politics: How Americans Produce Apathy in Everyday Life* (New York: Cambridge University Press, 1998), 61.

20. U.S. Commission on Organization of the Executive Branch of the Government, *General Management of the Executive Branch* (Washington, D.C.: Government Printing Office, 1949), 1; James Q. Wilson, "Reinventing Public Administration," *PS* 27 (Dec. 1994): 668; Al Gore, *From Red Tape to Results—Creating a Government That Works Better and Costs Less: Report of the National Performance Review* (Washington, D.C.: National Technical Information Service, 1993), 43.

21. Fritz Morstein Marx, *The Administrative State* (Chicago: University of Chicago Press, 1957), 44.

22. Steven Cohen and William Eimicke, *The New Effective Public Manager* (San Francisco: Jossey-Bass, 1995), chap. 10.

23. Will Kymlicka and Wayne Norman, "The Return of the Citizen: A Survey of Recent Work on Citizenship Theory," *Ethics* 104 (Jan. 1994): 352.

24. Tom Brokaw, *The Greatest Generation* (New York: Random House, 1998).

25. For influential explanations along these lines, see Robert B. Putnam, "The Strange Disappearance of Civic America," *American Prospect* 7 (Winter 1996): 34–48; Robert N. Bellah, Richard Madsen, William M. Sullivan, Ann Swidler, and Steven M. Tipton, *Habits of the Heart: Individualism and Commitment in American Life* (Berkeley: University of California Press, 1985); Lawrence Mead, *Beyond Entitlement: The Social Obligations of Citizenship* (New York: Free Press, 1986).

26. Putnam, "Strange Disappearance of Civic America," 34–48; "Bowling Alone: America's Declining Social Capital," *Journal of Democracy* 6, no. 1 (January 1995): 65–78.

27. Robert D. Putnam, *Bowling Alone* (New York: Simon and Schuster, 2000), 128–31.

28. Peter Riesenberg, *Citizenship in the Western Tradition: Plato to Rousseau* (Chapel Hill: University of North Carolina Press, 1992), xvii.

29. Thucydides, *The History of the Peloponnesian War,* trans. Sir Richard Livingstone (New York: Oxford University Press, 1960), 117.

30. Otto Hintze, "Military Organization and State Organization," in *The Historical Essays of Otto Hintze,* ed. Felix Gilbert (New York: Oxford University Press, 1975), 196, 211. See also Edward W. Fox, *The Emergence of the Modern European World: From the Seventeenth to the Twentieth Century* (Cambridge: Blackwell, 1993), 189.

31. Derek Sayer, "A Notable Administration: English State Formation and the Rise of Capitalism," *American Journal of Sociology* 97 (Mar. 1992): 1382–1415; David H. Sacks, "The Paradox of Taxation: Fiscal Crises, Parliament and the Liberty of England," in *Fiscal Crises, Liberty and Representative Government, 1450–1789,* ed. Philip T. Hoffman and Kathryn Norberg (Stanford: Stanford University Press, 1994), 7–66.

32. Charles Tilly, *Coercion, Capital and European States* (Cambridge: Blackwell, 1992), 74–75; Kathryn Norberg, "The French Fiscal Crisis of 1788," in Hoffman and Norberg, *Fiscal Crises,* 253–98.

33. Rogers Brubaker, *Citizenship and Nationhood in France and Germany* (Cambridge: Harvard University Press, 1992), 41; Sayer, "Notable Administration," 1398–99.

34. Shefter, *Political Parties and the State,* 75–81.

35. Ruth O'Brien, "Taking the Conservative State Seriously: Statebuilding and Restrictive Labor Practices in Postwar America," *Journal of Labor Studies* (Winter 1997): 33–63; Ronald A. Cass, "Models of Administrative Action," *Virginia Law Review* 377 (1986).

36. O'Brien, "Taking the Conservative State Seriously," p. 50.

37. Ibid., 61; Susan Sterett, "Legality in Administration in Britain and the United States: Toward an Institutional Explanation," *Comparative Political Studies* 25 (July 1992): 210–11.

38. R. Shep Melnick, *Regulation and the Courts: The Case of the Clean Air Act* (Washington, D.C.: Brookings Institution, 1983).

39. Jeffrey M. Berry, "Citizen Groups and the Changing Nature of Interest Group Politics in America," *Annals of the American Academy of Political and Social Science* 528 (July 1983): 31–32. The phrase *advocacy explosion* is also Berry's. See *The Interest Group Society,* 2d ed. (Glenview, Ill.: Scott, Foresman, 1989), 16. On government and founda-

tion funding of interest groups, see Michael S. Greve, "Why 'Defunding the Left' Failed," *Public Interest*, no. 89 (Fall 1987): 93–99; Theda Skocpol, "Associations without Members," *American Prospect*, no. 45 (July–Aug. 1999): 66–73.

40. Mary Ann Glendon, *Rights Talk: The Impoverishment of Political Discourse* (New York: Free Press, 1991), 171.

41. Andrew Koshner, *Solving the Puzzle of Interest Group Litigation* (Westport, Conn.: Greenwood Press, 1998).

42. Steven E. Schier, *By Invitation Only: Contemporary Party, Interest Group and Campaign Strategies* (Pittsburgh: University of Pittsburgh Press, 2000).

43. Skocpol, "Associations without Members," 68.

44. Matthew Crenson and Francis Rourke, "American Bureaucracy since World War II," in *The New American State: Bureaucracies and Policies since World War II*, ed. Louis Galambos (Baltimore: Johns Hopkins University Press, 1987).

45. Richard Cloward and Frances Fox Piven, *Regulating the Poor: The Functions of Public Welfare* (New York: Pantheon, 1971), 275–76; Robert Kerstein and Dennis R. Judd, "Achieving Less Influence with More Democracy: The Permanent Influence of the War on Poverty," *Social Science Quarterly* 61 (Sept. 1980): 208–20; Matthew A. Crenson, "Organizational Factors in Citizen Participation," *Journal of Politics* 36 (May 1974): 356–78.

46. Theodore J. Lowi, *The End of Liberalism* (New York: Norton, 1969), 234–35.

47. Timothy Conlan, *From New Federalism to Devolution: Twenty-Five Years of Governmental Reform* (Washington, D.C.: Brookings Institution, 1998), chap. 8.

T W O : Governance Principles

1. Martin Diamond, *The Founding of the Democratic Republic* (Itasca, Ill.: F. E. Peacock Publishers, 1981).

2. *The Federalist Papers*, ed. Clinton Rossiter and Charles R. Resler (New York: Mentor, 1999).

3. There are only two indirect references to the question of administrative organization in the Constitution; namely, that the president "require the Opinion, in writing, of the principal Officer in each of the executive Departments, upon any subject relating to the duties of their respective Offices," and that "the Congress may by Law vest the Appointment of such inferior Officers, as they think proper, in the President, alone, in the Courts of Law, or in the Heads of Departments," art. 2, sec. 2, cl. 1–2.

4. Organization for Economic Cooperation and Development (OECD), *Distributed Public Governance: Agencies, Authorities, and Other Autonomous Bodies* (Paris: OECD, 2002); B. Guy Peters and John Pierre, "Governance without Government? Rethinking Public Administration," *Journal of Public Administration Research and Theory* 8 (Apr. 1998): 223–43.

5. See, for example: Barry Bozeman, *All Organizations Are Public: Bridging Public and Private Organization Theories* (San Francisco: Jossey-Bass, 1987); David Osborne and Ted Gaebler, *Reinventing Government: How the Entrepreneurial Spirit Is Transforming the Public Sector* (Reading, Mass.: Addison-Wesley, 1992; L. J. O'Toole, "The Implications for Democracy in a Networked Bureaucratic World," *Journal of Public Administration Research and Theory* 7 (July 1997): 443–60.

6. Ronald C. Moe, "The Importance of Public Law: New and Old Paradigms of

Government Management," in *Handbook of Public Law and Administration,* ed. Phillip J. Cooper and Chester A. Newland (San Francisco: Jossey-Bass, 1997), 41–58.

7. David H. Rosenbloom, *Building a Legislative-Centered Public Administration: Congress and the Administrative State, 1946–1999* (Tuscaloosa: University of Alabama Press, 2000); Robert S. Gilmour and Alexis A. Halley, eds., *Who Makes Public Policy? The Struggle for Control between Congress and the Executive* (Chatham, N.J.: Chatham House Press, 1994).

8. George C. Edwards III and Stephen J. Wayne, *Presidential Leadership: Politics and Policy Making,* 4th ed. (New York: St. Martin's Press, 1997).

9. Richard E. Neustadt, *Presidential Power: The Politics of Leadership* (New York: John Wiley and Sons, 1960), 6.

10. Ibid., 10.

11. U.S. Library of Congress, Congressional Research Service (CRS), *General Management Laws: A Selective Compendium,* ed. Ronald C. Moe, CRS report RL30267 (Washington, D.C.: CRS, 2001).

12. Justice Louis Brandeis, in his dissent in the 1926 *Myers* case, expressed what has become the conventional wisdom: "The doctrine of separation of powers was adopted by the Convention of 1787, not to promote efficiency but to preclude the exercise of arbitrary power." *Myers v. United States,* 272 U.S. 52, 293 (1926).

13. Louis Fisher, "The Efficiency Side of Separated Powers," *Journal of American Studies* 5 (Aug. 1971): 115.

14. The executive branch has never been a pristine unity. From the decision in the first Congress to give the Treasury's comptroller substantial legal autonomy within the department down to today's uneasy relationship between "independent counsels" and the executive branch, not all officers have been directly accountable to the president. These exceptions notwithstanding, the prevailing norm has historically been an executive accountable to the president.

15. Stephen Skowronek, *Building a New American State: The Expansion of National Administrative Capacities, 1877–1920* (Cambridge: Cambridge University Press, 1982); Leonard D. White, *Republican Era, 1869–1901: A Study in Administrative History* (New York: Macmillan, 1958).

16. For a bibliography of congressional inquiries into the conduct of business of executive departments through World War I, consult Gustavus Weber, *Organized Efforts for the Improvement of Methods of Administration* (New York: Appleton, 1919).

17. Peri E. Arnold, *Making the Managerial Presidency: Comprehensive Reorganization Planning, 1905–1996,* 2d ed. (Lawrence: University Press of Kansas, 1998).

18. U.S. Commission on the Organization of the Government of the United States, *Hoover Commission Report* (New York: Macmillan, 1949), viii, 7–8.

19. Ronald C. Moe and Robert S. Gilmour, "Rediscovering Principles of Public Administration: The Neglected Foundation of Public Law," *Public Administration Review* 55 (Mar.–Apr. 1995): 135–46.

20. Herbert Emmerich, *Federal Organization and Administrative Management* (Tuscaloosa: University of Alabama Press, 1971), 17.

21. Ronald C. Moe, "At Risk: The President's Role as Chief Manager," in *The Managerial Presidency,* ed. James P. Pfiffner, 2d ed. (College Station: Texas A&M University Press, 1999), 265–84; Paul C. Light, "The Incredible Shrinking Budget Office," *Government Executive* (Jan. 2002): 66.

22. Paul C. Light, *The True Size of Government* (Washington, D.C.: Brookings Institution, 1999); Mark L. Goldstein, *America's Hollow Government* (Homewood, Ill.: BusinessOneIrwin, 1992).

23. Ronald C. Moe, *Administrative Renewal: Reorganization Commissions in the 20th Century* (Lanham, Md.: University Press of America, 2003), 131–38.

24. Christopher Lee, "Overhaul of Federal Workforce Sought," *Washington Post,* June 8, 2003, A1; Stephan Barr, "In Relaxing Civil Service Rules, the Issue Becomes Where to Draw the Line," *Washington Post,* May 12, 2003, B2.

25. Dan Eggan, "For a Premium, INS to Expedite Visa Processing," *Washington Post,* May 31, 2001, 1.

26. OECD, *Governance in Transition: Public Management Reforms in OECD Countries* (Paris: OECD, 1995).

27. Donald F. Kettl, *The Global Public Management Revolution: A Report on the Transformation of Governance* (Washington, D.C.: Brookings Institution, 2000).

28. Allen Schick, *The Spirit of Reform: Managing the New Zealand State Sector in a Time of Change* (Wellington: New Zealand State Services Commission, 1996).

29. Dennis Mueller, ed., *Public Choice: A Handbook* (London: Cambridge University Press, 1997), 1.

30. Osborne and Gaebler, *Reinventing Government.*

31. U.S. National Performance Review, *From Red Tape to Results: Creating a Government That Works Better and Costs Less* (Washington, D.C.: GPO, 1993). For a critical history of the reinvention exercise, consult Michael E. Norris, *Reinventing the Administrative State* (Lanham, Md.: University Press of America, 2000).

32. It is not clear whether these "new principles" for government management constitute any kind of comprehensive theory (propositions subject to disproof) or if they are merely aphorisms, calls to good behavior. Is "casting aside red tape," a metaphor usually employed to signal an undesired law or regulation, really a useful guide for organizational design and management, or is "red tape" simply a symptom of some other and more fundamental theoretical problem? Ronald C. Moe, "The 'Reinventing Government' Exercise: Misinterpreting the Problem, Misjudging the Consequences," *Public Administration Review* 54 (Mar.–Apr. 1994): 111–22.

33. Donald F. Kettl noted the anticongressional bias of the reinventing government exercise: "First, 'reinventing government' seeks the transfer of power from the legislative to the executive branch. . . . Almost all of what the NPR recommends, in fact, requires that Congress give up power." "Beyond the Rhetoric of Reinvention: Driving Themes of the Clinton Administration's Management Reforms," *Governance* 7 (July 1994): 309.

34. Pauline Vaillancourt Rosenau, ed., *Public-Private Policy Partnerships* (Cambridge, Mass.: MIT Press, 2000).

35. Harold Seidman, "The Quasi World of the Federal Government," *Brookings Review* 2 (Summer 1988): 23–27.

36. Ronald C. Moe, "The Emerging Federal Quasi Government: Issues of Management and Accountability," *Public Administration Review* 61 (May–June 2001): 276–98.

37. In the United Kingdom and some other countries the terms *quango* and *quago* are employed to refer to hybrid entities. A quango is essentially a private organization that is assigned some, or many, of the attributes normally associated with the governmental sector. A quago, on the other hand, is essentially a government organization

that is assigned some, or many, of the attributes normally associated with the private sector. Under this schema, for instance, the Red Cross would be a quango, while the Legal Services Corporation would be a quago. Matthew Flinders, *The Politics of Accountability in the Modern State* (London: Ashgate, 2001); Paul Hirst, "Quangos and Democratic Government," *Parliamentary Affairs* 65 (Apr. 1995): 341–59.

38. Ronald C. Moe, "Congressionally Chartered Corporate Organizations (Title 36 Corporations): What They Are and How Congress Treats Them," *Federal Lawyer* 46 (July 1999): 35–41.

39. There are presently six GSEs. Four are investor owned: Federal National Mortgage Association (Fannie Mae), Federal Home Loan Mortgage Corporation (Freddie Mac), Student Loan Marketing Association (Sallie Mae), and the Federal Agricultural Mortgage Corporation (Farmer Mac). Two are owned cooperatively by their borrowers: the Federal Home Loan Bank System and the Farm Credit System. GSEs are among the largest financial institutions in the United States.

40. Ronald C. Moe and Thomas H. Stanton, "Government-Sponsored Enterprises as Federal Instrumentalities: Reconciling Private Management with Public Accountability," *Public Administration Review* 49 (July–Aug. 1989): 321.

41. There is a sizable literature on GSEs; see Thomas H. Stanton, *Government-Sponsored Enterprises: Mercantilist Companies in the Modern World* (Washington, D.C.: AEI Press, 2002); Thomas H. Stanton and Ronald C. Moe, "Government Corporations and Government Sponsored Enterprises," chap. 3 in *Tools of Government: A Guide to the New Governance,* ed. Lester M. Salamon (New York: Oxford University Press, 2002); Peter Wallison, ed., *Serving Two Masters, Yet Out of Control* (Washington, D.C.: AEI Press, 2001).

42. "Fannie Mae Enron?" Editorial, *Wall Street Journal,* Feb. 20, 2002, A22; Alison Leigh Cowan, "Big-City Paydays at 'Farmer Mac,'" *New York Times,* Apr. 28, 2002, 3:1.

43. All is not roses for the mortgage GSEs, however, as recent management failures may have placed these institutions, and the mortgage finance market generally, at risk. Jenny Wiggins and Vincent Boland, "Freddie Mac Hit by Management Crisis," *Financial Times,* June 10, 2003, 1; Patrick Barta et al., "Freddie Mac Ousts Top Officials as Regulators Prepare Inquiries," *Wall Street Journal,* June 10, 2003, 1; Thomas H. Stanton, "A Fannie and Freddie for the 21st Century," *Wall Street Journal,* June 17, 2003, B2.

44. U.S. Congressional Budget Office (CBO), *Assessing the Public Costs and Benefits of Fannie Mae and Freddie Mac* (Washington, D.C.: CBO, 1996), 37. See also CBO, *Federal Subsidies and the Housing GSEs* (Washington, D.C.: CBO, 2001).

45. A study of governmentally appointed directors on instrumentality boards, in this instance emphasizing the Union Pacific Railroad in the 1870s and COMSAT experiences, led Herman Schwartz to conclude: "Both the practicalities of life and the lessons of history lead to the conclusion that the appointment of government directors to a private board cannot protect the public interest against private abuse. Moreover, such directors may even reinforce the belief that the Government assures the profitability of the corporation." "Governmentally Appointed Directors in a Private Corporation: The Communications Satellite Act of 1962," *Harvard Law Review* 79 (Dec. 1965): 363.

46. Harold Seidman, *Politics, Position, and Power: The Dynamics of Federal Organization,* 5th ed. (New York: Oxford University Press, 1998), 213.

47. Hugh Stretton and Lionel Orchard, *Public Goods, Public Enterprise, Public Choice: Theoretical Foundations of the Contemporary Attack on Government* (New York: St. Martin's Press, 1994); Mark Schneider, Paul Teske, and Michael Mintrom, *Public Entrepreneurs: Agents for Change in American Government* (Princeton, N.J.: Princeton University Press, 1995).

48. *NPR Report,* 68.

49. Harlan Cleveland, "The Future Is Uncentralized," *Public Administration Review* 6 (July–Aug. 2000): 293–97.

50. David Ignatius, "The CIA as Venture Capitalist," *Washington Post,* Sept. 29, 1999, A1. Apparently, the reporter misunderstood the name of the corporation, which is In-Q-Tel, not In-Q-It. By June 2001 the corporation had invested in sixteen companies. "In typical unbureaucratic fashion, In-Q-Tel decided to invest $1 million in Triangle Boy's development after one of its representatives struck up a conversation with a SafeWeb executive at a Silicon Valley bar." Vernon Loeb, "CIA's Adventures in Venture Capital," *Washington Post,* June 3, 2001, A5. The point is: The CIA, when it buys one company's stock, rather than another, is sending a signal to the market that the government has selected a "winning" company for others to invest in. It is little wonder, then, that In-Q-Tel's CEO, Gilman Louie, states that his "biggest problem is keeping people away." Qtd. in Rick E. Yannuzi, "In-Q-Tel: A New Partnership between the CIA and the Private Sector," *Defense Intelligence Journal* 9 (Winter 2000): 25–38.

51. Anne Laurent, *Entrepreneurial Government: Bureaucrats as Businesspeople* (Washington, D.C.: PriceWaterhouseCoopers Endowment, 2000).

52. Steve Vogel, "Pentagon Recruits New Business: Military Turns to Private Enterprise to Help Pay Bills," *Washington Post,* Aug. 8, 1998, B1.

53. For a full case study of the antidemocratic bias allegedly built into the practice of executive departments creating, without statutory authority, private, state-chartered nonprofit organizations to perform functions normally reserved to federal executive agencies as agents of the sovereign, see A. Michael Froomkin, "Wrong Turn in Cyberspace: Using ICANN to Route Around the APA [Administrative Procedure Act] and the Constitution," *Duke Law Journal* 50 (2000): 17–143.

54. No element of the meshing of the governmental and private sectors has generated more debate and heat than the efforts to privatize prisons and corrections. The premise underlying most legal criticisms of privatization of corrections is that a fundamental difference exists between "state actions" and "private actions" and this difference is to be found in law, not economic functions. "The Fifth and Fourteenth Amendments, which prohibit the government from denying federal constitutional rights and which guarantee due process of law, apply to acts of the state and federal governments, and not to acts of private parties and entities." Ira Robbins, "Privatization of Corrections: Defining the Issues," *Federal Bar News and Journal* 3 (May–June 1986): 196; U.S. Department of Justice, Office of Justice Programs, Bureau of Justice Assistance, *Emerging Issues on Privatized Prisons,* by James Austin and Garry Coventry (Washington, D.C.: GPO, 2001).

55. The Supreme Court in a 1995 case faced the issue of distinguishing between a governmental and private corporation. The National Railroad Passenger Corporation (AMTRAK) established by Congress (45 U.S.C. 451) was sued by Michael Lebron for rejecting, on political grounds, an advertising sign he had contracted with them to display. Lebron claimed that his First Amendment (free speech) rights had been abridged

by AMTRAK because it is a government corporation and, therefore, an agency of the United States. AMTRAK argued, on the other hand, that its legislation provides that it "will not be an agency or establishment of the United States Government" and thus is not subject to constitutional provisions governing freedom of speech. The Court decided that, while Congress can determine AMTRAK's governmental status for purposes within Congress's control (e.g., whether it is subject to statutes such as the Administrative Procedure Act), Congress cannot make the final determination of AMTRAK's status as a government entity for purposes of determining constitutional rights of citizens affected by its actions. To do so, in the Court's view, would mean that the government could evade its most solemn constitutional obligations by simply resorting to the corporate form of organization. *Michael A. Lebron v. National Railroad Passenger Corporation,* 513 U.S. 374 (1995).

THREE: Inherently Governmental Functions and the New Millennium

1. Harold Seidman, "Notes on Privatization," MS, May 21, 1987.

2. The terms *public, private,* and *government* are used here with less rigor than likely required. The end of the Cold War, and the related renewal of interest in alternative forms of governance, provides cause and opportunity for reflection on the conventional dichotomy between *public* and *government* (or *state*), on the one hand, and *private* or *market,* on the other. For historical perspective, see, for example, Jeff Weintraub, "The Theory and Politics of the Public/Private Distinction," in *Public and Private in Thought and Practice,* ed. Jeff Weintraub and Krishan Kumar (Chicago: University of Chicago Press, 1997).

3. See Paul C. Light, *The True Size of Government* (Washington D.C.: Brookings Institution, 1999), 1. ("As of 1996, this 'shadow of government,' . . . consisted of 12.7 million full-time equivalent jobs, including 5.6 million generated under federal contracts, 2.4 million created under federal grants, and 4.6 million encumbered under mandates to state and local governments.") A more recent analysis by the Department of the Army of its contractor workforce suggests that the number of contract employees may be substantially smaller than Brookings estimated but the average cost per employee correspondingly greater. See Peckenpaugh, "Army Has Fewer Contractors but They Cost More, Study Shows," *Gov. Exec. Com.,* July 17, 2001.

4. Locus of the debate is the agency-by-agency review of the official workforce to determine which jobs are "inherently governmental," as provided for by OMB policy and codified in the Federal Activities Inventory Reform Act of 1998, and which jobs are "commercial" and may be contracted out. See Ellen Nakashima, "Bush Opens 40,000 Jobs for Competition," *Washington Post,* June 8, 2001; Christopher Lee, "Army Weighs Privatizing Close to 214,000 Jobs," *Washington Post,* Nov. 3, 2002; Richard Stevenson, "Government Plan May Make up to 850,000 Jobs Private," *New York Times,* Nov. 15, 2002.

5. As discussed later in the chapter, the term *diffusion of sovereignty* is owed to Don Price.

6. See "Federalist 1" in *The Federalist Papers,* ed. Clinton Rossiter (New York: Mentor Books, 1961); the question posed by the debate over ratification of the Constitution, per Hamilton, is "whether societies of men are really capable or not of establishing

good government from reflection and choice or whether they are forever destined to depend for their political constitutions on accident and force".

7. For a more complete story of this development, see Daniel Guttman and Barry Willner, *The Shadow Government* (New York: Pantheon, 1976); Guttman, "Public Purpose and Private Service: The Twentieth Century Culture of Contracting Out and the Evolving Law of Diffused Sovereignty," *Administrative Law Review* (Summer 2000).

8. See Walter A. McDougall, *The Heavens and the Earth: A Political History of the Space Age* (New York: Basic Books, 1985), 67; Vannevar Bush, *Pieces of the Action* (New York: Morrow, 1970), 56–64.

9. See Merton J. Peck and Frederick Scherer's classic study of weapons contracting; *The Weapons Acquisition Process: An Economic Analysis* (Cambridge: Harvard University Press, 1962), 97.

10. See Staff of Senate Committee on Governmental Affairs, 96th Cong., *Oversight of the Structure and Management of the Department of Energy* (Washington, D.C.: Comm. Print, 1980), 303.

11. S. S. Hecker, "Nuclear Weapons Stewardship in the Post–Cold War Era: Governance and Contractual Relationships," http://www.lanl.gov/orgs/pa/News/goco3 .html, Apr. 15, 1997.

12. See *Lodge 1858 American Federation of Government Employees v. Webb*, 580 F. 2d 496 (D.C. Cir. 1978).

13. See Don K. Price, *The Scientific Estate* (Cambridge: Belknap Press of Harvard University Press, 1965), 75.

14. See John J. Corson, *Business in the Humane Society* (New York: McGraw-Hill, 1971), iv.

15. Ibid., 74.

16. "Farewell Radio and Television Address to the American People," Pub. Papers Par. 421 (Jan. 17, 1961).

17. "Report to the President on Government Contracting for Research and Development," Apr. 30, 1962, Executive Office of the President, Bureau of the Budget. The report was accompanied by congressional hearings on "systems development and management" by nonprofits such as RAND and Aerospace.

18. The panel delicately observed the interlocking relationships within the contract bureaucracy:

> There is a significant tendency to have on the boards of trustees and directors of the major universities, not-for-profit and profit establishments engaged in federal research and development work, representatives of other institutions involved in such work. . . . Certainly it is in the public interest that organizations on whom so much reliance is placed for accomplishing public purposes, should be controlled by the most responsible, mature, and knowledgeable men available in the Nation. However, we see the clear possibility of conflict-of-interest situations developing . . . that might be harmful to the public interest.

On this account, as Don Price observed, during the 1950s "no Congressmen chose to make political capital out of an investigation of the interlocking structure of corporate and government interests in the field of research and development." *Scientific Estate*, 51.

19. The rules applicable to employees were under wholly distinct review by another

blue ribbon panel (chaired by Roswell Perkins, a Wall Street lawyer who would take a high position in the Kennedy defense department). See *Conflict of Interest and the Federal Service; The Association of the Bar of the City of New York Special Committee on the Federal Conflict of Interest Laws* (New York: Association of the Bar of the City of New York, 1960).

20. Paul Light, in *True Size of Government*, provides a catalog of the personnel ceilings. See Guttman and Willner, *Shadow Government*, for a description of the third-party predicated social reform efforts that ran from the Kennedy to the Nixon administrations.

21. "Federal Political Personnel Manual," in *Presidential Campaign Activities of 1972, Senate Resolution 60: Executive Session Hearings before the Senate Select Committee on Presidential Campaign Activities*, 93d Cong., 8903, 8976 (1974).

22. David Osborne and Ted Gaebler, *Reinventing Government: How the Entrepreneurial Spirit Is Transforming the Public Sector* (Reading, Mass.: Addison-Wesley, 1992), 30.

23. Ibid., 39–40.

24. The failure of the privatized U.S. Enrichment Corporation (USEC) to abide by the statutory purposes that were a condition of its creation has been well chronicled. See, for example, Matthew Weinstock, "Meltdown," *Government Executive* (Feb. 2001); Thomas L. Neff, "U.S./Russia Uranium Deal," in "Decision Time for the HEU Deal: U.S. Security vs. Private Interests," *Arms Control Today* (June 2001). In March 2001 a federal judge found the USEC privatization to be a "model" of what not to do when privatizing. See *Oil, Chemical and Atomic Workers vs. Department of Energy*, District Court of District of Columbia, Mar. 16, 2001. On Harvard's role in administering Russian aid, see Janine Wedel, "Tainted Transactions: Harvard, the Chubais Claim, and Russia's Ruin," *National Interest* (Spring 2000).

25. In a summer 2001 White Paper in support of the initiative, the White House explained: "The Federal Government . . . has little idea of the actual effect of the billions of social service dollars it spends directly or sends to State and local governments." See "Barriers: A Federal System Inhospitable to Faith-Based and Community Organizations." The report appears at http://www.whitehouse.gov/news/releases/2001/08/unlevelfield3.html.

26. The Management Agenda appears at http://www.whitehouse.gov/omb/budget/fy2002/mgmt.pdf. The 1998 Federal Activities Reform Act, 31 U.S.C Sec. 501(2)(a) requires agencies to review their workforces and identify those jobs that are "inherently governmental," with the remaining jobs subject to outsourcing. The fulcrum of the outsourcing requirement of the Bush Management Agenda is the provision that agencies will be graded on the percentage of such jobs that they put up for competition each year.

27. See "DOE Contract Management," *Hearings before the Subcommittee on Oversight and Investigations of the House Committee on Energy and Commerce*, 103d Cong. 92, 111 (1993); "DOE's Fixed-Price Cleanup Contracts: Why Are Costs Still Out of Control?" *Hearings before the Subcommittee on Oversight and Investigations of the House Committee on Energy and Commerce*, 106th Cong., June 22, 2000, serial no. 106–137, GPO stock no. 552–070–25962–7.

28. See Department of Energy Workforce Analysis, July 2001, at http://www

.ma.mbe.doe.gov/pol/WFAnal.pdf; also see the report of the "Commercial Activities Panel," at http://www.gao.gov/a76panel/dcap0201.pdf.

29. See Jason Peckenpaugh, "Army Secretary Announces Massive Outsourcing Plan," Government Executive Online, Oct. 10, 2002, http://207.27.3.29/dailyfed/1002/101002p1.htm.

30. Memorandum for Under Secretary of Defense (Acquisition, Technology and Logistics), Under Secretary of Defense (Comptroller/Chief Financial Officer), Under Secretary of Defense (Preparedness and Readiness), from Thomas E. White, Secretary of the Army; Subject: Accounting for the Total Force: Contractor Workforce, Mar. 8, 2002.

31. See Richard Stevenson, "Government Plan May Make up to 850,000 Jobs Private," *New York Times,* Nov. 15, 2002.

32. See DARPA (Defense Advanced Research Projects Agency) Web site, at http://www.darpa.mil/body/overtheyears.html; and http://www.darpa.mil/ipto/Solicitations/faq/general"; also see Center for Public Integrity, "Outsourcing Big Brother," http://www.publicintegrity.org/dtaweb/report.asp?ReportID=484&L1=10&L2=10&L3=0&L4=0&L5=0.

33. See, for example, Center for Public Integrity, "The Business of War," at http://www.publicintegrity.org/dtaweb/ICIJflBOW.ASP?L1=10&L2=65&L3=0&L4=0&L5=0&State=; see also, for example, Gordon L. Campbell, United States Army Combined Arms Support Command, "Contractors on the Battlefield: The Ethics of Paying Civilians to Enter Harm's Way and Requiring Soldiers to Depend upon Them, a paper prepared for presentation to the Joint Services Conference on Professional Ethics 2000, Jan. 27–28, 2000, http://www.usafa.af.mil/jscope/JSCOPE00/Campbell00.html.

34. 436 U.S. 149 (1978). The court majority surveyed tradition and precedent to determine whether "binding conflict resolution" was an "exclusive public function" and, therefore, a warehouseman's sale of goods under the Uniform Commercial Code would be subject to constitutional protections.

35. The *Flagg Brothers* decision speaks in terms of "exclusive public functions," not "inherently governmental functions," but the distinction would not seem to make a difference for present purposes.

36. See letter from Charles A. Bowsher, comptroller general to Hon. David Pryor, Dec. 29, 1989; and "Use of Consultants and Contractors by the Environmental Protection Agency and the Department of Energy," *Hearing before the Subcommittee on Federal Services, Post Office, and Civil Service, Committee on Governmental Affairs,* U.S. Senate, 101st Cong., 1 (1989).

37. "Are Service Contractors Performing Inherently Governmental Functions?" GAO/GGD–92–11; quotation at 4.

38. See note 26 on the FAIR Act.

39. See http://www.whitehouse.gov/omb/circulars/index-procure.html. By its terms, however, the modification might be read and employed to leave virtually no activity as inherently governmental, since it provides that contractors can exercise even substantial discretion on behalf of the government as long as the discretion is bounded by existing law or even guidance and subject to "final approval or regulatory oversight by agency officials." Since laws and guidance apply to most government activities, and since officials typically necessarily retain rights of final approval, this test appears to

permit contractors to exercise discretion as long as the form, without regard to evidence of substance, or official oversight exists. See definition of *inherently governmental activity* at B1b.

40. For a more complete treatment of these developments, see Guttman, "Public Purpose and Private Service."

41. See Bruce L. R. Smith, *The Rand Corporation: Case Study of a Nonprofit Advisory Corporation* (Cambridge: Harvard University Press, 1966).

42. The "hardware ban" story is told in H. L. Neiburg, *In the Name of Science* (Chicago: Quadrangle Books, 1966), chap. 11.

43. See Dan Guttman, "Organizational Conflict of Interest and the Growth of Big Government," 15, *Harvard Journal of Legislation* 297 (1978).

44. See, for example, Court rejection of requests by Public Citizen for access to privately created expert (PSRO) data even where the data was admittedly "conclusive" to government Medicare Medicaid reimbursements. *Public Citizen Health Research Group v. Dept of HEW,* 668 F. 2d 537 (D.C. Cir. 1981).

45. The Shelby Amendment, enacted as part of the Fiscal Year 1999 Omnibus Appropriations Bill, directed OMB to "require Federal awarding agencies to ensure that all data produced under an award will be made available to the public . . . under the Freedom of Information Act." Pub. L. No. 105–277, 112 Stat. 2681 (1998).

46. *Lebron* dealt with Amtrak's refusal to permit an artist to post his work in a station. Amtrak is a government corporation, created pursuant to the Government Corporation Control Act. In creating Amtrak, Congress took pains to free it from constraints otherwise applicable to agencies (e.g., federal procurement law) and declared that Amtrak "will not be an agency or establishment of the United States Government." Justice Scalia, for the majority, explained that the Amtrak statute is "assuredly dispositive of Amtrak's status as a Government entity for purposes of matters that are within Congress's control"—such as procurement laws. But, he explained, "it is not for Congress to make the final determination of Amtrak's status for purposes of determining the constitutional rights of citizens affected by is actions." On review of the circumstances surrounding Amtrak's creation, including the public purposes mandated by the Amtrak statute, the Court majority held that Amtrak "is an agency or instrumentality of the United States for the purpose of individual rights guaranteed against the Government by the Constitution."

47. Compare *Board of County Commissioners v. Umbehr,* 518 U.S. 668 (1996) (which found that a contractor alleging retaliation is entitled to the same first amendment protections as a civil servant, because contractors and civil servants are essentially fungible) with *Richardson v. McKnight,* 521 U.S. 399 (1997) (which found that a private prison guard charged with assault is not entitled to the same limited immunity as civil servants because, per Justice Breyer, "the most important special government immunity producing concern—unwarranted timidity—is less likely present, or at least is not special, when a private company subject to competitive market pressures operates a prison"). Justice Scalia issued valuable (and colorful) dissents in both cases. These cases, in turn, might be compared with *Boyle v. United Technologies Corp.,* 487 U.S. 500 (1988) (where injured party sues a defense contractor for defective design under state tort law, the contractor is entitled to the same "discretionary function," immunity from suit as government because of the proximity of the contractor to official decisions).

48. See, for example, *Forsham v. Harris,* 445 U.S. 169 (1980).

49. The "study of policies and procedures for transfer of commercial activities" was mandated by Section 832 of the National Defense Authorization Act, Fiscal Year 2001, and chaired by Comptroller General Walker. The final report of the "Commercial Activities Panel" appears at: http://www.gao.gov/a76panel/.

50. See *Munn v. Illinois,* 94 U.S. 113 (1876).

51. See, for example, the discussion of the Blackstone codified concept of the legislature's inability to alienate sovereign power permanently in *U.S. v. Winstar,* 518 U.S. 839 (1996).

52. See, for example, the survey of precedent in "Validity of Proposal for Board to Assist in Dairy Income Maintenance Program," American Law Division, Library of Congress, Congressional Research Service, July 19, 1991.

53. For example, courts may perceive that, in contrast to officials, contractors present special and unaddressed conflict of interest problems. See, for example, *Sierra Club v. Sigler,* 695 F. 2d 957, fn. 3 (5th Cir. 1983), which involved court review of a contractor-prepared Army Corps of Engineers' environmental impact statement.

54. The concept has been used to: (1) define the identity of those to whom statutes apply; (2) examine claims to "intergovernmental immunity," for example, whether a state or local government can tax a federally related entity that is not clearly an official body; (3) analyze whether alleged anticompetitive conduct is immune from the antitrust laws because it has been, to the requisite degree, dictated by the state; (4) assess whether an entity is sufficiently governmental as to implicate constitutional protections; (5) determine the bounds of sovereignty in international law and treaties. In a lead case on the status of government contractors as "state actors," *Alabama v. King and Boozer,* 314 U.S. 1 (1941), the Supreme Court found that a cost-plus government contractor was not immune from state taxation even though the government was, in essence, the purchaser. See also Ronald C. Moe and Thomas H. Stanton, "Government Sponsored Enterprises as Federal Instrumentalities: Reconciling Private Management with Public Accountability," *Public Administration Review* (July–Aug. 1989).

55. The term *business affected with the public interest* fell into disuse when Progressive and New Deal regulation came close to defining all businesses as subject to police power.

56. *Standard Oil v. United States,* 221 U.S. 1 54–60 (1911).

57. Under this tradition third parties can seek enforcement of government contracts in cases in which the intent of the contracting parties—whether expressed in the contract or expressed in its context—is sufficiently particular to the third-party claimants. See, for example, *Bossier Parish Sch. Bd. v. Lemon,* 370 F. 2d 847 (5th Cir. 1967), which found that federally funded school board in military installation could not refuse to integrate schools: "Defendants by their contractual assurances have afforded rights to these federal children as third party beneficiaries." Also see *Holbrook v. Pitt,* 643 F. 2d 1261 (7th Cir. 1981), which established that federal housing program tenants are third-party beneficiaries of contracts between HUD and developers.

58. 214 F. 3d 1379 (D.C. Cir. 2000).

FOUR: The Cabinet Officer as Juggler

This chapter draws on a longer study published as Beryl A. Radin, *The Accountable Juggler: The Art of Leadership in a Federal Agency* (Washington, D.C.: CQ Press, 2002).

1. Harold Seidman, *Politics, Position, and Power: The Dynamics of Federal Organization*, 2d ed. (New York: Oxford University Press, 1977), 309.

2. Paul H. Appleby, *Policy and Administration* (University: University of Alabama Press, 1949), quoted in John J. Kirlin, "The Big Questions of Public Administration in a Democracy," *Public Administration Review* 56, no. 5 (Sept.–Oct. 1996): 417.

3. Garry Wills, *A Necessary Evil: A History of American Distrust of Government* (New York: Simon and Schuster, 1999), 17–18.

4. Ibid., 18.

5. Martha Derthick, *Agency under Stress: The Social Security Administration in American Government* (Washington, D.C.: Brookings Institution, 1990), 171

6. Ibid., 200–201.

7. Herbert Kaufman, *The Administrative Behavior of Federal Bureau Chiefs* (Washington, D.C.: Brookings Institution, 1981), 176.

8. Ibid., 176–77.

9. Richard Danzig, Secretary of the Navy, Webb Lecture, National Academy of Public Administration, Washington, D.C., November 17, 2000.

10. Ibid.

11. Ibid.

12. See Donna E. Shalala, "Are Large Public Organizations Manageable?" *Public Administration Review* 58, no. 4 (July–Aug. 1998): 284–89.

13. HHS is not the only cabinet agency that contains diverse elements. The size and scope of the programs within HHS, however, make the job of the secretary incredibly demanding.

14. Executive secretariats have been created in a number of cabinet departments as a way to deal with this process. These offices vary in terms of their influence on the decision-making process, depending on the style of the secretary and the personal relationship between the person heading that office and the secretary.

15. Some of these issues were discussed in Beryl A. Radin, *The Challenge of Managing across Boundaries: The Case of the Office of the Secretary in the U.S. Department of Health and Human Services*, PWC Endowment for the Business of Government, Nov. 2000; and *Managing in a Decentralized Department: The Case of the U.S. Department of Health and Human Services*, PWC Endowment for the Business of Government, Oct. 1999.

16. See discussion in James Q. Wilson, *Bureaucracy: What Government Agencies Do and Why They Do It* (New York: Basic Books, 1989), 149.

17. See discussion of policy communities in John W. Kingdon, *Agendas, Alternatives, and Public Policies*, 2d ed. (New York: HarperCollins, 1995), 117–19.

18. Ibid., 119.

19. Ibid., 222, 224.

F I V E : The Future of the Postal Service

1. Executive Order No. 11341, dated April 8, 1967.

2. Sometimes mischaracterized as a dissent, here is Meany's "Comment," as he called it: "I agree with the goal of modernizing the postal system and improving working conditions and job opportunities for its employees. However, the status of the Post Office as a Cabinet Department has a positive value that should not be discarded lightly." The President's Commission on Postal Organization, *Towards Postal Excellence (The Kappel Commission Report)*, June 1968, 2.

3. David Whitman, "Selling the Reorganization of the Post Office," Center for Press, Politics and Public Policy, Harvard University, John F. Kennedy School of Government, Case No. C14–84–610; and sequel, Case No. C14–84–610.1 (both 1984), published in *How the Press Affects Federal Policy Making* (New York: W. W. Norton, 1986).

4. P.L. 91–375, Title 39, U.S. Code.

5. Whitman, *How the Press Affects Federal Policy Making*, sequel, 6.

6. Rick Merritt, letter, *Federal Times*, Mar. 18, 2002.

7. United States Postal Service, Press Release 02–083, app. 1.

8. By Senator Susan Collins (R-ME) and Representative John McHugh (R-NY), Feb. 12, 2003.

9. Disclosure is appropriate here: a major mailer is a client of the writer.

10. Commission Report, *Towards Postal Excellence*, 34

11. Quoted in *Government Executive*, Feb. 2002.

12. *Business Mailers Review*, Mar. 18, 2002.

13. The President's Commission on the United States Postal Service, *Embracing the Future: Making the Tough Choices to Preserve Universal Mail Service*, Washington, D.C., 2003.

s i x : Professionalism as Third-Party Governance

1. For a portrait of the current state of affairs in Medicare administration, see *Statement of William J. Scanlon, Director, Health Care Issues, United States General Accounting Office, Testimony before the Committee on Finance, United States Senate, June 19, 2001;* hereafter *Scanlon Statement.* Scanlon notes that "Medicare ranks second only to Social Security in federal expenditures for a single program. Medicare spending totaled over $220 billion in fiscal year 2001; covers about 40 million beneficiaries; enrolls and pays claims from nearly 1 million providers and health plans; and has contractors that annually process about 900 million claims" (2–3)

2. See *Scanlon Statement:* "Because of Medicare's vast size and complex structure, in 1990 . . . [GAO] designated it as a high-risk program—that is, at risk of considerable losses to waste, fraud, abuse and mismanagement—and it remains so today. . . . HCFA's ability to manage has been diminished by frequent turnover in leadership, a relatively sparse cadre of senior executives, human capital challenges that threaten to worsen in the near future, the lack of a performance-based approach to management, constraints on its contracting authority that limit its flexibility to choose claims administration contractors and assign administrative tasks, and archaic information technology systems incapable of providing critical, timely management information" (1).

3. For a sympathetic account of the American public's affection for Medicare, see

Theda Skocpol, "Pundits, People, and Medicare Reform" in *Medicare: Preparing for the Challenges of the 21st Century,* ed. Robert D. Reischauer, Stuart Butler, and Judith R. Lave (Washington, D.C.: National Academy of Social Insurance, 1998), 19–27 (hereafter *Preparing*).

4. U.S. Constitution, art. 1, sec. 8, cl. 1, provides: "The Congress shall have Power To lay and collect taxes, . . . to pay the Debts and provide for the common Defence and general Welfare of the United States."

5. Robert M. Ball, *Reflections on How Medicare Came About,* in *Preparing,* 27–37.

6. This chapter uses the term *distributed governance* to describe the entire pattern of the distribution of powers in the Medicare program. Each of these distributions to nonfederal entities qualifies as an instance of "third-party governance" within the meaning of that term as coined by Lester Salamon. See Lester M. Salamon, "Rethinking Public Management: Third-Party Government and the Tools of Government Action," *Public Policy* 29, no. 1 (Summer 1981): 255–75.

7. For historical and descriptive information about Medicare, this chapter draws on the reports and publications of the National Academy of Social Insurance's *Restructuring Medicare for the Long Term Project.* In addition to the *Preparing* book, the following National Academy of Social Insurance (NASI) reports have been consulted in the preparation of this chapter: *Final Report of Study Panel on Medicare's Governance and Management, Matching Problems with Solutions: Improving Medicare's Governance and Management* (Washington, D.C.: National Academy of Social Insurance, July 2002); *Report of the Medicare Steering Committee, Restructuring Medicare: Next Steps* (Washington, D.C.: National Academy of Social Insurance, Jan. 2000); Study Panel on Medicare Management and Governance, *Reflections on Implementing Medicare* (Washington, D.C.: National Academy of Social Insurance, Jan. 2001); *Final Report of Study Panel on Medicare's Larger Role, Medicare and the American Social Contract* (Washington, D.C.: National Academy of Social Insurance, Feb. 1999); *Final Report of Study Panel on Fee-for-Service Medicare, from a Generation Behind to a Generation Ahead: Transforming Traditional Medicare* (Washington, D.C.: National Academy of Social Insurance, Jan. 1998). All are available from the National Academy of Social Insurance Web site, http://www.nasi.org.

8. The term *physicians* used in this context is intended to refer to the organized medical profession; the views of individual physicians may differ from the positions taken by official representatives of the profession.

9. See Eliot Friedson, *Professional Dominance: The Social Structure of Medical Care* (New York: Atheron Press, 1970); Donald A. Schon, *The Reflective Practitioner* (New York: Basic Books, 1983).

10. The text of the 1933 Principles of Medical Ethics of the American Medical Association (AMA), chap. 3, art. 6, sec. 2, published in *American Medical Directory,* 15th ed.(Chicago: AMA, 1938), reads as follows:

Contract practice per se is not unethical. However, certain features or conditions if present make a contract unethical, among which are: 1. When there is solicitation of patients, directly or indirectly. 2. When there is underbidding to secure the contract. 3. When the compensation is inadequate to assure good medical service. 4. When there is interference with reasonable competition in a community. 5. When free choice of a physician is prevented. 6. When the conditions of employment make it impossible to render adequate service to the patients. 7. When the contract because of any of its provisions or practical results is contrary to sound public policy.

Each contract should be considered on its own merits and in the light of surrounding conditions. Judgment should not be obscured by immediate, temporary or local results. The decision as to its ethical or unethical nature must be based on the ultimate effect for good or ill on the people as a whole.

11. For a history of the group health associations, see William A. MacColl, *Group Practice and Prepayment of Medical Care* (Washington, D.C.: Public Affairs Press, 1966). See also *American Medical Association v. United States,* 317 U.S. 519 (1943).

12. See Rosemary Stevens, *American Medicine and the Public Interest* (New Haven, Conn.: Yale University Press, 1971); Kenneth R. Wing, Michael S. Jacobs, and Patricia C. Kuszler, *The Law and American Health Care* (New York: Aspen Publishers, 1998), 14–18.

13. In calling fee-for-service Medicare a "voucher" system, I am disagreeing with the typology argued for by C. Eugene Steuerle and Eric C. Twombly, authors of the *Tools of Government* chapter on "Vouchers." See Lester Salamon, ed., *The Tools of Government: A Guide to the New Governance* (New York: Oxford University Press, 2002); hereafter *Tools.* Steuerle and Twombly characterize as a voucher in the context of Medicare only a defined contribution payment made to an insurer to buy coverage for a Medicare beneficiary and contrast this with Medicare fee-for-service, which they characterize as being not a voucher program because Medicare acts as an insurer and pays claims directly (446 n. 4), and is an "open-ended subsidy" (456). This distinction results from their definition of *voucher,* which they define as "not open-ended; the amount of purchasing power a voucher provides is limited" (446).

In contrast to Steurle and Twombly, who discuss the voucher tool as a method of controlling government financial responsibilities, I think it analytically useful to distinguish between (1) the extent of the government's financial obligation, which may range from open-ended to minimalist; and (2) the legal relationships between and among the parties involved in the program. According to this analysis fee-for-service Medicare has exactly the structure of a voucher program. Moreover, although the purchasing power it provides is subject to uncertainty in forecasting, it is not in principle unlimited: it is confined to the cost of "medically necessary" services, which is in effect a delegation to the provider to determine the limit on the patient's purchasing power in the particular circumstance.

14. Robert Ball, in *Reflections on How Medicare Came About,* observes that Medicare Part B, which pays fees to physicians, was modeled on an Aetna plan offered through the Federal Employees' Health Benefit Program. It was a last-minute addition; the primary thrust of Medicare was to pay for hospitalization.

15. *Final Report of Study Panel on Medicare's Governance and Management.*

16. Government payers have rearranged the professional configuration of the social services sector. See Steven Rathgeb Smith and Michael Lipsky, *Nonprofits for Hire: The Welfare State in the Age of Contracting* (Cambridge: Harvard University Press, 1993).

17. Delegating difficult decisions to professionals to be made silently has been recommended as a solution to the general problem of medical rationing. See Guido Calabresi and Phillip Bobbitt, *Tragic Choices* (New York: W. W. Norton, 1978).

18. *Tools,* 32.

19. *Final Report of Study Panel on Medicare's Governance and Management.*

20. *Goldfarb v. Virginia State Bar,* 421 U.S. 773 (1975), was the case in which the United States Supreme Court decided that there was no "learned professions" exception to the federal antitrust laws.

21. See *American Medical Association v. Federal Trade Commission,* 638 F.2d 443 (2d Cir. 1980), affirmed 455 U.S. 676 (1982).

22. A National Institutes of Health (NIH)–funded clinical trial of hormone replacement therapy (HRT) was stopped because the medical risk to the patients of taking HRT was demonstrated so conclusively that it seemed medically irresponsible to continue to give it to them. Even more stunning is the information that HRT had never been subjected to clinical trial *prior* to being recommended to millions of women by their allopathic physicians. What stands revealed is not only an unanticipated fact about the risks of HRT but an even more unanticipated fact about the method by which allopathic physicians decide on courses of treatment, which turns out, in this area at least, not to rest on "science": the absence of scientific validation of the claims made by the manufacturer of the particular drug tested in the NIH clinical trial had not troubled the thousands of clinicians who had prescribed it to their patients. This revelation undermines the allopaths' claim of superiority on the ground of their close association with science and does so in exactly the area—women's health—in which that authority has been under intellectual attack for decades. See Writing Group for the Women's Health Initiative Investigators, "Risks and Benefits of Estrogen Plus Progestin in Healthy Postmenopausal Women," *Journal of the American Medical Association* 288, no. 3 (July 17, 2002): 321–33.

23. See John E. Wennberg, Elliott S. Fisher, and Jonathan S. Skinner, *Geography and the Debate over Medicare Reform, Health Affairs* Feb. 13, 2002, Web edition at http://www.healthaffairs.org/1130_abstract_c.php?ID=http://www.healthaffairs.org/Library/v21n2/s3.pdf.

24. See Robert H. Miller and Harold S. Luft, "HMO Plan Performance Update: An Analysis of the Literature, 1997–2000," *Health Affairs* 21, no. 4 (July–Aug. 2002): 63–86.

25. See Molly Joel Coye, "No Toyotas in Health Care: Why Medical Care Has Not Evolved to Meet Patients' Needs," *Health Affairs* 20, no. 6 (Nov.–Dec. 2001): 44–56.

26. Kenneth J. Arrow, "Uncertainty and the Welfare Economics of Medical Care," *American Economic Review* 18, no. 5 (Dec. 1963): 851–83.

27. See John Holland, *Adaptation in Natural and Artificial Systems* (Ann Arbor: University of Michigan Press, 1975).

28. See Elliott Sclar, *You Don't Always Get What You Pay For: The Economics of Privatization* (Ithaca, NY: Cornell University Press, 2000).

29. See Peter D. Fox, "The Medicare Fee-for-Service System: Applying Managed Care Techniques," in *Preparing,* 185–206.

SEVEN: Organization and Management of Federal Departments

This chapter is based partly on the author's personal experience in organizing and managing executive departments and large independent agencies and partly on the work and conclusions of various study groups, beginning in 1948 with the first Hoover Commission and continuing through 2002 with the assessment by the National Academy of Public Administration's (NAPA) Standing Panel on Executive Organization and Management of President Bush's recommendation to create a Department of Homeland Security.

Many aspects of departmental management described or suggested in this chapter have been, and remain, subject to controversy. These include the need for and effectiveness of major purpose departments, decentralized field organizations, unified centers of leadership for administrative management, the current value of inspectors general, and the need for and role of strengthened management analysis staff. It is often difficult to prove which management approach would work best in a particular department, but, in the author's view, practical experience and the recommendations of well-led and well-staffed groups should be given considerable weight in reforming existing departments and designing new ones.

Many helpful suggestions provided by the staff of the academy and members of the Standing Panel on Executive Organization and Management have been incorporated in this chapter and have positively influenced its content. The author is indebted to these contributors for their support and encouragement.

1. Commission on Organization of the Executive Branch of the Government, which conducted its studies from 1947 to 1949 and issued a number of important reports. A second Hoover Commission undertook similar work from 1953 to 1955, but it had less impact than its predecessor.

2. Legislation establishing a Department of Veterans Affairs was approved in 1988 and took effect March 15, 1989. No action was taken on President Reagan's recommendation that the Departments of Energy and Education be abolished or converted to nondepartmental status. Nor did the Ninety-ninth Congress follow through on its plans to eliminate at least two departments. Currently, the executive departments are State, Treasury, Defense, Interior, Agriculture, Justice, Commerce, Labor, Health and Human Services, Housing and Urban Development, Transportation, Education, Energy, Veterans Affairs, and Homeland Security.

3. This figure excludes the nearly 861,000 employees of the U.S. Postal Service, a self-supporting government enterprise. *Budget of the United States Government for Fiscal Year 2001* (Washington, D.C.: Government Printing Office), table S-13, 418.

4. *Independent agency* is used here to mean any entity of the Executive Branch created outside the departments and, in theory, accorded a direct reporting relationship to the president. It also includes independent regulatory agencies such as the Securities and Exchange Commission, the National Labor Relations Board, and the Consumer Product Safety Commission, which are headed by Senate-confirmed presidential appointees serving fixed terms and which perform quasi-legislative and quasi-judicial functions.

5. For example, the attorney general was included in the cabinet beginning with President Washington's administration, but the Department of Justice was not established until 1870. Also, President George W. Bush found in 2001 that withdrawing cabinet status for the U.S. trade representative proved too controversial to accomplish.

6. The current DOT includes elements and programs previously placed in the Department of Commerce, HUD, the former Civil Aeronautics Board, the former Interstate Commerce Commission, the then-independent Federal Aviation Administration, the Treasury Department, and NASA.

7. HEW was established by reorganization plan in 1953 through the conversion of

the Federal Security Agency into a department. HUD was a departmental version of its predecessor, the Housing and Home Finance Agency.

8. President's Advisory Council on Executive Organization (1969–71), chaired by Roy L. Ash. Members were George P. Baker, John B. Connally, Frederick R. Kappel, Richard M. Paget, and Walter N. Thayer. Murray Comarow was executive director from July 1969 to July 1970. Andrew M. Rouse was deputy executive director during that period and executive director from July to November 1970.

9. These features were included in the recommendations of the first Hoover Commission and the Ash Council. They also reflected the experience of existing departments, such as DOT and HUD.

10. The drafts of legislation and the analytic reports that described in detail how the departments would be organized and administered were published by OMB in a volume titled *Papers Relating to the President's Departmental Reorganization Program,* issued as a revised edition in Feb. 1972.

11. For example, the Energy Department was structured to place policy and operating control in a group of program assistant secretaries. This produced an over-centralized management that handicapped the functioning of such elements as the Naval Petroleum and Oil Shale Reserves, the Bonneville Power Administration, and the disposal of nuclear waste.

12. The Department of Education now contains approximately forty-seven hundred employees. The next in size is HUD with a staff of about nine thousand. The Nixon Departmental Reorganization Program called for the abolition of the Labor Department. Most of its functions were to be moved to the proposed Department of Economic Affairs.

13. *Papers Relating to the President's Departmental Management Program.*

14. This reorganization was launched by the National Security Act of 1947 and completed by amendments enacted in 1949.

15. One of the best-known scandals is Teapot Dome, which took place during the 1920s, and the administrative failures of Indian programs continue to this day.

16. The civil works projects of the Army Corps of Engineers have little to do with the national defense. The current location was determined by the fact that originally virtually all of the government's engineers came from West Point.

17. Seidman, *Politics, Position, and Power,* 11.

18. Many efforts, largely unsuccessful, have been made to foster cooperation in river basin matters through the use of interagency committees. The Federal Interagency River Basin Committee (known as "Firebrick"), the Interagency Committee on Water Resources (called "Icewater"), and the Water Resources Council successively failed over forty years to bring about significant improvements in natural resources development matters. The Air Coordinating Committee, which preceded the Federal Aviation Administration, provides another instance of a largely ineffective effort to foster interagency coordination.

19. Except for the Consumer Product Safety Commission, the term *independent agency* as used here does not include regulatory agencies headed by commissions or boards, such as the Federal Communications Commission and the Securities and Exchange Commission.

20. In 1978 urban mass transportation functions were transferred from HUD to

DOT by a reorganization plan. The maritime functions of the Commerce Department were moved to DOT in 1981.

21. These are, respectively, the Federal Highway Administration, the National Highway and Traffic Safety Administration, and the Federal Motor Carrier Safety Administration, the last of which was created pursuant to the Motor Carrier Safety Act of 1999.

22. There recently have been attempts—occasionally successful—to establish funding limits for each assistant secretary's office. Any such practice could severely impair the secretary's authority to move resources within his office. The current appropriations act is free of such restrictions.

23. These functions include policy formulation, human resources management, management analysis, and the budget, which affect most or all departmental activities.

24. The author, in association with Harold Seidman, conducted three National Academy of Public Administration studies of major Energy Department programs. In each instance the department's centralized management seemed to be more of an impediment than a help to these entities.

25. The adage that one cannot serve two masters is arguably applicable to inspectors general.

26. The Executive Committee of the Academy's Standing Panel on Executive Organization and Management sent Presidential Transition Memorandum No. 4, entitled "Inspectors General: Relationships with Agency Head," to a number of administration officials on January 30, 2001.

27. The Social Security Administration was a part of HHS until it became an independent agency in 1995.

28. For example, prior to World War II the chief clerk of the War Department individually approved appointments and promotions of all civil servants subject to the Classification Act of 1923.

29. The statute creating ASAs in these departments continued to place the appointment authority in secretaries, but the selections were subject to presidential approval.

30. In DOT this official was initially responsible for the budget, human resources, management analysis, financial operations, audits and investigations, internal security, and all common services administered through the working capital fund.

31. The Chief Financial Officers Act of 1990 (P.L. 101–576).

32. See National Academy of Public Administration (NAPA) reports on *Revitalizing Federal Management* (1983); and *Renewing HUD: A Long-Term Agenda for Effective Performance* (1994).

33. Secretary Weinberger and Undersecretary Carlucci had no need for a COO in HEW. This also was true of Secretary Volpe and Deputy Secretary Beggs in DOT.

34. Congress struck out the funding of DOT's secretary's representatives as a part of the Fiscal Year 1989 Appropriations Act.

35. The initial Cisneros reorganization left eighty-one small field offices reporting directly to several headquarters offices.

36. It required four years (1961–65) to complete the successful Federal Aviation Administration decentralization, but continuity of leadership and a strong management analysis and engineering staff made full implementation possible. A similar multiyear effort at HEW (1971–75) collapsed with a change in departmental leadership.

37. OMB replaced the Bureau of the Budget in 1970. The Office of Personnel Management replaced the Civil Service Commission in 1978.

38. A principal aide to President Nixon is reported to have said, "When the White House asks a secretary to jump, the only question should be 'How high?'"

39. Letter from Murray Comarow, vice chairman, NAPA Standing Panel on Executive Organization and Management, to Senator Fred Thompson, chairman, Senate Committee on Governmental Affairs, June 12, 2000.

E I G H T : Modernizing Federal Field Operations

1. One of the exceptions was a set of hearings in 2001 on federal regional offices held by the House Subcommittee on Government Efficiency, Financial Management and Intergovernmental Relations, chaired by Rep. Steve Horn (R-CA).

2. Because of the number and diversity of programs involved in the Department of Homeland Security, designing an optimal field structure that facilitates interagency and intergovernmental coordination will be a demanding task.

3. The organization of the Environmental Protection Agency also involved interaction with many other agencies, and its field organization was somewhat similar to that of HUD.

4. When Secretary Cisneros of HUD abolished his department's regions, some eighty-one field offices remained in direct reporting relationships with Washington. HUD has also used service centers to help meet some field needs.

5. Final Staff Report, President Carter's Personnel Management Project, 1977, 1:193.

6. An exception is the Inter-Modal Surface Transportation Efficiency Act (ISTEA), under which DOT tried to help states and local governments with urban land planning that crosses jurisdictional lines. DOT has also recently established several metropolitan service centers.

7. Legislation was passed that authorized the doubling of the size of the rebuilt small boat harbors, for example, and highways rebuilt to modern standards rather than replacing the old ones. Areas totally destroyed were rebuilt according to new carefully designed community plans that were often very different from what had existed before.

8. From 1969 to 1971 hundreds of domestic programs were flowcharted both before and after decentralization, often resulting in the 75 percent or more savings in staff effort and time mentioned in the earlier section on "Modernizing Management Systems." No comparable effort has been made since the Nixon New Federalism initiative to determine what the potential advantages of a renewed decentralization program might be.

N I N E : Technocracies

Based on a revision by J. B. Rundell, 1869.

1. Harold Seidman, *Politics, Position and Power: The Dynamics of Federal Organization*, 5th ed. (New York: Oxford University Press, 1998), 132.

2. Frederick C. Mosher, *Democracy and the Public Service* (New York: Oxford University Press, 1982), 142.

3. Ronald C. Moe, *The United States: A Country Study in Organization and Governance* (Washington, D.C.: Library of Congress, 2001), 2.

4. Ibid., 3.

5. Department of Homeland Security Web site, http://www.dhs.gov, Feb. 8, 2003.

6. David Garrison, "Interagency Collaborations: Are There Best Practices or Just Good Practices?" Report to the President's Management Council, 2001.

7. National Academy of Public Administration (NAPA), *Revitalizing Federal Management: Managers and Their Overburdened Systems* (Washington, D.C.: NAPA, 1983).

8. Paul C. Light, "The Incredible Shrinking Budget Office," *Government Executive* (Jan. 2002), http://www.govexec.com/features/0102/0102lastword.htm.

9. William Clinger, memorandum to Vice President Richard Cheney, July 24, 2001.

10. G. Edward DeSeve, Dwight Ink, and Herb Jasper, *Presidential Transition Memorandum No. 5, NAPA, Office of Management and Budget—Operational Issues,* Feb. 5, 2001, 15.

11. But see Light, "Incredible Shrinking Budget Office."

12. *The President's Management Agenda,* Executive Office of the President, Office of Management and Budget, Fiscal Year 2002, 11–30.

13. Paul C. Light, "Security, Proliferation, and Federal Services," testimony, Mar. 19, 2002.

14. Joel D. Aberbach and Bert A. Rockman, *In the Web of Politics: Three Decades of the U.S. Federal Executive* (Washington, D.C.: Brookings Institution Press, 2000), 77.

15. Moe, *United States,* 18.

16. Aberbach and Rockman, *In the Web of Politics,* 75.

17. Moe, *United States,* 18.

18. Don Zauderer, "The Benefit of Dialogue in Public Management," *Public Manager* (Winter 2000–2001): 28.

T E N : Program Design and the Quest for Smaller and More
Efficient Government

The author would like to thank Murray Comarow, Alan Dean, and Dan Guttman for providing insights with respect to earlier drafts of this research and would also like to express gratitude to the Ripon Society Educational Fund for sponsoring this work. Portions of an earlier version of this chapter were published in the *Ripon Quarterly* (now the *Ripon Forum*) 34, no. 2 (Fall 1999).

1. Charles A. Bowsher, "An Emerging Crisis: The Disinvestment of Government," Webb Lecture, National Academy of Public Administration, Washington, D.C., 1988.

2. United States Commission on National Security/21st Century, *Road Map for National Security: Imperative for Change,* Feb. 15, 2001, 47, 16.

3. "Crisis Facing HCFA and Millions of Americans: An Open Letter to Congress and the Executive," *Health Affairs* 18, no. 1 (Jan.–Feb. 1999): 8–10.

4. United States Commission on National Security/21st Century, *Road Map for National Security,* xiv.

5. See, for example, Thomas H. Stanton, "Lessons Learned: Obtaining Value from Federal Asset Sales," *Public Budgeting and Finance* (Spring 2003): 22–44.

6. This issue is explored in greater detail in Thomas H. Stanton, *Understanding Fed-*

eral Asset Management: An Agenda for Reform, IBM Center for the Business of Government, Arlington, Va., July 2003.

7. See Thomas H. Stanton, *Moving Toward More Capable Government: A Guide to Organizational Design,* IBM Center for the Business of Government, Arlington, Va., June 2002.

8. Thomas H. Stanton, "Opportunities for Reducing Delinquencies and Defaults in Federal Mortgage Credit Programs: A Review of New Technologies and Promising Practices," *Journal of Public Budgeting, Accounting and Financial Management* 13, no. 2 (Summer 2001).

9. U.S. General Accounting Office, *Highlights of a GAO Forum, Mergers and Transformation: Lessons Learned for a Department of Homeland Security,* GAO–03–293SP, Nov. 2002, 4.

10. See Terry M. Moe, "The Politics of Bureaucratic Structure," in *Can the Government Govern?* ed. John E. Chubb and Paul E. Peterson (Washington, D.C.: Brookings Institution Press, 1989).

Contributors

Murray Comarow, a Washington, D.C., attorney, is a director and senior fellow of the National Academy of Public Administration. He was executive director of President Lyndon Johnson's Commission on Postal Organization in 1967–68, executive director of President Richard Nixon's Advisory Council on Executive Organization in 1970–71, and served as senior assistant postmaster general. He was Distinguished Adjunct Professor in Residence at the American University from 1975 to 1995 and acting dean of its College of Public and International Affairs.

Matthew A. Crenson is professor of political science at the Johns Hopkins University who specializes in urban politics and American political development. Crenson is the author of *The Un-Politics of Air Pollution* (1971), *The Federal Machine: Beginnings of Bureaucracy in the Age of Jackson* (1975), *Neighborhood Politics* (1983), and *Building the Invisible Orphanage: A Prehistory of the American Welfare System* (1998). He is coauthor of *Models in the Policy Process* (1976) and *Downsizing Democracy: How America Sidelined Its Citizens and Privatized Its Public* (2002), which he wrote with Benjamin Ginsberg.

Alan L. Dean has devoted over fifty-five years to the study of how best to organize and manage federal executive departments, independent agencies, and government enterprises. He is the former chairman of the Board of Trustees of the National Academy of Public Administration. He has held numerous senior positions in the executive branch, including vice president for administration of the U.S. Railway Corporation; management advisor to the secretary and undersecretary of the Department of Health, Education, and Welfare; deputy assistant director for management of the Office of Management and Budget; assistant secretary for administration of the Department of Transportation; and associate administrator for administration of the Federal Aviation Agency.

Benjamin Ginsberg is the David Bernstein Professor of Political Science and director of the Center for the Study of American Government at the Johns Hopkins University. He is the author or coauthor of a number of books, including *Downsizing Democracy: How America Sidelined Its Citizens and Privatized Its Public* (2002), *Politics by Other Means* (1990), *The Fatal Embrace: Jews and the State* (1993), *The Consequences of Consent* (1982), *American Government: Freedom and Power* (1990), *We the People* (1997), and *The Captive Public* (1988).

Dan Guttman, a fellow at the Center for Study of American Government at the Johns Hopkins University and of the National Academy of Public Administration, served as special counsel to Senator David Pryor in the oversight of "government by third party" and coauthored *The Shadow Government* (1976). Now an attorney in private practice in Washington, D.C., he also served as executive director of the Presidential Advisory Commission on Human Radiation Experiments and commissioner of the U.S. Occupational Safety Health and Review Commission.

Dwight Ink is president emeritus and former president of the Institute of Public Administration. He has held numerous executive positions in the federal government, including assistant administrator, Bureau for Latin America and the Caribbean, U.S. Agency for International Development; acting administrator, General Services Administration; director, U.S. Community Services Agency; and assistant director for executive management of the Office of Management and Budget, assistant secretary, HUD, and director of several presidential task forces.

Ronald C. Moe is presently a fellow at the Washington Center for the Study of American Government of Johns Hopkins University. In 2002 he retired after thirty years as the specialist in government organization and management at the Congressional Research Service of the Library of Congress. During this period he worked closely with lawmakers and staff on governmental management issues. In support of this responsibility, he wrote scholarly books and articles and four times received the Brownlow Award for the best management article to appear in the *Public Administration Review*. Moe is also a fellow of the National Academy of Public Administration.

Sallyanne Payton is the William W. Cook Professor of Law at the University of Michigan Law School. Prior to her career as an academic, she served as chief counsel of the Urban Mass Transportation Administration in the U.S. Department of Transportation and before that as staff assistant to the president of the United States. She specializes in administrative law, presently concentrating on the health care sector. She is past chair of the Section on Administrative Law of the Association of American Law Schools, a past senior fellow of the Administrative Conference of the United States, and is presently a fellow of the National Academy of Public Administration. She served on the National Academy of Social Insurance's Study Panel on Medicare's Governance and Management.

Beryl A. Radin is professor of government and public administration at the University of Baltimore. A fellow of the National Academy of Public Administration, she is the managing editor of the *Journal of Public Administration Research and Theory*. She has written a number of books and articles on public policy and public management issues, focusing on management issues in the federal government. Her latest book is *The Accountable Juggler: The Art of Leadership in a Federal Agency* (2002). She served as a special advisor and consultant to the assistant secretary for management and budget in the Department of Health and Human Services from 1995 to 1999. She is also a former president of the Association of Public Policy Analysis and Management.

Harold Seidman served five years in the government of New York City and twenty-five years in the U.S. Bureau of the Budget. He played a key role in implementing the Alaska and Hawaii Statehood Acts and the Government Corporation Control Act and in establishing a modern Panama Canal Company. He also provided significant support for the first Hoover Commission and the task force that created the U.S. Department of Transportation. His book, Politics, Position, and Power: The Dynamics of Federal Organization (1970), now in its fifth edition, is a public administration classic. Seidman was professor at the University of Connecticut from 1971 to 1984 and visiting professor at the University of Leeds from 1972 to 1975. In 1995 the United States Supreme Court, in the constitutional case of Lebron v. National Railroad Passenger Corporation, characterized Seidman as "a perceptive observer" and quoted at length a passage from his written work in support of the Court's decision.

Thomas H. Stanton is a Washington, D.C., attorney. He provides legal and policy counsel on improving the design and capacity of public institutions. Stanton is a former member of the federal Senior Executive Service. He chairs the Standing Panel on Executive Organization and Management of the National Academy of Public Administration and is a fellow of the Center for the Study of American Government at Johns Hopkins University. His writings on government include two books and many articles. The concerns he expressed in A State of Risk (1991) helped lead to enactment of legislation and the creation of a new federal financial regulator in 1992.

Barbara S. Wamsley, a former member of the federal Senior Executive Service, advises a wide range of organizations, including research institutes; military, domestic, federal, state, and local agencies; and foreign governments. She has extensive experience in policy setting, research and assessment, reengineering processes, strategic planning and management, and leading organizations through change. Her federal experience includes service as deputy assistant secretaries with responsibility for management and budget, information resources, grants and procurement policy, and management and organizational analysis. She is a fellow of the National Academy of Public Administration and a fellow of the Center for the Study of American Government at Johns Hopkins University.

Index

Page numbers in *italics* refer to tables.

AARP, 17–18
accountability: delegation and, 199; expectations of, 70–71; in HHS, 76, 85; as juggling process, 72–74
activism, community, 4, 5, 9, 19–20
Administrative Procedure Act (1946), 15–16, 26
Advisory Commission on Electronic Commerce, 103
advocacy explosion, 5–6, 16–18
Aerospace, 58
agencies: collaboration between, x; complexity of, 69–70; disaggregation of, 29; dual-hat appointment in, 209; fragmentation of, 179, 192–93; independent, 147, 155, 269n. 19; overview of, 25–26; performance of, improving, 231; preconditions for making smaller, more efficient, 238–42. *See also specific agencies*
Agriculture, Department of: business process improvement in, 234–35; Interior and, 153; organization of, xvii, 157, 165, 189
Akaka, Daniel, 106
Alabama v. King and Boozer, 262n. 54
Alaska earthquake and field coordination, 193–96
Alaskan Field Committee, 194, 195
allopathic medicine, 131–32
Alloway, Robert, 241
American Postal Workers Union, 95–96
Americorps, 10
Anderson, Clinton, 194
anthrax scare, 86, 87
antitrust law, 62

Appleby, Paul, 71
appointees, political: field operations and, 190–91; Nixon administration and, 144–45, 169; training for, 224; transience of, 220
arbitration, binding, 91–93, 95–96
Aristotle, 14, 15
army, secretary of, 52
Army Corps of Engineers, 153
Arrow, Kenneth, 134–35
Ash, Roy, 269n. 8
Ash Council, 104, 149, 170–71
assistant secretary for administration (ASA): Executive Officers Group, 169; Hoover Commission and, 161; HUD and, 181; recommendation for reestablishment of, 223–24; replacement of, 144–45; role of, 218–19
Atomic Energy Commission, 43, 189–90
audit function, 159
automaticity, 127–28, 129

baggage checkers, 52–53
Bailar, Benjamin, 100
Baker, George, 89, 269n. 8
Bell, David, 46, 89
Bell report, xxii, 46–48
Biller, Moe, 96
bioterrorism, 79
block grants, 79, 176, 193
Blount, Winton, 91–92, 101, 109
Blue Cross, 118–19, 122, 125
Board of County Commissioners v. Umbehr, 261n. 47
Bossier Parish Sch. Bd. v. Lemon, 262n. 57
boundary issues, 129–30
Bowsher, Charles, 230–31

Boyd, Alan, 160, 184, 185
Boyle v. United Technologies Corp., 261n. 47
Brandeis, Louis, 253n. 12
Brokaw, Tom, 12
Brownlow Commission, 104, 170–71
Budgeting and Accounting Act (1922), 42
bureaucracy, changes in, 70
Bureau of Budget: Alaskan reconstruction and, 195; career staff and, 169; Circular A-49, 43; inherently governmental function concept and, 40–41. *See also* Office of Management and Budget (OMB)
Bush, George W., address to nation after September 11, 4
Bush administration: competitive outsourcing and, 41–42; Faith-Based Initiative, 50–51, 59; Management Agenda, xxix, 50–51, 197, 198, 217–18, 220; market-based competition and, x–xi; Postal Service commission, 110
business, adopting new ways of doing, 234–35
Business in the Humane Society (Corson), 45
buyouts, employee, 241

cabinet, xvii–xviii, 147. *See also* departments, executive; secretaries
Cain, D. Jamison, 89
Califano, Joseph, Jr., 88, 164, 188
career civil servant: as "chief clerk," 161, 205; downsizing and, 240–41; field offices and, 166, 189–90; importance of, 146; replacement of, 196–97; role of, 168–70; statutory positions and, 210. *See also* assistant secretary for administration (ASA)
Carlucci, Frank, 166, 186–87
Carter, Jimmy, 152, 169
Carter administration and inspector general concept, 157–59
"catalytic government," xxvi
Center for the Study of American Government, Johns Hopkins University, xiii, xiv
Centers for Disease Control, 83
Centers for Medicare and Medicaid Services (CMS), xxvi, 124, 128–29
Central Intelligence Agency, 35–36
"chief clerk," 161, 205
chief financial officer (CFO), 161–62, 209, 212
chief human capital officer, 210

chief operating officer (COO), 162, 163
Cisneros, Henry, 165, 185
citizens: access to political process by, 4–5; customers compared to, 10–11; declining importance of, 3–4, 14; demobilization of, 15–20; mobilization of, 5–7; political conduct of, 11–14; taxpayers as, 13. *See also* citizenship
Citizens Committee for Postal Reform, 102
Citizens for a Postal Corporation (CIPCO), 101–2
citizenship: interest in concept of, 11–12; social capital and, 12–13; state and, 13–14; transformation of political into personal, 8–10. *See also* citizens
civic education in public schools, 8
Civil Aeronautics Administration, 199
Civil Service Commission, 271n. 37
Civil Service Reform Act (1978), 190
Civil Service Retirement System, 97
Cleveland, Harlan, 35, 49
Clinger, William, 215, 218
Clinger-Cohen Act (1996), 162, 209
Clinton administration: downsizing of government by, 229; HHS and, 82, 86, 87; National Performance Review and, 10; Office of Management and Budget (OMB) and, 216; President's Management Council of, 163; "reinventing government" program of, 49, 197, 198, 217; training of personnel and, 190
Cochran, Thad, 106
Colson, Charles, 92, 93
Comarow, Murray, 171, 269n. 8
Commerce, Department of, 164
Commercial Government Enterprise, 107
commissions: characteristics of effective, 100–101, 171–72; execution and, 101–2; reorganization and, 170–71. *See also specific commissions*
commodification in health care, 116
common law tradition, 61–62, 63
Community Action Program, 18
compromise, need for, 242–43
conflict of interest in health insurance, 116
Congress: centrality of to political system, 23–24; departmental positions established by,

209–12; downsizing by, 229; oversight capacity of, 218; prescription of management functions by, 205. *See also* general management laws

Connally, John, 269n. 8

Consolidated Rail Corporation, xxx, 233

Constitution of 1787: Article I, 23; Article II, 24; executive departments and, 143, 146; organization, governance, and, 22–23, 37

contracts and contracting: delegation of work and, xxi–xxii; management and operating (M&O), 43–44; Medicare and, 124–27; overview of, xxvi; Project RAND, 57–58. *See also* outsourcing; third party government

coordination, interagency and intergovernmental, 192–97

corporations, as furnishing medical services, 116, 131

corrections, privatization of, 256n. 54

Corson, John, 45

crisis: management reform and, 213–14; structural choices decided by, ix

Critelli, Michael, 110

customer: citizen compared to, 10–11; dealing with government as, 5; interest of government as, 129–30; screening of by private sector, 238

Dahl, Robert, 6

Daley, Richard, 181

Danzig, Richard, 74–75

Dean, Alan, 205

decentralization: of departments, 145; of FAA, 166, 190, 199–201; of field officials, 165–66; of HEW, 188; overview of, 197–99; of programs, 191–92; of Transportation, 160, 183

Defense, Department of, xvii, xxvii, 53, 157

delegation doctrine, 60–61

democracy: fundamental question of, ix; personal, 5, 15–20; political, neoclassical theory of, 6

departmentalism, 28

Department of Transportation Act (1966), xxvii, 156

departments, executive: career staff, role of, 168–70; Constitution and, 146; criteria for establishment of, 151–54, 172–74; evolution of, 147–51; future of, 170–72; internal administration of, 160–63; list of, 268n. 2; major purpose concept and, 154–55; management capacity of, 218–19, 223–24; management of, 144–46; management systems and, 166–68; overview of, 143–44; reorganization of, 146; secretaries, role of in, 160; senior responsibility, level of in, 210–12, *211*; structuring of, 156–59; White House and, 170

Derthick, Martha, 71–72

Desautels, Claude, 102

devolution, 233–34

disaggregation of government: dimensions of, xviii–xix; in executive branch, 29–30; executive organization and management and, xix–xxii; into private decisions, 19; technocracies and, xxix–xxx

distributed governance, 265n. 6

downsizing: conditions for effective, 232–37; essential preconditions for, 238–42; numbers-driven, 229; OMB and, 218; problems with, 230–32

due diligence, components of, 64

Dunlap, William, 102

DuPont, Clyde, 100

Duverger, Maurice, 6

economic developments, 237–38

Education, Department of, 150, 152, 235–36

education and political participation, 5

Eisenhower, Dwight, 40, 45–46, 104

Eliasoph, Nina, 9

elites, 5–8

Elk Hills Naval Petroleum Reserve, xxx, 233, 240–41

end-of-life care, 135

Energy, Department of (DOE), xxi, xxviii, 43, 51–52, 157

Environmental Protection Agency, 147

equality ethic and Medicare, 126–27

executive branch: disaggregation of, 29–30; management leadership capacity in, 214–17; organization and management of, 28–29

executive departments. *See* departments, executive

Executive Office of the President, xix, 170

Federal Activities Inventory Reform (FAIR) Act (1998), 41, 51–52, 56, 259n. 26

Federal Aviation Administration (FAA): decentralization of, 165, 166, 190, 199–201; secretarial offices and, 160; technological developments and, 167; Transportation and, 183

Federal Clean Water Act (1987), 234

Federal Emergency Management Agency, xvii, 155

federal examiner staff, 230–32

Federal False Claims Act, 62–63

Federal Highway Administration (FHWA), 165, 184, 185–86

Federal Home Loan Mortgage Corporation (Freddie Mac), 32, 34, 255n. 39

Federal Housing Administration (FHA), 181, 238, 239–40, 243

Federalist Papers (Madison and Hamilton), 22

Federal Loan Agency, 154

Federal National Mortgage Association (Fannie Mae), 34, 255n. 39

federal power administrations, 243

Federal Reconstruction and Development Planning Commission, 194

Federal Regional Councils (FRCs), 184–85

Federal Transit Administration (FTA), 185, 186

Federal Works Agency, 154

FedEx, 95, 99

fee-for-service provider payment system, 114–20, 131

field operations: coordination of, 192–97; decentralization and, 197–201; HEW and HHS, 186–88; homeland security and, 175, 178, 197, 203; HUD, 180–83; importance of, 175–76, 201–2; organization of, 145, 163–66; recommendations for, 202–3; role of, 176–78; structure of, 178–80, 189–92; Transportation, 183–86

Flagg Bros. v. Brooks, 55, 58

Fleischli, George, 95–96

Food and Drug Administration, 83

foreign policy and third-party governance, 49–50

fragmentation: of federal agencies and programs, 179, 192–93; of HHS, 83–84; inspectors general and, 159; of leadership, 222–23; of policy, 84

France, 13

Freddie Mac. *See* Federal Home Loan Mortgage Corporation (Freddie Mac)

Freedom of Information Act, 58

Gaebler, Ted, xxvi, 49

Gardner, John, 222–23

General Accounting Office (GAO): audit responsibility of, 24, 159; inherently governmental function test and, 55–56; IRS and, 102–3; USPS and, 88, 105–6

general management laws: growth in, *208*; list of, 226–28; overview of, 26–27; technocracies and, 207, 209

General Management Laws: A Selective Compendium (Congressional Research Service), 207

General Services Administration, 209

Ginsberg, Benjamin, xiii

Ginsburg, David, 89, 99

Glendon, Mary Ann, 17

Goldberg, Stephen, 96

Gore, Al: on management, 35; National (Labor/Management) Partnership Council, 206; National Performance Review, 10, 31, 217; reinventing government and, 197

governance: accountability task of, 70–74; concerns of, 21; Congress and, 23–24; constitutionalist paradigm of, 28–29, 34–35, 37, 38; distributed, 265n. 6; entrepreneurial paradigm of, 35–37; executive power of president and, 24–25; government-sponsored enterprises (GSEs) and, 33–34; hybrid organizations and, 34–37, 38; legal authority and, 22–23; of Medicare, 113–14, 119–20, 139–40; president as unitary executive and, 27–28; principles of, 37–39; public choice theory and, 30–31; quasi-government and, 31–32; separation of powers doctrine and, 27–28; of USPS, 98–99, 108–9

government: disinvestment in, 230–31; political principles of, xx; private, 205; purpose and function of, 237–38. *See also* disaggregation of government; reconstitution of federal government; third party government

Government Performance and Results Act (1993), 168

government-sponsored enterprises (GSEs), xviii, 33–34

Grace Commission, 217

graduate programs, 222, 225

Great Society, 180

guilds, professional, 205

Guttman, Dan, 233

Halaby, Najeeb, 199–200

Hamilton, Alexander, 22

Hardesty, Robert, 99

Harris, David, 99

headquarters offices, 177–78

Health, Education, and Welfare (HEW), Department of: field operations of, 186–88; management of, 86–87; regional directors of, 164; separation of, 152

Health and Human Services (HHS), Department of: accountability expectations and, 85; federal government as partner to, 81–82; field operations of, 178–79, 186–88; fragmentation of, 83–84; nature of issues and programs of, 79, 80–81; organization of, 157; overview of, xxiii–xxiv, 75–77; post-September 11 environment and, 85–87; professionals within, 82–84; staff-line competition and, 78–79

Health Care Financing Administration, 231. *See also* Centers for Medicare and Medicaid Services (CMS)

health maintenance organizations (HMOs). *See* managed care

health policy: controversy over, 115, 117–19; managed care and, 130–39; partnership and, 138–39

Hecker, S. S., 44

Heineman Task Force, 104

HEW. *See* Health, Education, and Welfare (HEW), Department of

HHS. *See* Health and Human Services (HHS), Department of

Hintze, Otto, 13

Holbrook v. Pitt, 262n. 57

hollowness of organizations, xxvi, 29, 128, 129, 229

homeland security: field operations and, 175, 178, 197, 203; inherently governmental function concept and, 52–54; streamlining and, 192

Homeland Security, Department of: assessing, 150–51; chief human capital officer in, 210; creation of, x, xvii–xviii, 150–51; employee buyouts and, 241; field structure of, 179–80, 202; flexibility given, 219; Transportation and, 154

Hoover Commission, first: on accountability, 10; assistant secretary for administration and, 161, 169; departmental organization and, 147–48; on executive branch, 28; lines of authority and, x; recommendations of, 104–5; success of, 170–71

Hoover Commission, second, 104

hormone replacement therapy, 267n. 22

Horn, Steve, 223, 271n. 1

hospitals, voluntary, and Medicare, 120–22

Housing and Urban Development (HUD), Department of: field operations of, 178–79, 180–83, 240; loan asset sales of, 236; management of, 148; regional directors and, 163; secretary's representative and, 165

HUD. *See* Housing and Urban Development (HUD), Department of

Hughes, Phillip "Sam," 196

hybrid organizations, 31–33, 34–37, 38

Ickes, Harold, 153

improving executive organization and management, xxvi–xxxii

Indian Health Service, 81

Information Technology Management Reform Act (1996), 162

inherently governmental function concept: emergence of, 42–44; homeland security and, 52–54; overview of, 40–42; test of, 54–56

In-Q-Tel (Central Intelligence Agency), 35–36

Inspector General Act (1978), 157–58, 209

inspector general concept, 157–59
institutions of higher learning, 222, 225
instrumentality, government, 61
insurance, health: controversy over, 115–16, 117–19; fee-for-service medicine and, 131; hospitals and, 120–21; regulation of, 136–37. *See also* managed care
intercontinental ballistic missile (ICBM) program, 58
Interior, Department of, 153, 157, 165
Internal Revenue Service, 102–3, 165, 167
Internet Sales Taxes Commission, 103
"Is Government Manageable?" conference, xiv

Johnson, James, 110
Johnson, Lyndon, 88, 120, 180, 194

Kappel, Frederick, 88, 269n. 8
Kappel commission, 88–89, 90–91, 108–9
Kennedy, John F., 9, 46
Kennedy, Robert, x
Kerrey, Bob, 102
Key, V. O., 6
Kingdon, John, 84, 85
Klassen, Elmer, 94

Labor, Department of, 150, 151–52
law and technocracies, 206–12
lawsuits, public interest, 16–17
leadership: disparity between levels of within departments, 211–12; executive branch and, 214–17; improving quality of, 224–25; politicization of in field operations, 190–91; secretaries and, 74–75; support for redesign of agency by, 238–40; technocracies and, 206, 219–20
Lebron v. National Railroad Passengers Corporation, 58–59, 61, 256–57n. 55
Letter Carriers Branch, 36, 91–93
Lieberman, Joseph, 106, 171
loan asset sales, 236
Louis, Gilman, 36
Lowi, Theodore, 18
Low-Income Home Energy Assistance Program, 79
Lujan v. Defenders of Wildlife, 62–63

Madison, James, 22
Mailing Industry CEO Council, 110
managed care: as commercialism *vs.* professionalism, 132–35; medical profession and, 131–32; Medicare and, 130–31, 133, 135–36; trustworthiness and, 133–34
managed competition, 137–38
management: accountability expectations of, 73–74; agencies and, 25–26; Congress and, 23–24; constitutionalist paradigm of, 28–29, 34–35, 37, 38; entrepreneurial paradigm of, 35–37; of executive branch, 28–29; of executive departments, 144–46; of field staff, 163–66; general management laws, 26–27, 207, *208*, 209, 226–28; of HHS, 75–84, 85–87; impact of organization and program design on, xxiii–xxvi; in leadership capacity in executive branch and, 214–17; need for reform in, 213–14; OMB and, 202, 203, 210, 214–17; of Post Office Department, 89–90; of USPS, 95–99
management systems: field operations and, 189; modernizing, 191–92; overview of, 166–68
market: Bush administration and, x–xi; managed care and, 130–31, 132–33, 134–35, 136–38; superiority of, arguments for, 30
Marshall Space Center, 44
Marx, Fritz Morstein, 11
Maternal and Child Health, 81
"maximum feasible participation," 18
McGee, Gale, 93
Meany, George, 89, 92
medical profession: managed care and, 131–32, 136–37; Medicare and, 115–17, 139–40
Medicare: administration of, 127–31; administrative functions in, *123*; automaticity and, 127–28; Blue Cross and, 118–19, 122, 125; contracting-out by, 124–27; design of, 113–14, 118–19, 122, 124; insurance principle and, 136–37; legislative compromise and, 120–24; managed care and, 130–31, 133, 135–36; managed competition and, 137–38; overview of, xxv–xxvi, 112–13; partnership and, 138–39; problems with, 114–20; robustness and rigidity in, 139–40; self-regulation in, 113, 119, 126–27

Merritt, Rick, 95
metropolitan expediters, 182
military-industrial complex, 40, 45–46
Model Cities Program, 18
modernization of management systems, 191–92
Moe, Ronald, 56, 207, 222
Morton, Thurston, 102
Mosher, Frederick, 206
Mueller, Dennis, 30
Munn v. Illinois, 61, 62

National Academy of Public Administration (NAPA): assistant secretary for administration (ASA) and, 144–45; on internal management, 162; Senate Committee on Governmental Affairs and, 150, 171; Standing Panel on Executive Organization and Management, xiii–xiv
National Aeronautics and Space Administration (NASA), 44, 147, 189–90
National Association of Letter Carriers, 95–96
National Community Service Act (1990), 9–10
National Health Service (Britain), 120
National Institutes of Health, 83
National (Labor/Management) Partnership Council, 206
National Labor Relations Board, 15
National Oceanic and Atmospheric Administration, 153
National Performance Review, xix, 10, 31, 217
National Rifle Association, 17–18
Naval Petroleum Reserves, Office of, 240–41
Neustadt, Richard, 24–25
New Deal, 15
New Federalism, 192
New Public Management paradigm, 30, 31
New Zealand, 30
Nixon administration: assistant secretary for administration (ASA) and, 144; career staff and, 205; Community Development, Department of, 148, 182; departmental reorganization and, 149, 152, 161, 169; Federal Regional Councils (FRCs), 184–85; New Federalism, 192; Personnel

Manual, 48–49; Postal Reorganization Act, 91; postal strike and, 92; regional concept and, 196
(non)delegation doctrine, 60–61

O'Brien, Larry, 100, 101, 102
Office of Federal Financial Management, 212
Office of Federal Procurement Policy, 41, 56, 212
Office of Information and Regulatory Affairs, 212
Office of Management and Budget (OMB): field operations and, 175–76; management component of, 202, 203, 210, 214–17; Nixon administration and, 149; offices within, 212; reorganization of, 196–97; Resource Management Offices, 216; scorecard of, 218; weakening of management role of, 29, 218. *See also* Bureau of Budget
Office of Personnel Management, 190, 198–99, 271n. 37
Oil, Chemical and Atomic Workers International Union v. Richardson, 63–64
O'Leary, Hazel, 51
OMB. *See* Office of Management and Budget (OMB)
organization: agencies and, 25–26; of executive branch, 28–29; federal management, impact on of program design and, xxiii–xxvi; of field staff, 145, 163–66; importance of, xxxi–xxxii; improving, xxvi–xxxii; legal authority and, 22–23; political environment and, 242–43. *See also* reorganization
Organization for Economic Cooperation and Development, 30
organizations: hollowness of, xxvi, 29, 128, 129, 229; hybrid, 31–33, 34–37, 38
Osborne, David, xxvi, 49
outsourcing: Bush administration and, 41–42; selective and intelligent, xxxi, 235–37. *See also* third party government

Paget, Richard, 269n. 8
partnership and Medicare, 138–39
Pearce, Harry, 110
Pell Grant program, 119
performance, improving, 231

Pericles, 13, 14
personal democracy, 5, 15–20
personnel ceilings, 48
Petersen, John, 234
physicians. *See* medical profession
policy expectations, 72–73
policy fragmentation, 84
policy role of headquarters offices, 177–78
political democracy, neoclassical theory of, 6
political expectations, 73
political theory, American, 22
politics: citizen in, 3–4; in nineteenth century, 3
Portman, Bob, 102
Postal Rate Commission, 91, 93–94
Postal Reorganization Act (1970), xxiv–xxv, 91
postal services, foreign, 109
postmaster general, 89–90
Post Office Department, 89–90. *See also* U.S. Postal Service (USPS)
Potter, John, 97, 99–100, 106
power: executive, of president, 24–25; popular support and, 7–8; secretaries and, 160; secretary's representatives and, 185
president: as chief manager, 28–29; executive power of, 24–25; management capacity of, 223; secretaries and, 170; as unitary executive, 27–28. *See also* Executive Office of the President
Presidential Power (Neustadt), 25
President's Commission on Postal Organization, 88–89, 170–71
President's Committee on Administrative Management, x
President's Management Agenda, xxix, 50–51, 197, 198, 217–18, 220
Price, Don, 45
private sector: government-sponsored enterprises (GSEs) and, 33–34; quasi-government and, 32–33; screening of customers by, 238; as separate and legally distinctive from government, 37–39
privatization, 232–34, 256n. 54. *See also* third party government
program delivery. *See* field operations
Progressive era, 15
Pryor, David, 43, 55

public administration, new science of, 10–11, 30–31
public choice theory, 30–31
Public Health Service, 81
public interest, third-party enforcement of, 62–64
public law tradition, 32–33, 37–39, 56, 60–64
Public Service Consortium, 206
public utility regulation, 62
Putnam, Robert, 12–13

quago, 254–55n. 37
quango, 254–55n. 37
quasi-government, emergence of, 31–33
Quesada, Elwood "Pete," 199
qui tam litigation, 62

Rademacher, James, 92–93
rationalization in health care, 116, 132
Reagan, Ronald, 169, 217
Reagan administration: tax cuts, community action, and, 18; Veterans Affairs, Department of, 149–50
reconstitution of federal government: muddling through, 56–59; overview of, 56; reviving public law tradition, 60–64; viewing workforce as whole, 59–60
redesign of programs and downsizing, 232–37
reform: leadership vacuum and, 219–20; management agendas and, 217–18; need for, 213–14; oversight, evaluation capacity, and, 214–17; preconditions for making agencies smaller, more efficient, 238–42; of procurement rules, 221–22; recommendations for, 222–25; technocracies and, 204, 212. *See also* reorganization
regional directors: HEW, 187–88; HUD, 181–82; role of, 163–65
regional offices, 179, 181, 196
regularity, presumption of, 63
"reinventing government": decentralization and, 197, 198; disaggregation and, 29; HHS and, 82; as New Public Management, 31; overview of, 217
Reinventing Government (Osborne & Gaebler), 49
reorganization: commissions and, 170–72; de-

sign and implementation of, 150–51; Nixon administration and, 149, 152, 161, 169. *See also* decentralization; reform

Reorganization Act (1949), 154–55

Resolution Trust Corporation, 236

resources, commitment of, and downsizing, 241–42

Richardson, Elliot, 164, 186–87

Richardson v. McKnight, 261n. 47

Rider, Robert, 106

Riesenberg, Peter, 13

rights, language of, 17

Rouse, Andrew, 269n. 8

rule making, opening of to public, 15–16, 18

Rural Housing Service, 235, 240–41, 242

Salamon, Lester, x, xi, 127

savings and loan industry, 230–32

Scalia, Antonin, 62–63

Schattschneider, E. E., 6

Schein, Edgar, 222

Schudson, Michael, 5

Schultz, George, 92

The Scientific Estate (Price), 45

secretaries: accountability of as juggling process, 72–74; deputy secretaries and, 160–61, 162–63; of executive departments, 144; expectations of, 70–71; as leaders, 74–75; president and, 170; role of, 70, 160

secretary's representatives, 165, 179, 185

Seidman, Harold: Bureau of Budget and, 43; on cabinet officials, 70; conference honoring, xiv; on government-sponsored enterprises, 34; inherently governmental function concept and, 40–41, 62; panel membership of, 46; studies by, 270n. 24

self-interestedness and citizenship, 13

self-regulation in Medicare, 113, 119, 126–27

Senate Governmental Affairs Committee, 106, 150, 171

Senior Executive Service, 190, 209, 214–15, 220–22, 224–25

separation of powers doctrine, 27–28

Shalala, Donna, xxiv, 75, 86, 87

Shelby amendment, 59

Sherman Act, 61–62

Skinner, Sam, 186

Small Business Administration, 143, 155, 236

social capital, 12–13

Social Security Act (1935), 81

Social Security Administration: as independent agency, xxi, 147; management of, 71–72; Medicare and, 126; secretarial office of, 160

Sombrotto, Vincent, 92

stakeholders, 128–29, 239–40

Stanton, Thomas, xiii

State, Department of, 231

state and citizenship, 13–14

statecraft, 242–43

Stimson, Henry Lewis, 170

strikes, 91–93, 107–8

student service learning, 8–10

systems design and implementation, 145–46

Taft-Hartley Act (1947), 15, 16

technocracies: components of, 205; description of, xviii–xix, xxix, 204–5; influence of, 205–6, 220–22; law and, 206–12; leadership and, 206, 219–20; management leadership and, 216–17; tension between management reform and, 212–20

technological developments, 237

Temporary Assistance for Needy Families, 81

Tennessee Valley Authority, 108, 147

terrorism: baggage checkers and, 52–53; HHS and, 79. *See also* homeland security; Homeland Security, Department of

Thayer, Walter, 269n. 8

third party government: Bush administration and, 50–51; Clinton administration and, 49–50; conflict of interest rules and, 46, 57–58; control over, 47–48, 51–52; cumulative effects of, 46–47; design of, 45–46; development of, 42–44; foreign policy and, 49–50; history of, 48–49; hollowness of organizations and, 128, 129; homeland security and, 53–54; management challenges of, xi; Medicare claim payment and, 124–27; openness to bureaucracy, 58–59; performance issues and, 235–36; size of, 41

Thompson, Fred, 106, 171

Thompson, Tommy, xxiv, 85, 86–87

Title 5, U.S. Code, 25, 32

Tools of Government (Salamon), 127

training: downsizing and, 240; of field personnel, 190
Transportation, Department of (DOT): career
staff and, 189–90; creation of, 148–49; decentralization of, 160; field operations of,
183–86; as model of major purpose department, 153–54; organization of, 156–57; secretary's representative and, 165
Transportation Security Administration, xvii
Treasury Department, 164
Truman, Harry, 103, 161

U.S. Agency for International Development,
53
U.S. Commission on National Security/21st
Century, 231
U.S. Enrichment Corporation, xxx, 233, 259n.
24
U.S. Postal Service (USPS): creation of, xxiv,
152; critical issues for, 109–11; effects of 1970
reform, 94; future of, 88; GAO and, 104–5;
governing board and, 108–9; as independent agency, 147; Kappel commission and,
88–89, 90–91, 108–9; leadership and, 243;
management of, 95–99; minimalist approach of, 104–5; Postal Rate Commission
and, 93–94; presidential commission for,
100–104; problems in, 99–100; strike
against, 91–93; transformation plan of,
106–8
Undersecretaries Group, 196, 197
United Parcel Service (UPS), 95, 99

*Vermont Agency of Natural Resources v. United
States,* 63
Veterans Affairs, Department of, 149–50, 172–
74, 234
Volcker Commission, 191
Volpe, John, 160, 166, 183, 185
voter participation, 3–4, 5
voucher programs: analyst esteem for, 127;
benefits of, 242–43; citizenship and, 19;
Medicare as, xxv, 119

Walker, David, xiii
Washington, George, 27
Webster, William, 102
Weinberger, Caspar, 164, 166, 186–87
welfare block grant, 79. *See also* Temporary
Assistance for Needy Families
Wennberg, John, 135
White, Edward Douglas, 62
White, Lee, 88
Whitman, David, 90
Willhite, Deborah, 104
Wills, Gary, 71
Wilson, James, 6
Wilson, James Q., 10
withdrawal from program, 232–34
Witt, James Lee, 155
workforce issues in downsizing, 240–41

Year 2000 computer problem, 214